After Sex

edited by
Edna Bonhomme
and Alice Spawls

SILVER PRESS

CONTENTS

INTRODUCTION

It is easy to ignore how difficult we find sex and its after-math when many sexual acts are no longer criminal or taboo. We are no longer coy about pre-coital courtship and its consequences; we know what is meant by the misty trance on the dance floor, the exchange of selfies, the one-night stand, the walk of shame, the morning-after pill. These interactions have become an index of our intimate lives. We know more than Dr Kinsey could have dreamed about the sex lives of others, their fetishes and peccadillos, their self-fashioning and their self-labelling: hetero-, homo-, poly-, pan-, bi-, a-, queer, sub, dom, bottom, throuple . . . We have a thousand ways of talking about what we like and how we like to get it. It's harder, though, to talk about what happens when sex doesn't go the way we want. We know, even if we don't voice it, that sex doesn't always live up to our efforts or expectations. We know that when it is non-consensual, the violation of the body can rend the soul. And we know that what results from sex can change our lives in ways we never desired or imagined.

The emotional and physical aftermath of sex has histor-ically centred on two outcomes: pregnancy and disease. Good, bad, consensual, drunken, spousal, unwanted, un-thought-through, illicit, paid for – no matter the nature of the encounter, the attempt or not at contraception, life-altering disease and the possibility of pregnancy have shaped human behaviours and understandings of sex. And long before people understood the science of conception, they sought ways to end pregnancies. Terminations take place in all societies and most societies regard them as legal, moral or religious transgressions, but for those that seek them, they are practical and necessary events. 'No matter what men think,' the African-American feminist Shirley Chisholm wrote in 1970, 'abortion is a fact of life. Women have always had them . . . they always will.' The degree to which societies condone and/or assist in abortions is determined less by anxiety about the procedure – though illegality often shrouds it in horror – than by apprehension over sex. The availability of contraception and of information about contraception runs parallel to abortion access, as does the diminishment of stigma and increased freedoms for women. As bell hooks puts it in *Feminism Is for Everybody*, the women's liberation movement of the 1960s started with 'the rights of women to choose when and with whom they would be sexual'. What this meant, in practice, was that 'there could be no genuine sexual liberation for women and men without better, safer contraceptives – without the right to a safe, legal abortion.'

The oldest identifiable condoms date to 1642 and were found at Dudley Castle in the English West Midlands. They were made of animal membranes, a technique that goes back thousands of years: ancient sources describe the use of goats' bladders and intestines as well as linen sheaths, silk pockets, shells, plants and leather. These early condoms worked up to a point. But they were often expensive and impractical, more commonly employed to prevent the wearer from catching a disease than creating a pregnancy. Few people in human history had access to safe, reliable contraceptives. Unsurprisingly, there is written evidence of

II

abortion from two thousand years before the Dudley Castle condoms. Traditional approaches, which are still employed wherever abortion is illegal, were often violent. Injury to the pelvis, whether external or internal, in the hope of dislodging the pregnancy, has taken extreme forms: pounding the lower abdomen with a pestle, inserting a stick of mallow into the uterus, sitting over boiling water, jumping from a height or exposing the belly to blows. The women of Lacedaemon were said to leap vigorously into the air, kicking at their buttocks each time until the desired outcome was achieved. Herbal methods were not always less harmful – or more effective. The 11th-century physician Macer Floridus believed that Italian catnip, savory, sage, soapwort and black hellebore could induce an abortion. The unidentified plant silphium was used across the ancient world and was said to be worth its weight in silver. Early sources also describe instruments we might recognise today – frames for dilation, blades for curettage, hooks for extraction – but the skill and knowledge required to use these instruments was far from widespread.

As medical understanding advanced, legislation followed close behind. But the laws of the 19th-century English-speaking world attest to an ambivalence about abortion that continues today. When did life begin? Was abortion just a procedure or was it murder? And what was fair and practical at a time when, as one estimate has it, a fifth of pregnancies ended this way? The first law explicitly forbidding abortion was passed in Britain in 1803. Punishment extended even to death. The common law distinction of quickening – the point at which the woman was able to sense movement in her womb – was introduced into law and then removed in the following decades; the death penalty was also removed. In both Britain and the US (though with distinctions between states), criminalisation increased in the second half of the 19th century. The Comstock Laws of 1873 were the most far-reaching: it became, in effect, a federal crime to supply information or materials pertaining to abortion, contraception or the prevention of venereal disease. What began as an attempt to censor pornography became something much greater. It took a full century for the effects of Anthony Comstock's campaign to be nullified, if, indeed, we can say they have.

Despite this, many, many abortions took place. Abortifacients were widely, if discreetly, advertised – 'renovating pills', 'women's friend', 'female aliments' – and prosecution was haphazard. As the middle classes grew, so did the number of 'respectable' women who sought abortions. These women, as Patricia Knights writes, were nearly always married, often with two or more children. Married women continued to constitute the majority of those seeking abortion throughout the 20th century, as both Andrea Dworkin (writing in 1983) and Joanna Biggs (writing in 2017) point out. This did not in itself, however, lead to a reassessment of abortion laws in either country, and many late 19th-century campaigners for women's rights feared the legalisation of abortion would only facilitate irresponsible men and incontinent husbands.

It was women, however, who fought to make abortion legal and accessible, along with contraception, specialist clinics and family planning services. We remember some of their names, though not all: Stella Browne, Margaret Sanger, Emily Stowe, Frida Laski, Janet Chance, Alice Jenkins, Joan Malleson – the list goes on and is long. It has often proved difficult for pro-legalisation feminists to make space for the beliefs and experiences, including forced termination, non-consensual contraception and sterilisation, that have made abortion a symbol of the violence exacted by the medical profession on some women in society, just as it has been a tool denied to others. The debates over Margaret Sanger's legacy, and that of Marie Stopes, to which we cannot do justice in this introduction, form just one part of this complex history – a history that we must face openly. Abortion, like sex, is not a universal good. In the extract from *Heart of the Race* (1985) included here, the Brixton Black Women's Collective, represented by authors Beverley Bryan, Stella Dadzie and Suzanne Scafe, outline some aspects of medicalised coercion and force in the reproductive lives of women of colour in the UK. That this history is still not widely known shows how far we still have to go.

While the essays, poems, stories and other texts in this collection share a concern with the bodily freedom and personal agency of those who become pregnant, the attitudes on display are wide-ranging. For a good number, abortion – along with contraception (in particular, the pill) – was and remains essential to female emancipation. What use is fair pay if childbearing and child-rearing prevents you from working? What use is access to male spaces or equal standing in society and before the law when these new freedoms cannot be exercised be of the demands of pregnancy and the unequal burden of childcare? For others, however, abortion was only ever a solution of brutal expediency, the recourse of the poor and powerless, a failure of society to allow women to flourish *and* procreate. Others still, including some of those nurses and doctors recorded in the documentary *Kind to Women* (2018), understood abortion as a social reality that, when hidden and illegal, caused indescribable suffering. Their attitude – and it was far from the attitude of all health workers – was that terminations were consistent with their commitment to ameliorate harm. As many of the writers here show, illegality does not prevent people from seeking abortions.

It does, though, make them far more likely to die or endure life-changing injuries. Before abortion was legal in the US, radical feminists in Illinois formed the Abortion Counselling Service of Women's Liberation, known as the Jane network, which operated as an underground collective providing abortions: first via co-operative doctors, and later by the Janes themselves. The late 1960s saw a number of American states liberalise their abortion laws, but fundamental change came in the form of two major, if inherently limited, pieces of legislation: the first in the UK, in 1967, and the second in the US, in 1973. Both the Abortion Act and *Roe v.Wade* have been called 'bad law'; feminist legal scholars argued from the start that the compromises and convolutions required to secure some access to abortion meant that the resulting legislation fell short of providing a clear and unequivocal right to terminate a pregnancy. Conservative and religious factions began at once to impose restrictions in whatever fashion they could, though even here we find the history is not straightforward – consider the shift of Republican Party members, for instance, from largely pro-choice (more so than Democrats) in the 1970s to less than a quarter so today, or the importance of Church of England bishops in securing the passage of the Abortion Act.

Anti-abortion violence began to rise in the late 1970s. The documented attacks include more than two hundred cases of arson, fire-bombing or bombing of abortion clinics; scores of murders or attempted murders of abortion providers and their staff; thousands of threats and acts of intimidation. For reasons discussed in this collection, the US has seen the most extreme anti-abortion movement in the English-speaking world. But it is important to note that violence and intimidation has not defined most people's experience of legal abortion even in the US, nor has it dented collective organising. We invoke it here as one of the threats faced by pregnant people and to commend those who have risked their lives and liberties to provide information and assistance. Laws limiting or forbidding access to abortion and contraception disproportionately harm people of colour, who are on average three times as likely to die during childbirth as their white counterparts (this is true in both Britain and the US). Such statistics come after the event: they have never been needed by those whose communities are most affected. It has always been clear to them that reproductive rights and healthcare have never been equally distributed, and it is from their experiences that the demand for 'reproductive justice' emerged. As the SisterSong collective defines it, 'reproductive justice' is 'the human right to maintain personal bodily autonomy, have children, not have children, and parent the children we have in safe and sustainable communities'.

Reproductive justice is hard won, and in the US, recent decades have seen more losses than gains. 2019 was a turning point. That year, 25 state-wide laws were passed – including bans on abortions after six weeks of pregnancy in Mississippi, Kentucky, Ohio, Georgia and Alabama. In 2021, the governor of Texas, Greg Abbott, signed Senate Bill Eight, the most draconian anti-abortion law in the US, restricting all abortions after six weeks (so before most women know they are pregnant), including in cases of rape and incest. Within a few weeks of the Supreme Court's decision in *Dobbs v. Jackson Women's Health Organisation*, which in 2022 overturned *Roe v. Wade*, Alabama, Arkansas, Idaho, Kentucky, Louisiana, Mississippi, Missouri, Oklahoma, South Dakota, Tennessee, Texas and West Virginia banned abortion with limited exceptions. The slow and concerted effort by the anti-abortion lobby to capture the Republican Party and criminalise abortion is tracked across many pieces in this collection. While those in the UK might think of America as an exception, or at any rate the product of specific circumstances, fifty years of double standards over Northern Ireland should shake our complacency.

Nor can we expect the law to stand still. Advances in medical care, which in some cases enable the survival of babies as young as 22 weeks, offer a new challenge to a long-established upper limit, as does an increasingly vocal contingent in the Conservative Party – and society at large – protesting abortion with American-style rhetoric. Changing ideas about and experiences of disability will prompt new reckonings. For now, the majority of people in both the US and the UK support abortion under some circumstances, and between a half and two-thirds under any circumstances in the first three months. But this book is not a catalogue of policies and statistics. In 1969, as Maggie Doherty describes here, the Redstockings – a radical feminist group – disrupted judicial hearings on the further liberalisation of New York State's abortion laws. The committee of experts convened by the state consisted of fourteen men and a nun: it is with this in mind that we have sought texts that cleave close to the experiences of pregnant people.

The American context dominates much writing and thinking about reproduction in the English-speaking world and beyond. Changes to American laws affect international aid, and thus greatly impact the lives of women in many countries. American money and American lobbyists influence policies and public opinion around the world. But the trajectory of US politics is not echoed everywhere. Since 2010, for instance, Chile has expanded access to the morning-after pill. The Philippines enshrined in law access to contraception and maternal care. Uruguay legalised abortion in the first trimester. Ireland made abortion legal

when a woman's life was at risk, and then – after a remark-
able referendum – repealed the Eighth Amendment of the
constitution, which gave the unborn as equal a right to life
as the mother. Malta approved the sale of emergency contraception without a prescription. Elsewhere, France imposed and then abolished a 'cooling-off' period for people
seeking an abortion. Poland restricted access to emergency
contraception. South Korea's highest court ruled the criminalisation of abortion unconstitutional. Honduras made
its abortion ban constitutional. Hungary passed a law in-
sisting women listen to the foetal heartbeat before terminating a pregnancy. Colombia decriminalised abortion in
the first 24 weeks of pregnancy. Benin legalised abortion in most circumstances. The Supreme Court of India
ruled that 'every pregnant woman has the intrinsic right
to choose to undergo or not to undergo abortion without any consent or authorisation from a third party' and
removed the distinction between married and unmarried
pregnant women.

Even where laws stay the same, changing political attitudes and the influence of religious leaders can dramatically affect availability and acceptability. Tunisia, famous for
its progressive reproductive policies, became an increasingly difficult place to seek or speak of abortion after the
revolution of 2011. Abortion has not yet become illegal
in Turkey, but access is so limited as to almost make it so.
Further, where pregnancies are policed, women who think
they might be pregnant, and don't wish to be, risk their
health in other ways by avoiding prenatal care. Both China
and Russia, where abortion has long been widespread and
abused by the state, are attempting to reduce abortion rates
as their populations decline.

Many of those who have written openly about their
experiences of sex, pregnancy, unwanted pregnancy and

AFTER SEX

abortion have done so from a position of vulnerability.
Their openness gives courage to others and advances our
shared understanding; it can be the basis of a political
demand but it can also be misused as propaganda or ap-
propriated for the agendas of others. There are narratives
in this collection that invoke or mirror the experiences
of their authors, and these are only a tiny proportion of
an ever-expanding corpus, fictional and non-fictional, realistic and speculative. To give one example, in her novel
The Tenth Month (1970), Laura Z. Hobson created a version
of her own life in the story of Theodora Gray, a divorced
woman in her forties who becomes pregnant after an affair with a married lover. It is not the affair that causes
suffering so much as 'the shame factor' that shapes its
repercussions. If the shame factor were absent, she won-
ders, 'how few young lives would be wrecked, how few
hideous abortions there would be, the awful self-inflicted
ones, the filthy unsterile ones, the slicing agony at the
hands of the doctor who would not risk an anaesthetic?'
The problem, for Gray, isn't the procedure itself but society's fears about losing control – of women, of the sanctity
of paternity, of traditional morality. And the effect of these
fears is to compel the completion of pregnancies. As bell
hooks writes, 'many of us were the unplanned children of
talented, creative women whose lives had been changed
by unplanned and unwanted pregnancies. We witnessed
their bitterness, their rage, their disappointment with their
lot in life.' Children don't preclude meaningful work (they
often constitute it) but not being able to choose when to
have children – or not to have children – often does. And
that curtailment limits another freedom: the freedom to
establish a satisfying sex life, something straight men have
often taken for granted and others have had to learn not
to seek.

***

We began discussing this collection in the months following *Dobbs v. Jackson Women's Health Organisation*. The overthrow of *Roe v. Wade* was the work of decades, but even the inevitable has its moment of arrival, and those of us living in more liberal, secular societies come to understand the power of the law at such moments. Something like eighty million American women – more than the entire population of the UK – saw a half-century-old right struck down. Of course where access is limited and stigma high, a legal right means little. Women, particularly poor women, in many American states saw their options narrowing long before *Dobbs*. But it would be naïve to think that the ruling simply formalised an existing situation, that it made little difference. Law is much stronger and stranger than that. The year since *Dobbs* has seen the cessation of what limited provision was still available in many states. It has seen the religious right grow more ambitious and the police more punitive. The arrest and imprisonment of women who seek reproductive care is no longer a wild exaggeration or dystopian fantasy.

Around 22 million American women live in states that actively punish women seeking terminations, and in doing so, these states criminalise healthcare, turning doctors into felons or informants. Human Rights Watch has recorded the difficulties women now face in accessing abortion in cases of miscarriage; the denial of care in cases of ectopic pregnancy; the delay of care until the woman's health has sufficiently deteriorated to constitute 'risk to life'; the withholding of information – including basic health information – out of fear of violating anti-abortion laws; reduced access to other forms of healthcare, such as chemotherapy, while pregnant; complications for adolescents and children forced to carry pregnancies to term; reduced access to other forms of reproductive care including contraception; increased violence against pregnant people, particularly those in abusive relationships; the avoidance of prenatal care to escape surveillance. Even before *Dobbs*, prosecutors in some states charged pregnant women whose actions were deemed injurious to their foetus – actions including taking prescription or recreational drugs, inciting a brawl, drinking alcohol and accidentally falling down stairs.

The expansion of surveillance technology offers ever more ways of invading the pregnant body: evidence now available to both corporations and prosecutors includes photographs and video footage, social media posts and electronic communications, location data, internet searches, fertility and menstrual apps. Those most affected by the denial of medical care, most likely to face arrest or to suffer the psychological and physical harms of forced pregnancy and unassisted miscarriage, are people of colour, immigrants, people with disabilities and those living in poverty. At the intersections of these categories, we see the greatest vulnerability and the greatest harm.

We initially intended to make this collection international in scope. There is much to be learned from the experiences and struggles of people outside the English-speaking world, and such a collection would have the advantage of showing just how varied and socially configured ideas about reproduction and abortion are. But we soon realised that such an edition would be too vast to be wieldy, or so selective as to be eccentric. Even after limiting our remit to post-1945 works written in English, there is so much we couldn't include. It is worth saying that this collection is not intended as a textbook for students of reproductive rights in the contemporary Anglosphere. Philosophy, medicine, feminism, theology, sociology, history and other disciplines have their own genealogies of thought; there are vast libraries of oral histories, newspaper articles and TV debates; there are many representations – and many more suggestions and coded omissions – in literature, poetry and drama. Surveying this vast field, we recognised that any selection would have arbitrary outlines. We don't, therefore, seek to defend ours as definitive – only to recommend it as useful. These are the texts that we have found most helpful in working through these vexed questions; many of them are canonical, but we include them here because without them we would know less, feel less, think less well. Many have challenged us in some way, and though we did not wish to include any texts engaged in faulty reasoning, or which did not foreground the pregnant person, we found that even the most agreeable polemic cannot provide a full picture of human experience. Nor were we satisfied by stereotypical narrative forms, coloured by atmospheric shame or recurrent regret. We have sought writing, whether provocation or meditation, that is free from the trappings of dogma.

Many of the texts in this collection refer to laws that have since changed. This context will, we hope, be familiar to readers and add to the historical resonance and, in some cases, the pathos. There is an arbitrariness to the laws and dominant cultural attitudes under which any of us lives. Rights can be accrued and denied within our lifetimes, and while we can see from many pieces in this collection the very real gains made by campaigners and activists, the difference made to the lives of many by the interventions of some, we also acknowledge the helpless, loneliness and ambivalence that often accompany experiences of sex and its aftermath. It is because of this – and because of their anarchic political potential – that we have included some texts that made us laugh.

Such a collection inevitably contains repetitions. Many of

the texts reflect on, draw on, critique or otherwise make use of earlier texts also included here. We have found these connections and lineages immensely thought-provoking and hope you do too. The juxtapositions and unruly energies of such a collection can offer new lines of inquiry and new historical understanding. No story of reproductive rights in the West can be written without reference to *Dirty Dancing*, Pope Sixtus, thalidomide and knitting needles. While we might be glad not to rely on rabbit tests to determine whether we are pregnant or suffer quinine blindness in our attempts to terminate a pregnancy, we gain nothing from forgetting those who did or confining them to an unenlightened past. They were our grandmothers and great-grandmothers; they may be our daughters and their daughters (and sons). Some of the most important texts not represented here are guides written by women for women and information provided by healthcare professionals. These texts do not receive plaudits; they are found in women's magazines and doctors' surgeries, in community centres and households. They are free and they are essential. At the opposite end, we have chosen not to include legal texts or religious edicts. These can be found online.

There are many texts that could not be included here because they have not been written (or are not yet accessible). The people who would have written them were illiterate, poor, sick or disabled; they did not think of their experiences or thoughts as worthy of record; they felt themselves to be outside the realm of legitimacy or looked to others and found that there was no one to represent them. Queer, trans, Black and brown accounts, accounts that centre on the psychological suffering of the pregnant person, the experiences of the extremely young or those pregnant as a result of incest or rape, are still occluded and much, much more work needs to be done to change this.

Many of the texts here are extracted from longer works and we refer readers to the bibliographic information at the end of the book: only by reading these works in full can we understand their full significance (and, in some cases, their strangeness). We have also limited footnotes to those most immediately helpful to the comprehension of a given text; for details of sources and so on we refer readers to the original published works. Because the majority of our readers will be in the UK, we have anglicised spellings throughout.

We began by calling this book 'In Search of Reproductive Justice'. *After Sex* is more provocative, and nods both to the bodily realities and intellectual upheaval that accompany and follow from the sexual encounter. Nonetheless, the previous title runs through this book and is its submerged raison d'etre. We are in search of reproductive justice – in our reading, to know how we might articulate it; in our actions, to know what forms it might take; in publishing this book, in the hope that others will join us. Like Amia Srinivasan, we wonder what it would mean to have a politics that does not flee from vulnerability and dependency, that does not take as its implicit starting point the sovereign, perfectly autonomous individual. SisterSong broke this ground and while we do not claim to build on that work, we offer the book to that cause.

EDNA BONHOMME AND ALICE SPAWLS
OCTOBER 2023

What It Was Like
Ursula K. Le Guin
(2004)

My friends at NARAL (National Association for the Repeal of Abortion Laws) asked me to tell you what it was like before *Roe v.Wade*. They asked me to tell you what it was like to be twenty and pregnant in 1950 and when you tell your boyfriend you're pregnant, he tells you about a friend of his in the army whose girl told him she was pregnant, so he got all his buddies to come and say, 'We all fucked her, so who knows who the father is?' And he laughs at the good joke.

They asked me to tell you what it was like to be a pregnant girl – we weren't 'women' then – a pregnant college girl who, if her college found out she was pregnant, would expel her, there and then, without plea or recourse. What it was like, if you were planning to go to graduate school and get a degree and earn a living so you could support yourself and do the work you loved – what it was like to be a senior at Radcliffe and pregnant and if you bore this child, this child which the law demanded you bear and would then call 'unlawful', 'illegitimate', this child whose father denied it, this child which would take from you your capacity to support yourself and do the work you knew it was your gift and your responsibility to do: What was it like?

I can hardly imagine what it's like to live as a woman under Fundamentalist Islamic law. I can hardly remember now, 54 years later, what it was like to live under Fundamentalist Christian law. Thanks to *Roe v. Wade*, none of us in America has lived in that place for half a lifetime.

But I can tell you what it is like, for me, right now. It's like this: If I had dropped out of college, thrown away my education, depended on my parents through the pregnancy, birth and infancy, till I could get some kind of work and gain some kind of independence for myself and the child, if I had done all that, which is what the anti-abortion people want me to have done, I would have borne a child for them, for the anti-abortion people, the authorities, the theorists, the fundamentalists; I would have borne a child for them, their child.

But I would not have borne my own first child, or second child, or third child. My children.

The life of that foetus would have prevented, would have aborted, three other foetuses, or children, or lives, or whatever you choose to call them: my children, the three I bore, the three wanted children, the three I had with my husband – whom, if I had not aborted the unwanted one, I would never have met and married, because he would have been a Fulbright student going to France on the Queen Mary in 1953 but I would not have been a Fulbright student going to France on the Queen Mary in 1953. I would have been an 'unwed mother' of a three-year-old in California, without work, with half an education, living off her parents, not marriageable, contributing nothing to her community but another mouth to feed, another useless woman.

But it is the children I have to come back to, my children Elisabeth, Caroline, Theodore, my joy, my pride, my loves. If I had not broken the law and aborted that life nobody wanted, they would have been aborted by a cruel, bigoted and senseless law. They would never have been born. This thought I cannot bear. I beg you to see what it is that we must save, and not to let the bigots and misogynists take it away from us again. Save what we won: our children. You who are young, before it's too late, save your children.

the mother
Gwendolyn Brooks
(1945)

Abortions will not let you forget.
You remember the children you got that you did not get,
The damp small pulps with a little or with no hair,
The singers and workers that never handled the air.
You will never neglect or beat
Them, or silence or buy with a sweet.
You will never wind up the sucking-thumb
Or scuttle off ghosts that come.
You will never leave them, controlling your luscious sigh,
Return for a snack of them, with gobbling mother-eye.

I have heard in the voices of the wind the voices of my
                                        dim killed children.
I have contracted. I have eased
My dim dears at the breasts they could never suck.
I have said, Sweets, if I sinned, if I seized
Your luck
And your lives from your unfinished reach,
If I stole your births and your names,
Your straight baby tears and your games,
Your stilted or lovely loves, your tumults, your marriages,
                                        aches, and your deaths,
If I poisoned the beginnings of your breaths,

Believe that even in my deliberateness I was not deliberate.
Though why should I whine,
Whine that the crime was other than mine?–
Since anyhow you are dead.
Or rather, or instead,
You were never made.
But that too, I am afraid,
Is faulty: oh, what shall I say, how is the truth to be said?
You were born, you had body, you died.
It is just that you never giggled or planned or cried.

Believe me, I loved you all.
Believe me, I knew you, though faintly, and I loved, I loved

you

All.

Our Bodies, Ourselves:
Reproductive Rights
bell hooks
(2000)

When the contemporary feminist movement began the issues that were projected as most relevant were those that were directly linked to the experiences of highly educated white women (most of whom were materially privileged). Since the feminist movement followed in the wake of civil rights and sexual liberation it seemed appropriate at the time that issues around the female body were foregrounded. Contrary to the image the mass media presented to the world, of a feminist movement starting with women burning bras at a Miss America pageant and then later images of women seeking abortions, one of the first issues which served as a catalyst for the formation of the movement was sexuality – the issue being the rights of women to choose when and with whom they would be sexual. The sexual exploitation of women's bodies had been a common occurrence in radical movements for social justice whether socialist, civil rights etc.

When the so-called sexual revolution was at its peak, the issue of free love (which usually meant having as much sex as one wanted with whomever one desired) brought females face to face with the issue of unwanted pregnancy. Before there could be any gender equity around the issue of free love women needed access to safe, effective contraceptives and abortions. While individual white women with class privilege often had access to both these safeguards, most women did not. Often individual women with class privilege were too ashamed of unwanted pregnancy to make use of their more direct access to responsible health care. The women of the late 1960s and early 1970s who clamoured for abortions had seen the tragedies of illegal abortions, the misery of forced marriages as a consequence of unwanted pregnancies. Many of us were the unplanned children of talented, creative women whose lives had been changed by unplanned and unwanted pregnancies; we witnessed their bitterness, their rage, their disappointment with their lot in life. And we were clear that there could be no genuine sexual liberation for women and men without better, safer contraceptives – without the right to a safe, legal abortion.

In retrospect, it is evident that highlighting abortion rather than reproductive rights as a whole reflected the class biases of the women who were at the forefront of the movement. While the issue of abortion was and remains relevant to all women, there were other reproductive issues that were just as vital which needed attention and might have served to galvanise masses. These issues ranged from basic sex education, prenatal care, preventive health care that would help females understand how their bodies worked, to forced sterilisation, unnecessary caesareans and/or hysterectomies, and the medical complications they left in their wake. Of all these issues, individual white women with class privilege identified most intimately with the pain of unwanted pregnancy. And they highlighted the abortion issue. They were not by any means the only group in need of access to safe, legal abortions. As already stated, they were far more likely to have the means to acquire an abortion than poor and working-class women. In those days poor women, black women included, often sought illegal abortions. The right to have an abortion was not a white-women-only issue; it was simply not the only or even the most important reproductive concern for masses of American women.

The development of effective though not totally safe birth control pills (created by male scientists, most of whom were not anti-sexist) truly paved the way for female sexual liberation, more so than abortion rights. Women like myself who were in our late teens when the pill was first widely available were spared the fear and shame of unwanted pregnancies. Responsible birth control liberated many women like myself who were pro-choice but not necessarily pro-abortion for ourselves from having to personally confront the issue. While I never had an unwanted pregnancy in the heyday of sexual liberation, many of my peers saw abortion as a better choice than conscious, vigilant use of birth control pills. And they did frequently use abortion as a means of birth control. Using the pill meant a woman was directly confronting her choice to be sexually active. Women who were more conscientious about birth control were often regarded as sexually loose by men. It was easier for some females just to let things happen sexually then take care of the 'problem' later with abortions. We now know that both repeated abortions or prolonged use of birth control pills with high levels of oestrogen are not risk-free. Yet women were willing to take risks to have sexual freedom – to have the right to choose.

The abortion issue captured the attention of mass media because it really challenged the fundamentalist thinking of Christianity. It directly challenged the notion that a woman's reason for existence was to bear children. It called the nation's attention to the female body as no other issue could have done. It was a direct challenge to the church.

Later all the other reproductive issues that feminist thinkers called attention to were often ignored by mass media. The long-range medical problems from caesareans and hysterectomies were not juicy subjects for mass media; they actually called attention to a capitalist patriarchal male-dominated medical system that controlled women's bodies and did with them anything they wanted to do. To focus on gender injustice in these arenas would have been too radical for a mass media which remains deeply conservative and for the most part anti-feminist.

No feminist activists in the late 1960s and early 1970s imagined that we would have to wage a battle for women's reproductive rights in the 1990s. Once the feminist movement created the cultural revolution which made the use of relatively risk-free contraceptives acceptable and the right to have a safe, legal abortion possible, women simply assumed those rights would no longer be questioned. The demise of an organised, radical feminist mass-based political movement coupled with anti-feminist backlash from an organised right-wing political front which relies on fundamentalist interpretations of religion placed abortion back on the political agenda. The right of females to choose is now called into question.

Sadly the anti-abortion platform has most viciously targeted state-funded, inexpensive, and, when need be, free abortions. As a consequence women of all races who have class privilege continue to have access to safe abortions – continue to have the right to choose – while materially disadvantaged women suffer. Masses of poor and working-class women lose access to abortion when there is no government funding available for reproductive rights health care. Women with class privilege do not feel threatened when abortions can be had only if one has lots of money because they can still have them. But masses of women do not have class power. More women than ever before are entering the ranks of the poor and indigent. Without the right to safe, inexpensive, and free abortions they lose all control over their bodies. If we return to a world where abortions are only accessible to those females with lots of money we risk the return of public policy that will aim to make abortion illegal. It's already happening in many conservative states. Women of all classes must continue to make abortions safe, legal and affordable.

The right of women to choose whether or not to have an abortion is only one aspect of reproductive freedom. Depending on a woman's age and circumstance of life the aspect of reproductive rights that matters most will change. A sexually active woman in her twenties or thirties who finds birth control pills unsafe may one day face an unwanted pregnancy and the right to have a legal, safe, inexpensive abortion may be the reproductive issue that is most relevant. But when she is menopausal and doctors are urging her to have a hysterectomy that may be the most relevant reproductive rights issue.

As we seek to rekindle the flames of a mass-based feminist movement, reproductive rights will remain a central feminist agenda. If women do not have the right to choose what happens to our bodies we risk relinquishing rights in all other areas of our lives. In the renewed feminist movement the overall issue of reproductive rights will take precedence over any single issue. This does not mean that the push for legal, safe, inexpensive abortions will not remain central, it will simply not be the only issue that is centralised. If sex education, preventive health care and easy access to contraceptives are offered to every female, fewer of us will have unwanted pregnancies. As a consequence the need for abortions would diminish.

Losing ground on the issue of legal, safe, inexpensive

11

abortion means that women lose ground on all reproductive issues. The anti-choice movement is fundamentally
anti-feminist. While it is possible for women to individ-
ually choose never to have an abortion, allegiance to feminist politics means that they still are pro-choice, that they
support the right of females who need abortions to choose
whether or not to have them. Young females who have
always had access to effective contraception – who have
never witnessed the tragedies caused by illegal abortions
– have no first-hand experience of the powerlessness and
vulnerability to exploitation that will always be the outcome if females do not have reproductive rights.

From *Fierce Attachments*
Vivian Gornick
(1987)

From out of nowhere she says to me, 'So tell me about your abortion.' She knows I had an abortion when I was thirty, but she has never referred to it. I, in turn, know that she had three abortions during the Depression, but I never mention them, either. Now, suddenly . . .'I had an abortion with my legs up against the wall in an apartment on West 88th Street, with Demerol injected into my veins by a doctor whose consulting room was the corner of 58th Street and Tenth Avenue.' She nods at me as I speak, as though these details are familiar, even expected. Then she says, 'I had mine in the basement of a Greenwich Village nightclub, for $10, with a doctor who half the time when you woke up you were holding his penis in your hand.' I look at her in admiration. She has matched me clause for clause, and raised the ante with each one. We both burst out laughing at the same moment.

Unpregnancy
Erin Maglaque
(2021)

The pro-choice case for abortion rights rests partly on the possessive pronoun. My body, my choice. Keep your rosaries off my ovaries. These slogans are predicated on the idea that a woman owns her internal organs, and that this ownership is what entitles her to make decisions about them. I once accepted this idea without much thought. Then I had an abortion. It was my abdomen under the ultrasound wand, my uterus on the grainy screen, my body anaesthetised on the clinic table; in some formal sense, my ownership of my ovaries had got me into this predicament and also allowed me to escape it. But the idea that I owned, controlled or chose anything about the procedure was so incongruous with the actual sensation of aborting that I had to remind myself, in between the waves of nausea and cramping, that I was exercising a right conceded to me, for which I should be grateful. Mostly it just hurt.

Now that I am pregnant again, bodily autonomy seems even more immaterial. As historians of reproduction have argued, the understanding that a woman can govern her pregnancy is a historically specific one, dateable to increasingly accurate home pregnancy tests and medical imaging. Women are encouraged to believe that the course of pregnancy is controllable, indeed that it's your responsibility to control it. I don't feel as though an invading alien has seized the levers of my body, which is the way some women describe pregnancy, but rather that the concept of control doesn't enter into the calculus of gestation at all. Nearly every week of pregnancy yields something stranger, generously interpreted by fellow pregnant people on the internet but only in the numinous way that one might interpret tea leaves or the flight patterns of birds.

The concept of body ownership is premised on dualism: the idea that one's thinking self can exercise rights over one's material self. This too is historically particular. In early modern Europe, mind and body were understood to be mingled, and this was a source of anxiety when it came to gestation. A pregnant woman who experienced a shock – being bitten by a dog, or confronted by a beggar – was in danger of giving birth to a deformed baby. A woman who longed for a particular food but couldn't fulfil her craving (for juicy strawberries out of season, perhaps) might deliver a child with a tell-tale strawberry-shaped birthmark. In inheritance disputes, a cuckolded husband's lawyers might argue in court that his wife had imagined her husband's face while having sex with her lover, so that the resulting infant would resemble her husband and her adultery remain concealed. There was a wild power in the maternal imagination.

The slightest disorder during pregnancy – badly aligned stars, stagnant air, intestinal gas, a sneeze – could shake loose a foetus 'like fruit [from] a tree', according to one 16th-century jurist. The body was not only shaped by the imagination and the senses, but by the environment and the heavenly spheres, as well as by one's neighbours and midwives. Elena Cocchi testified against her abusive husband in Rome in 1634, accusing him of causing her to miscarry. But she had been unsure about the pregnancy, even though it was not her first. 'When I began to know that I was pregnant, I had my midwife Dianora, who has [helped] deliver my other children, come and I told her I wondered whether I was pregnant and she looked at me and said I was and from that point I began to grow.' Pregnancy was partly conceived in the womb and partly conferred by others.

Pregnancy was also pathological. Maria, from a village outside Rome, had been involved with Superio, a wealthy legume dealer who was also her uncle. (He kept a mattress secreted in his bean storeroom for sex.) Her pregnancy threatened to reveal the scandal to their neighbours. Superio purchased an abortifacient from a toothless 89-year-old friar, who wandered the countryside practising both pharmacology and exorcism. The difference between being possessed by a demon and possessed by an unwanted foetus was a matter of degree, not kind. Pregnancy and abortion were not understood as the battleground for conflicts over bodily autonomy; rather, gestation revealed the vulnerability of existing in a body in which someone else lives and dies. The maternal body was responsive to the imagination, the stars, a fart, a midwife's touch. Pregnancy was a different kind of possession – not something one owned, but the fact of being possessed by another.

An aborted pregnancy was a *disgravidanza*, an unpregnancy, or might be described as a *parto acerbo*, an unripe birth. Judges described abortion in the language of corruption, waste, disorder and ruin. Women's language was more ordinary, and colder. Giving evidence to tribunals, they called an aborted foetus a *creatura*; an earlier-stage abortion a *pezzo di carne*, a piece of meat. Abortion was shared work, because men like Superio needed abortions to happen just as much as women did. Men procured herbal concoctions from physicians and apothecaries, arranged for blood-letting (from the 'vein of the mother', located on the foot), or – in truly desperate cases – beat their partners' backs and abdomens.

It's likely that the majority of abortions were sought by married couples who did not want any more children, but these were entirely private and so have gone unrecorded. In *Abortion in Early Modern Italy* (2021), John Christopoulos has meticulously pieced together a secret history not only from prescriptive sources but from the public records of trials, giving us for the first time a sense of the way early modern women and men experienced abortion. Trials inevitably centred on the most scandalous cases, but in the background of these tales of rape and incest, Christopoulos shows a more ordinary history: the quiet purchase of a bitter drink from an apothecary, the flux and the pain, burying the stained bedsheets out by the stable. The lifecycle of an abortion was completed in the spring. Men and women made confession once a year, at Easter, when they strung together their sins for the parish priest and waited for discreet absolution.

The Catholic Church claims to have held abortion to be a mortal sin since the first century. This is untrue. For most of the Church's history, Catholic theologians believed that the moral and physical gravity of abortion developed with gestation. An early pregnancy was easily lost and had not yet been endowed by God with a soul; animation was thought to take place at forty days for a male foetus and eighty days for a female. This aligned with contemporary medical thinking. According to Aristotelian and Galenic theory, these were the points at which foetuses achieved human shape (the female sex was colder and moister, so took longer to congeal into human form in the womb). Before the moment of animation, the unformed foetus might be aborted and the pregnant woman only incur mild sin; only at the later stage was it considered human, and its destruction equivalent to homicide. Most Italians, not just learned theologians and physicians, subscribed to this more nuanced understanding of abortion: one midwife in Rome reported in 1634 that her usual professional practice was to 'throw aborted foetuses that do not have a soul in the latrine, and I do not baptise them because they are not alive'.

This thinking was radically revised by Pope Sixtus V in his 1588 bull on abortion, the first the Catholic Church had ever issued. The bull was part of Sixtus's reformist campaign against sexual forms of moral deviance; he had issued harsh laws against adultery and incest in 1586 and 1587. In his abortion bull, he abolished the distinction between the pre and post-animate foetus and declared that life began at conception. All abortions were murder. Women who had abortions, and men who helped women procure them, would be subject to automatic excommunication from the Church and capital punishment. No longer could women privately confess their abortions to their parish priest and receive penance; now, only the pope himself could absolve them. The result was that most women decided to live excommunicate. Parish priests and bishops found the bull so impossible to implement and so out of step with the social need both for abortion and privacy that it was reversed three years later by a new pope. The Church's understanding of abortion once again cleaved closely to gestational development. This remained the status quo until 1869, when Pope Pius IX proclaimed that ensouled life began at conception.

Because the significance of abortion – and the severity of the consequences – developed along with the pregnancy, women had to be trusted to discern the gestational age of the foetus, to distinguish indigestion from early foetal movement, dropsy from the heaviness of pregnancy. As Christopoulos argues, this suggests 'a uniquely gendered experience of time, where a woman's days might be dominated by intense concentration on perceiving and evaluating physical sensations', waiting in hope or in fear. Maria da Brescia, a single servant woman in Bologna accused of abortion in 1577, thought she had eaten some bad onions, and took to bed with wind pains; when she got up to use the toilet, she explained to the judge, 'I expelled that creatura on the floor, dead, it did not cry . . . I had never been pregnant and I did not know what I had in my body. I thought I had a bubble in my body.' A woman in Tivoli had believed herself pregnant for fifteen months, before she finally 'passed a great amount of wind from her womb and her belly deflated'.

Equally difficult was determining the difference between an aborted foetus, a stillbirth and infanticide. Tribunals required evidence that a woman had intentionally terminated her pregnancy or had killed the infant shortly after birth. Midwives were enrolled by tribunals as forensics experts to examine the bodies of the mother and the foetus, assigned the near impossible task of assembling evidence of intent. In 1610, a young woman called Lucia from outside Bologna – she had concealed her pregnancy and intended to abandon the infant at Bologna's foundling hospital – delivered a stillborn baby at seven months. Two midwives examined her as part of the ensuing tribunal and evaluated the testimonies of witnesses. The midwives reported that Lucia had recently given birth and had not yet delivered the placenta; they could feel it throbbing dangerously in her uterus. The foetus was female, fully formed with hair and fingernails, and had still been warm when it was wrapped in Lucia's shirt. While there were no obvious signs of violence on the body, the midwives told the court that Lucia hadn't tied the umbilical cord in a knot but had torn it. This allowed the infant's breath fatally to escape its body, puff by puff. Lucia was defiant. 'It was not [born] alive, and I will never be able to say why it was not, and I cannot do anything about this, I cannot supersede the one who is the master of the whole world: it pleased God that it was born dead, and I don't know what to make of it.'

The ambiguities of pregnancy, miscarriage, stillbirth and abortion were the foundation for sympathetic tolerance as well as misogyny. The opacity of women's bodies and intentions could create sufficient uncertainty to allow judges and confessors to look the other way. This looks something like mercy when compared with the torture that goes on today in clinics in Kentucky, where women are required by law to view their foetus on an ultrasound screen and listen to its heartbeat before determining whether to come back for an abortion. But precisely because in the early modern period a gestating, miscarrying or aborting body was a mystery to be solved, women could be subject to invasive practices of a different sort. Pity Bianca Cappello, whose pregnancy could not be confirmed even after 'four or five of [Florence's] best physicians looked at and touched my body up to the meat.'

A pregnant woman could not always disguise her intentions. Maria was accused of aborting a foetus in 1614, after her incestuous relationship with Superio was made public. Dragged in front of the tribunal, she denied everything. She was tortured and maintained her innocence, claiming she had taken purgatives for a menstrual illness. But her body betrayed her. Three midwives examined Maria and found her genitals puffy and stretched, her belly 'flabby' and 'wrinkly', her breasts leaking milk. When she tried to claim she was lactating because of a menstrual disorder, the midwives scoffed: 'My girl, a young woman who has not been pregnant and who has not given birth cannot have milk the way you do.' They went on to ridicule her, asking if she thought her milk 'came from the heavens'. When Maria was examined in her prison cell, investigators noted a scar on her foot, evidence of bloodletting from the 'vein of the mother'. Maria's body gave her away more plainly than any confession by torture.

Put in front of tribunals, women knew to emphasise their vulnerability when faced by duplicitous men. In 1586, a widow called Aorelia was accused of either aborting a late-term foetus or murdering a new-born baby – the midwives couldn't tell which – and burying it under a chestnut tree. When questioned, she told the tribunal that her partner Pietro had lived with her openly, promising to look after her, providing her with money and food: 'Seeing as I am poor and that I cannot sustain my aforesaid family . . . he helped me and did what he could to help raise my children.' But Pietro remembered their relationship differently.

> I came and went, both day and night, from the said Aorelia's house, as I wanted and as it pleased me, and I slept there, and I screwed her at my convenience, and I gave her money, when I had it, and I screwed her like the whore that she is, as did other [men]. I cannot say who else screwed her, but I heard it said publicly that this woman is screwed by diverse people.

The scripts were well-worn. Men cast doubt on their partners' sexual past – whose baby was buried under that tree, anyway? – while women framed themselves as victims.

Most of the time, the judges' paternalism won out: they knew that economic need could be a powerful incentive to sex and so to abortion, and were inclined to leniency when presented with a compelling plea of fragilitas sexus. This might seem at first glance an admirable, even surprising, form of tolerance, but as Christopoulos persuasively argues, this discretionary mercy reinforced the misogyny of the judicial system empowered to grant it. Aorelia shaped her testimony to prick the judge's conscience. The pleas have changed, of course – our placards now argue that abortion is healthcare, healthcare is a human right – but a right conferred is a right that can be abruptly withdrawn. Aorelia knew that. So did Ruth Bader Ginsburg's mourners when they prostrated themselves in front of the Supreme Court.

'I am sometimes envious of the horrible circumstances of the past,' Anne Boyer wrote, 'because they are at least differently horrible and differently degraded than our era's own.' Christopoulos's accomplished account emphasises the ambiguities and ambivalences that surrounded pregnancy and its termination in early modern Italy. There is much that was differently horrible and differently degraded about abortion's past in his telling, but is there anything to covet? In 1593, Mattia, an impoverished agricultural worker in the Veneto who had been repeatedly raped by her father, was accused of aborting a foetus. She defended herself to the court. 'I did not know I was pregnant, and I was working in the fields. This harmed me, and I miscarried. The foetus slipped out like a slice of ham.' I am not envious of this past, not really. Abortion is safer now, after medicalisation and legalisation. But safer isn't safe, and safety isn't everything. If abortion is a right, it is a flimsy one, predicated on the whims of judges and a property relation to the body that obscures everything that is real and radical about gestation. Maybe there is something we can learn from a time when pregnancy was possession,

23

not of but by another; when an unwanted foetus was as precious as a slice of ham, and abortion as cleansing as an exorcism.

Reflecting on My Christian Past
R.O. Kwon
(2021)

As a former Christian who once believed abortions to be evil, and who is now convinced of the opposite, I have found heartbreaking, as so many have, the arguments about the Texas anti-abortion law. It's less that it's devastating to, once again, have our core reproductive rights up for Supreme Court debate – though it is, utterly so – and more that the people bent on overturning *Roe v. Wade* too vividly bring to mind the girl I used to be.

That girl was deeply, joyfully Christian. I grew up Catholic, at first; in junior high, I started veering towards more ecstatic, charismatic kinds of Protestantism. In high school, I believed myself on fire for the Lord: My idea of a riotous Friday night was an especially spirited youth group rally. I had block letter Bible verses printed on my public school textbook covers, so that I could silently proselytise while I walked around, like a one-girl billboard for Christ. I intended to be a pastor: I thought I'd give my life to the Lord. I believed too, as did almost everyone I knew, that life-curtailing abortions must be terribly sinful, a violence that, though legal, couldn't be right.

It's possible that, had I stayed in the faith, I'd have held onto this belief into adulthood. But instead, against my will, for a multitude of reasons – including the difficulty,

then impossibility, of believing that those who didn't wor-
ship as I did were to burn in hell – I lost my faith in God
when I was seventeen, a catastrophic loss whose enormity
I still have trouble conveying. It's a loss that's still happening, daily reshaping my life and mind around His ongoing
absence. It's always what I'm writing about, maybe because, as long as I'm writing about the Lord I lost, I can
still, in a way, be with Him.

And I do miss Christ. I miss Him so much. I would like
to be clear about that. The Christ I loved, the one who lifted up and valued the needy, suffering, poor, ill and outcast:
That Christ, He loved us not for our strength, not for
temporal success, wealth, power, nor even virtue, but just
because we were all children of God. Simply by merit of
existing, we deserved a love without end. Is there a more
capacious promise? I didn't think so before I left; years
later, I still don't think I've found a better pledge.

But in losing God, I didn't just lose a deity and faith.
Since my morals, my ethics, had been profoundly formed
by the logic of faith as I understood it, I also lost, and had
to rebuild, much of my previous understanding of what
was right. I questioned beliefs I'd long held; as a result, I
ended up looking into the origins of aspects of Christianity that the text, the Word, didn't necessarily support.

For instance, I learned that US politicians began focusing
on abortion rights, on reproductive rights, fairly recently.
It wasn't until the 1970s that abortions started becoming a
central voting issue for a lot of people: the voting issue, for
many. In 1976, presidential candidate Gerald Ford and his
strategists added 'right to life' language to the Republican
platform, hoping to tempt Catholics away from the Democratic Party. Until then, Republicans belonged to the party
of choice. It was political manoeuvring, in other words,
chicanery that made use of Christians for an American

political party's electoral gain. In which case, what was I doing, subscribing to an opinion established by 1970s political operatives?

If I was truly still interested in valuing human life – and I was, and am, deeply so – then the more ethically consistent, Christ-like position, or so I gradually discovered, was to fight and advocate for far better health care (Romans 15:1). An annulled death penalty (Romans 12:19). Tightened gun laws (Matthew 5:39). Universal childcare and paid parental leave to help all of God's children thrive, not just those whose parents can pay for full-time nannies (Mark 10:14). Borders opened to the migrants who come in need of welcome to the US – which is still, lest we forget, even almost two years into a disastrous pandemic, the richest country in the history of the world (Luke 6:30).

The Christ I knew and loved – and still love, really, since grief can be an obverse of love, love that has lost its object – cared, even more than He cared about everyone else, about the most vulnerable among us. I can see how that could be interpreted to mean He particularly cares about first-trimester foetuses, but He doesn't really say anything about foetuses in the Bible I used to memorise. What He did say a lot about, what He was repeatedly explicit about, was His love of the hungry, the poor, of living children, and of other fellow humans in need, for inasmuch as we have done to the least of His brethren, we have done unto Him (Matthew 25:40).

In part because of how close I still feel to the Christian I used to be, I ended up devoting ten years to writing my first novel, which is about domestic terrorists who bomb abortion clinics, health care clinics, in the name of God. While I was beginning this novel, unsure of what it would be but knowing the Christ I'd lost would play a starring role, I volunteered very briefly as a patient escort at a

27

Planned Parenthood. What this meant was that I put on an orange vest marking me as a volunteer, and I walked patients from their cars to the clinic entrance, past protesters. Most of the protesters were clearly Christian, their signs calling on Jesus, and as I walked patients back and forth, I experienced a nearly physical split in my body between who I used to be, and who I'd since become. In high school, I could have been one of them, convinced I had to protect lives; now, here I was on a Saturday afternoon, also certain I was protecting lives.

That split in my body, I think, has informed much of my fiction: I keep writing as if, through words, I might help bridge imaginative divides between very different worldviews. It's also why I'm writing this piece: I persist in believing there are people like the would-be pastor I was – or like my fervently religious parents, who have supported Republicans in the past and now, staunchly, do not. To be on the side of life is to care for existing people, the ones already here. No one should really believe otherwise, including Christians. No one, especially Christians.

Time for Change
Anne Enright
(2018)

Recently I spoke to a reasonable, sane Irish woman who said that she was against abortion and because she was so reasonable and sane, I was curious what she meant by that. Was she against the morning after pill? Certainly not. What about chemical abortifacients? They did not really worry her too much. So, what about terminations before twelve or thirteen weeks, the time when women are often given the all-clear to confirm their pregnancy to family and friends? This woman was not, all things considered, against terminations during this window, when pregnancy is not considered medically certain. She was also, just to make clear, in favour of abortion in cases of fatal foetal abnormality, rape and incest. In 1983 this woman might have voted 'against abortion', despite the fact that she is not against abortion, especially if it happens during those weeks when the natural loss of an embryo is called miscarriage. She just found abortion, in general, hard to vote 'for'. Had there been no referendum in 1983 – where people with a range of uncertainties were asked for a single 'yes' or 'no' – then limited abortion might well be available now in Ireland, in the way that the morning after pill is legally available and widely used.

The 1983 referendum was a little like the Brexit referendum – a population voting about something that seemed, on one side, clear, and on the other, contingent and hard to describe. As it turned out, the language problem worked both ways. In order to bring the issue to a vote, a new legal term had to be minted, one that did not appear in any previous laws. The Eighth Amendment to the Irish constitution acknowledges the right to life of 'the unborn' and this seemed to invent a new category of rights-holder, possibly a new kind of person. By acknowledging the 'equal right to life of the mother' an impregnated woman was changed from a human being into a relationship, that of motherhood, and a peculiar equivalence established. Pregnancy was a binary state, in which two souls temporarily shared the same blood supply. The question of who had it first was neither here nor there and a fertilised egg was a grown adult, temporarily inconvenienced by being a few hundred cells large.

In 2016, there were 63,897 live births in Ireland. The medical estimate, according to the American College of Obstetricians and Gynaecologists, is that up to a quarter of pregnancies end in miscarriage, which means that around 20,000 conceptions could have failed in Ireland last year due to natural causes. If all life is sacred, then all life did not get the memo.

The pro-life view is taken more from theology than biology. Its supporters in Ireland did not foresee, or did not care about, the medical consequences of their unnatural view – the decisions gone wrong, the danger to the life of the impregnated woman, such as the case of Savita Halappanavar who died of septic shock in a Galway hospital, when a miscarriage could not be treated until the foetal heartbeat stopped.

They did not care about the psychological consequences, and the cruelty of that indifference was hard, as a society, to live with. Arguments about suicide (how to believe her?), about rape (how to believe her?) reinforced the fact that 'a mother' could not be in charge of herself, because she had no self in the way we usually understand the word – this was set aside, for the duration. Once impregnated, a woman was reduced to a body, and that body was no longer hers. On the one side we have miracle, on the other, meat.

In March 2014, a refugee, Ms Y, arrived in Ireland and discovered that she was pregnant as the result of multiple rapes in her country of origin. She had no passport or papers and was turned back at a British port, when she tried to travel there for a termination. Back in Ireland and suicidal, she was told she could be detained under mental health legislation, and she agreed to stay in a maternity hospital instead. There, she went on hunger strike, until delivered by caesarean at thirty weeks. In the years since 1983 we have learned that there is no answer to the question: 'How much suffering is too much suffering?' The question is irrelevant because the psychology of the mother is irrelevant, as are social or practical concerns.

Unlike Ms Y, most women are not confined to Ireland and many make the decision to travel to Britain to avail themselves of abortion services there. This is not so much an Irish solution (pretend it isn't happening) as a middle-class one. It depends on people having literacy skills, cred-it cards, supportive parents if needs be, an amount of spare cash. It is not a solution for people in denial about what has happened to them – the woman who doesn't want it to be true; the couple who took a chance; the woman who has other issues, who has enough going on, who is de-pressed, or poor, who has three children already and no time. The girl impregnated by her stepfather, or her uncle, or her father, or by any man who has power over her, or over the people who might help her. The woman unsure of her visa. The woman who is alone, or feels herself to be suddenly and overwhelmingly alone, just now.

Conservative figures from the charity Rape Crisis reveal that 3265 Irish women went to Britain to procure abortions in 2016. This was down more than 50 per cent from a high of 6673 in 2001. The biggest shift happened among women in their twenties (those born after the referendum of 1983), with numbers declining more than 60 per cent, from 4089 to 1563. Figures may be disputed in this fiercely debated topic, but there is no doubting a significant reduction over the same years in which the general population rose by nearly 25 per cent. A more open and secular society has not resulted in more abortion, but less.

Pro-life campaigners don't seem to trust people much, though in my experience people do the best they can. They talk as though floodgates were about to burst open, as though women are naturally opposed to the rights of 'the unborn'. But having children is a complicated business, it is not a war. Many children are conceived by accident, or in a state of doubt, and their mothers bring them – half in dread, half in hope – into the world. Other babies are born after long months of their mother's anguish and incomprehension that her body should be so used – and after her body, her life.

The referendum on abortion was held in 1983, when contraception was also illegal in Ireland. Can you imagine how freaked out that made everyone I grew up with about sex? Do it once, and everything changes. Perhaps this informs the way pro-lifers think about mothers in general, perhaps even their own – that she is always trapped; that we must be saved from her rage, her sense of life's unfairness, her murderous intent.

There is an overlap of nine months, when the smaller

life depends on the bigger, and not the other way around. This is just true. If a foetus dies, the body surrounding it does not die, or not usually. The mother's life is the more powerful thing. This is very frightening, when you think about it. So, yes, women are very frightening, despite their almost universal willingness to please people, to smile and be nice.

The pro-life movement controlled the terms of the debate in Ireland, so it remained a religious discussion in which all conceptions are fully realised, as opposed to potential, human beings. This is something you either believe or you don't, but it is difficult to get outside their language, which has the weight of culture behind it. So I want to suggest two small shifts in the words we use. The first is to replace the word 'pregnant' with 'impregnated', to restore a sense of causality to a condition that is sometimes seen as self-enclosed. The other is to swap out the phrase 'unwanted pregnancy' with its echoes of unwanted gifts, or what used to be called 'unwanted advances' or 'attentions' (now called harassment), and to use the more radical 'pregnancy without consent'.

Sex without consent is a terrible thing, we are all agreed on that. We understand the horror of rape – to have someone inside you for thirty seconds, or ten minutes, to enter your body without your joyful invitation, this is known to be a terrible violation, a trauma from which it is hard to heal. We see the power dynamic here. We imagine, or remember, the pain inflicted and the pleasure taken, and we condemn the act absolutely. But this sense of drama – of a battle of wills – is also a distraction from an ethical argument that might be made about your body: who gets to use it, and on what terms.

If a conceived embryo is already, and instantly, a full human being, this raises questions about what human beings can do to each other, and why. This is not the way I usually think – my thoughts about abortion are always uncertain and, I hope, slow to judge – but if you want an absolute argument about all this, then here it is. What right does another human being have to be inside your body for the best part of a year, to make their way out of your private parts in a bloody, difficult and painful way, and then turn to you for nourishment, not to mention love – perhaps for the rest of your life?

In the nine months occupation that is a pregnancy, the embryo has no agency, it doesn't mean to be there and no intention to cause harm. But an absence of intention does not confer any rights. Just because someone does not mean to use you does not give them the right to use you. The fact that an embryo cannot ask for consent does not mean that consent must be given. An embryo takes no pleasure from its presence in your body, but this does not give it ownership of your body any more than a grown man has ownership over your body's interior. The hidden fact in the Eighth Amendment is that the term 'unborn' does not mean 'human being' as the mother is a human being – if it did then the mother's rights might also be asserted. The 'unborn' here is code for 'biology', 'happenstance' or 'life itself'.

It may be argued that when a woman consents to unprotected sex she is also consenting to carry any resulting pregnancy to term, but I do not know if you can make an agreement with someone who does not yet exist. The hidden power, in this contract-with-no one, lies not with the physically powerless embryo, or the legally powerless pregnant woman, it lies with the father, or with the father-as-state, who asserts control, from a sometimes indifferent distance, over both.

This argument may sound slightly absurd, not to mention harsh, but it is exactly as harsh and as absurd as the Eighth Amendment to the Irish constitution, which is widely understood without making any sense.

In 2016, people in Britain and the US voted for the tribal and the symbolic when they went for Brexit and for Trump. We know something about all this in Ireland because we had a tribal, symbolic vote in 1983. We saw the cruelty of that symbolic choice play out in our hospitals, and airports, and in our lives for more than thirty years. We know how debilitating it is to argue with the religious right and how wounding it is to face down their trolls.

If we, in Ireland, can repeal the Eighth Amendment, that shift will echo around the world. It will be heard in El Salvador, where women have been imprisoned for the natural loss of their babies; it will be heard in those Australian states where abortion is both available and illegal at the same time; it will be heard in Poland where 30,000 people marched against the further restriction of abortion laws, and won. It will be heard in the US, where state by state the rights conferred by *Roe v. Wade* are being whittled away to the especial detriment of poor women; women who own little or nothing, not even the body in which they walk around.

The message it will send is not just about women's right to choose, it is about how countries work. Democracies must also be allowed to change.

The Abortion
Alice Walker
(1981)

They had discussed it, but not deeply, whether they wanted the baby she was now carrying. 'I don't know if I want it,' she said, eyes filling with tears. She cried at anything now, and was often nauseous. That pregnant women cried easily and were nauseous seemed banal to her, and she resented banality.

'Well, think about it,' he said, with his smooth reassuring voice (but with an edge of impatience she now felt) that used to soothe her.

It was all she did think about, all she apparently could; that he could dream otherwise enraged her. But she always lost when they argued. Her temper would flare up, he would become instantly reasonable, mature, responsible, if not responsive precisely, to her mood and she would swallow down her tears and hate herself. It was because she believed him 'good'. The best human being she had ever met.

'It isn't as if we don't already have a child,' she said in a calmer tone, carelessly wiping at the tear that slid from one eye.

'We have a perfect child,' he said with relish, 'thank the Good Lord!'

Had she ever dreamed she'd marry someone humble

enough to go around thanking the Good Lord? She had not.

Now they left the bedroom, where she had been lying down on their massive king-size bed with the forbidding ridge in the middle, and went down the hall – hung with bright prints – to the cheerful, spotlessly clean kitchen. He put water on for tea in a bright yellow pot. She wanted him to want the baby so much he would try to save its life. On the other hand, she did not permit such presumptuousness. As he praised the child they already had, a daughter of sunny disposition and winning smile, Imani sensed subterfuge, and hardened her heart.

'What am I talking about,' she said, as if she'd been talking about it. 'Another child would kill me. I can't imagine life with two children. Having a child is a good experience to have had, like graduate school. But if you've had one, you've had the experience and that's enough.'

He placed the tea before her and rested a heavy hand on her hair. She felt the heat and pressure of his hand as she touched the cup and felt the odour and steam rise up from it. Her throat contracted.

'I can't drink that,' she said through gritted teeth. 'Take it away.'

There were days of this.

Clarice, their daughter, was barely two years old. A miscarriage brought on by grief (Imani had lost her fervidly environmentalist mother to lung cancer shortly after Clarice's birth; the asbestos ceiling in the classroom where she taught first graders had leaked for twenty years) separated Clarice's birth from the new pregnancy. Imani felt her body had been assaulted by these events and was, in fact, considerably weakened, and was also, in any case, chronically anaemic and run down. Still, if she had wanted the baby more than she did not want it, she would not have planned to abort it.

They lived in a small town in the South. Her husband, Clarence, was, among other things, legal adviser and defender of the new black mayor of the town. The mayor was much in their lives because of the difficulties being the first black mayor of a small town assured, and because, next to the major leaders of black struggles in the South, Clarence respected and admired him most.

Imani reserved absolute judgment, but she did point out that Mayor Carswell would never look at her directly when she made a comment or posed a question, even sitting at her own dinner table, and would instead talk to Clarence as if she were not there. He assumed that as a woman she would not be interested in, or even understand, politics. (He would comment occasionally on her cooking or her clothes. He noticed when she cut her hair.) But Imani understood every shade and variation of politics: she understood, for example, why she fed the mouth that did not speak to her; because for the present she must believe in Mayor Carswell, even as he could not believe in her. Even understanding this, however, she found dinners with Carswell hard to swallow.

But Clarence was dedicated to the mayor, and believed his success would ultimately mean security and advancement for them all.

On the morning she left to have the abortion, the mayor and Clarence were to have a working lunch, and they drove her to the airport deep in conversation about municipal funds, racist cops and the facilities for teaching at the chaotic, newly integrated schools. Clarence had time for the briefest kiss and hug at the airport ramp.

'Take care of yourself,' he whispered lovingly as she

walked away. He was needed, while she was gone, to draft the city's new charter. She had agreed this was important; the mayor was already being called incompetent by local businessmen and the chamber of commerce, and one inferred from television that no black person alive even knew what a city charter was.

'Take care of myself.' Yes, she thought. I see that is what I have to do. But she thought this self-pityingly, which invalidated it. She had expected him to take care of her, and she blamed him for not doing so now.

Well, she was a fraud, anyway. She had known after a year of marriage that it bored her. 'The Experience of Having a Child' was to distract her from this fact. Still, she expected him to 'take care of her'. She was lucky he didn't pack up and leave. But he seemed to know, as she did, that if anyone packed and left, it would be her. Precisely because she was a fraud and because in the end he would settle for fraud and she could not.

On the plane to New York her teeth ached and she vomited bile – bitter, yellowish stuff she hadn't even been aware her body produced. She resented and appreciated the crisp help of the stewardess, who asked if she needed anything, then stood chatting with the cigarette-smoking white man next to her, whose fat hairy wrist, like a large worm, was all Imani could bear to see out of the corner of her eye.

Her first abortion, when she was still in college, she frequently remembered as wonderful, bearing as it had all the marks of a supreme coming of age and a seizing of the direction of her own life, as well as a comprehension of existence that never left her: that life – what one saw about one and called Life – was not a facade. There was nothing behind it which used 'Life' as its manifestation. Life was itself. Period. At the time, and afterwards, and even now,

40

this seemed a marvellous thing to know.

The abortionist had been a delightful Italian doctor on the Upper East Side in New York, and before he put her under he told her about his own daughter who was just her age, and a junior at Vassar. He babbled on and on until she was out, but not before Imani had thought how her thousand dollars, for which she would be in debt for years, would go to keep her there.

When she woke up it was all over. She lay on a brown Naugahyde sofa in the doctor's outer office. And she heard, over her somewhere in the air, the sound of a woman's voice. It was a Saturday, no nurses in attendance, and she presumed it was the doctor's wife. She was pulled gently to her feet by this voice and encouraged to walk.

'And when you leave, be sure to walk as if nothing is wrong,' the voice said.

Imani did not feel any pain. This surprised her. Perhaps he didn't do anything, she thought. Perhaps he took my thousand dollars and put me to sleep with two dollars' worth of ether. Perhaps this is a racket. But he was so kind, and he was smiling benignly, almost fatherly, at her (and Imani realised how desperately she needed this 'fatherly' look, this 'fatherly' smile). 'Thank you,' she murmured sincerely: she was thanking him for her life.

Some of Italy was still in his voice. 'It's nothing, nothing.' he said. 'A nice, pretty girl like you; in school like my own daughter, you didn't need this trouble.'

'He's nice,' she said to herself, walking to the subway on her way back to school. She lay down gingerly across a vacant seat, and passed out.

She haemorrhaged steadily for six weeks. and was not well again for a year.

***

But this was seven years later. An abortion law now made it possible to make an appointment at a clinic, and for seventy-five dollars a safe, quick, painless abortion was yours.

Imani had once lived in New York, in the Village, not five blocks from where the abortion clinic was. It was also near the Margaret Sanger clinic, where she had received her very first diaphragm, with utter gratitude and amazement that someone apparently understood and actually cared about young women as alone and ignorant as she. In fact, as she walked up the block, with its modern office buildings side by side with older, more elegant brownstones, she felt how close she was still to that earlier self.

Still not in control of her sensuality, and only through violence and with money (for the flight, for the operation itself) in control of her body.

She found that abortion had entered the age of the assembly line. Grateful for the lack of distinction between her and the other women – all colours, ages, states of misery or nervousness – she was less happy to notice, once the doctor started to insert the catheter, that the anaesthesia she had been given was insufficient. But assembly lines don't stop because the product on them has a complaint.

Her doctor whistled, and assured her she was all right, and carried the procedure through to the horrific end.

Imani fainted some seconds before that.

They laid her out in a peaceful room full of cheerful colours. Primary colours: yellow, red, blue. When she revived she had the feeling of being in a nursery. She had a pressing need to urinate.

A nurse, kindly, white-haired and with firm hands helped her to the toilet. Imani saw herself in the mirror over the sink and was alarmed. She was grey, as if all her blood had leaked out.

'Don't worry about how you look,' said the nurse. 'Rest a bit here and take it easy when you get back home. You'll be fine in a week or so.'

She could not imagine being fine again. Somewhere her child – she never dodged into the language of 'foetuses' and 'amorphous growths' – was being flushed down a sewer. Gone all her or his chances to see the sunlight, savour a fig.

'Well,' she said to this child, 'it was you or me, Kiddo, and I chose me.'

There were people who thought she had no right to choose herself, but Imani knew better than to think of those people now.

It was a bright, hot Saturday when she returned.

Clarence and Clarice picked her up at the airport. They had brought flowers from Imani's garden, and Clarice presented them with a stout-hearted hug. Once in her mother's lap she rested content all the way home, sucking her thumb, stroking her nose with the forefinger of the same hand and kneading a corner of her blanket with the three fingers that were left.

'How did it go?' asked Clarence.

'It went,' said Imani.

There was no way to explain abortion to a man. She thought castration might be an apt analogy, but most men, perhaps all, would insist this could not possibly be true.

'The anaesthesia failed,' she said. 'I thought I'd never faint in time to keep from screaming and leaping off the table.'

Clarence paled. He hated the thought of pain, any kind of violence. He could not endure it; it made him physically ill. This was one of the reasons he was a pacifist, another reason she admired him.

She knew he wanted her to stop talking. But she continued in a flat, deliberate voice.

'All the blood seemed to run out of me. The tendons in my legs felt cut. I was grey.'

He reached for her hand. Held it. Squeezed.

'But,' she said, 'at least I know what I don't want. And I intend never to go through any of this again.'

They were in the living room of their peaceful, quiet and colourful house. Imani was in her rocker, Clarice dozing on her lap. Clarence sank to the floor and rested his head against her knees. She felt he was asking for nurture when she needed it herself. She felt the two of them, Clarence and Clarice, clinging to her, using her. And that the only way she could claim herself, feel herself distinct from them, was by doing something painful, self-defining but self-destructive.

She suffered the pressure of his head as long as she could. 'Have a vasectomy,' she said, 'or stay in the guest room. Nothing is going to touch me anymore that isn't harmless.'

He smoothed her thick hair with his hand. 'We'll talk about it,' he said, as if that was not what they were doing. 'We'll see. Don't worry. We'll take care of things.'

She had forgotten that the third Sunday in June, the following day, was the fifth memorial observance for Holly Monroe, who had been shot down on her way home from her high-school education ceremony five years before.

Imani always went to these memorials. She liked the re-assurance that her people had long memories and that those people who felt in struggle or innocence were not forgotten. She was, of course, too weak to go. She was dizzy and still losing blood. The white law givers attempted to get around assassination – which Imani considered extreme abortion – by saying the victim provoked it (there had been some difficulty saying this about Holly Monroe but they had tried) but were anti-abortionist to a man.

Imani thought of this as she resolutely showered and washed her hair.

Clarence had installed central air conditioning their second year in the house. Imani had at first objected. 'I want to smell the trees, the flowers, the natural air!' she cried. But the first summer of 110-degree heat had cured her of giving a damn about any of that. Now she wanted to be cool. As much as she loved trees, on a hot day she would have sawed through a forest to get to an air conditioner.

In fairness to him, she had to admit he asked her if she thought she was well enough to go. But even to be asked annoyed her. She was not one to let her own troubles prevent her from showing proper respect and remembrance towards the dead, although she understood perfectly well that once dead, the dead do not exist. So respect, remembrance was for herself and today herself needed rest.

There was something mad about her refusal to rest, and she felt it as she tottered about getting Clarice dressed. But she did not stop. She ran a bath, plopped the child in it, scrubbed her plump body on her knees, arms straining over the tub awkwardly in a way that made her stomach hurt – but not yet her uterus – dried her hair, lifted her out and dried the rest of her on the kitchen table.

'You are going to remember as long as you live what kind of people they are,' she said to the child, who, gurgling and cooing, looked into her mother's stern face with light-hearted fixation.

'You are going to hear the music,' Imani said. 'The music they've tried to kill. The music they try to steal.'

She felt feverish and was aware she was muttering. She didn't care.

'They think they can kill a continent – people, trees,

AFTER SEX

buffalo – and then fly off to the moon and just forget
about it. But you and me we're going to remember the
people, the trees and the fucking buffalo. Goddammit.'

'Buffwoe,' said the child, hitting at her mother's face
with a spoon.

She placed the baby on a blanket in the living room and
turned to see her husband's eyes, full of pity, on her. She
wore pert green velvet slippers and a lovely sea green robe.
Her body was bent within it. A reluctant tear formed beneath his gaze.

'Sometimes I look at you and I wonder "What is this
man doing in my house?"'

This had started as a joke between them. Her aim had
been never to marry, but to take in lovers who could be
sent home at dawn, freeing her to work and ramble.

'I'm here because you love me,' was the traditional
answer. But Clarence faltered meeting her eyes, and Imani
turned away.

It was a hundred degrees by ten o'clock. By eleven,
when the memorial service began, it would be ten degrees
hotter. Imani staggered from the heat. When she sat in the
car she had to clench her teeth against the dizziness until
the motor prodded the air conditioning to envelop them
in coolness. A dull ache started in her uterus.

The church was not of course air conditioned. It was
authentic Primitive Baptist in every sense.

Like the four previous memorials this one was designed
by Holly Monroe's classmates. All 25 of whom, fat and
thin, managed to look like the dead girl. Imani had never
seen Holly Monroe, though there were always photographs of her dominating the pulpit of this church where
she had been baptised and where she had sung in the choir
– and to her, every black girl of a certain vulnerable age
was Holly Monroe. And an even deeper truth was that

46

Holly Monroe was herself. Herself shot down, aborted on the eve of becoming herself.

She was prepared to cry and to do so with abandon.

But she did not. She clenched her teeth against the steadily increasing pain and her tears were instantly blotted by the heat.

Mayor Carswell had been waiting for Clarence in the vestibule of the church, mopping his plumply jowled face with a voluminous handkerchief and holding court among half a dozen young men and women who listened to him with awe. Imani exchanged greetings with the mayor, he ritualistically kissed her on the cheek and kissed Clarice on the cheek, but his rather heat-glazed eye was already fastened on her husband. The two men huddled in a corner away from the awed young group. Away from Imani and Clarice, who passed hesitantly, waiting to be joined or to be called back, into the church.

There was a quarter-hour's worth of music.

'Holly Monroe was five feet, three inches tall, and weighed one hundred and eleven pounds,' her best friend said, not reading from notes, but talking to each person in the audience. 'She was a stubborn, loyal Aries, the best kind of friend to have. She had black kinky hair that she experimented with a lot. She was exactly the colour of this oak church pew in the summer; in the winter she was the colour [pointing up] of this heart pine ceiling. She loved green. She did not like lavender because she said she also didn't like pink. She had brown eyes and wore glasses, except when she was meeting someone for the first time. She had a sort of rounded nose. She had beautiful large teeth, but her lips were always chapped so she didn't smile as much as she might have if she'd ever gotten used to carrying Chap Stick. She had elegant feet. Her favourite church song was 'Leaning on the Everlasting Arms.' Her favourite

47

other kind of song was 'I Can't Help Myself – I Love You and Nobody Else.' She was often late for choir rehearsal though she loved to sing. She made the dress she wore to her graduation in Home Ec. She hated Home Ec . . .'

Imani was aware that the sound of low, murmurous voices had been the background for this statement all along. Everything was quiet around her, even Clarice sat up straight, absorbed by the simple friendliness of the young woman's voice. All of Holly Monroe's classmates and friends in the choir wore vivid green. Imani imagined Clarice entranced by the brilliant, swaying colour as by a field of swaying corn.

Lifting the child, her uterus burning, and perspiration already a stream down her back, Imani tiptoed to the door. Clarence and the mayor were still deep in conversation.

She heard 'board meeting', 'aldermen', 'city council'. She beckoned to Clarence.

'Your voices are carrying!' she hissed.

She meant: How dare you not come inside.

They did not. Clarence raised his head, looked at her and shrugged his shoulders helplessly. Then, turning, with the abstracted air of priests, the two men moved slowly towards the outer door and into the churchyard, coming to stand some distance from the church beneath a large oak tree. There they remained throughout the service.

Two years later, Clarence was furious with her: What is the matter with you? he asked. You never want me to touch you. You told me to sleep in the guest room and I did. You told me to have a vasectomy I didn't want and I did. (Here there was a sob of hatred for her somewhere in the anger, the humiliation: he thought of himself as a eunuch and blamed her.)

She was not merely frigid, she was remote.

She had been amazed after they left the church that the anger she'd felt watching Clarence and the mayor turn away from the Holly Monroe memorial did not prevent her accepting a ride home with him. A month later it did not prevent her smiling on him fondly. Did not prevent a trip to Bermuda, a few blissful days of very good sex on a deserted beach screened by trees. Did not prevent her listening to his mother's stories of Clarence's youth as though she would treasure them forever.

And yet. From that moment in the heat at the church door, she had uncoupled herself from him, in a separation that made him, except occasionally, little more than a stranger.

And he had not felt it, had not known.

'What have I done?' he asked, all the tenderness in his voice breaking over her. She smiled a nervous smile at him, which he interpreted as derision – so far apart had they drifted.

They had discussed the episode at the church many times. Mayor Carswell – whom they never saw anymore – was now a model mayor, with wide biracial support in his campaign for the legislature. Neither could easily recall him, though television frequently brought him into the house.

'It was so important that I help the mayor!' said Clarence. 'He was our first!'

Imani understood this perfectly well, but it sounded humorous to her. When she smiled, he was offended.

She had known the moment she left the marriage, the exact second. But apparently that moment had left no perceptible mark.

They argued, she smiled, they scowled, blamed and cried as she packed.

Each of them almost recalled out loud that about this

time of the year their aborted child would have been a troublesome, 'terrible' two-year-old, a great burden on its mother, whose health was by now in excellent shape, each wanted to think aloud that the marriage would have deteriorated anyway, because of that.

From 'The Virtual Speculum in the New World Order' Donna Haraway (1997)

The foetus and the planet Earth are sibling seed worlds in technoscience. If NASA photographs of the blue, cloud-swathed whole Earth are icons for the emergence of global, national and local struggles over a recent natural-technical object of knowledge called the environment, then the ubiquitous images of glowing, free-floating human foetuses condense and intensify struggles over an equally new and disruptive technoscientific object of knowledge, namely 'life itself'. Life as a system to be managed – a field of operations constituted by scientists, artists, cartoonists, community activists, mothers, anthropologists, fathers, legislators, publishers, engineers, legislators, ethicists, industrialists, bankers, doctors, genetic counsellors, judges, insurers, priests, and all their relatives – has a very recent pedigree. The foetus and the whole Earth concentrate the elixir of life as a complex system, that is, of life itself. Each image is about the origin of life in a postmodern world.

Both the whole earth and the foetus owe their existence as public objects to visualising technologies. These technologies include computers, cameras, satellites, sonography optical fibre technology, video machines, television, microcinematography and much more. The global foetus and the spherical whole Earth both exist because of, and inside of, technoscientific visual culture. Yet, I think, both signify touch. Both provoke yearning for the physical sensuousness of a wet and blue-green Earth and a soft, fleshy child. That is why these images are so ideologically powerful. They signify the immediately natural and embodied, over and against the constructed and disembodied. These latter qualities are charged against the supposedly violating, distancing, scopic eye of science and theory. The audiences who find the glowing foetal and terran spheres to be powerful signifiers of touch are themselves partially constituted as subjects in the material-semiotic process of viewing. The system of ideological oppositions between signifiers of touch and vision remains stubbornly essential to political and scientific debate in modern Western culture. This system is a field of meanings that elaborates the ideological tension between body and machine, nature and culture, female and male, tropical and northern, traditional and modern, and lived experience and dominating objectification.

Sometimes complicitous, sometimes exuberantly creative, Western feminists have had little choice about operating in the charged field of oppositional meanings structured around vision and touch. Small wonder, then, that feminists in science studies are natural deconstructionists who resolutely chart fields of meanings that unsettle these oppositions, these setups that frame human and nonhuman technoscientific actors and sentence them to terminal ideological confinement. Because the fruit issuing from such confinement is toxic, let us try to reconceive some of the key origin stories about human life that congeal around the images of the foetus. In many domains in contemporary European and US cultures, the foetus functions as a kind of metonym, seed crystal or icon for configurations of person, family, nation, origin, choice, life and future. As the German historian of the body Barbara Duden put it, the foetus functions as a modern 'sacrum', that is, as an object in which the transcendent appears. The foetus as sacrum is the repository of heterogeneous people's stories, hopes and imprecations. Attentive to the wavering opposition of the sacred versus the comic, the sacramental versus the vulgar, scientific illustration versus advertising, art versus pornography, the body of scientific truth versus the caricature of the popular joke, the power of medicine versus the insult of death, I want to proceed here by relocating the foetal sacrum onto its comic twin.

This image, a cartoon by Anne Kelly that I have named *Virtual Speculum*, is a representation of Michelangelo's painting *Creation of Adam* on the ceiling of the Sistine Chapel. *Virtual Speculum* is a caricature in the potent political tradition of 'literal' reversals, which excavate the latent and implicit oppositions that made the original picture work. In Kelly's version, a female nude is in the position of Adam, whose hand is extended to the creative interface with not God the Father but a keyboard for a computer whose display screen shows the global digital foetus in its amniotic sac. A female Adam, the young nude woman is in the position of the first man. Kelly's figure is not Eve, who was made from Adam and in relation to his need. In *Virtual Speculum*, the woman is in direct relation to the source of life itself.

The cartoon seems to resonate in an echo chamber with a Bell Telephone advertisement that appeared on US television in the early 1990s, urging potential long-distance customers to 'reach out and touch someone.' The racial-ethnic markings of the cast of characters varied in different versions of the ad. The visual text showed a pregnant woman, who is undergoing ultrasonographic visualisation of her foetus, telephoning her husband, the father of the foetus, to describe for him the first spectral appearance of his issue. The description is performative: that is, the object described comes into existence, experientially, for all the participants in the drama. Fathers, mothers, and children are constituted as subjects and objects for each other and the television audience. Life itself becomes an object of experience, which can be shared and memorialised. Proving herself to be a literate citizen of technoscience, the pregnant woman interprets the moving grey, white, and black blobs on the televised sonogram as visually obvious, differentiated foetus. Family bonding is in full flower in Bell Telephone's garden of creation. Surrogate for the absent father, the mother touches the on-screen foetus, establishing a tactile link between both parents-to-be and child-to-be. Here are interactive television and video of a marvellous kind. The mother-to-be's voice on the phone and finger on the screen are literally the conduits for the eye of the father. These are the touch and the word that mediate life itself, that turn bodies and machines into eloquent witnesses and storytellers.

Through advertising, Bell Telephone puts us inside the dramatic scenarios of technology and entertainment,

twins to biomedicine and art. In the ad, reproductive technology and the visual arts – historically bound to the specific kinds of observation practised in the gynaecological
exam and the life-drawing class – come together through
the circles of mimesis built into communications practices
in the New World Order. Life copies art copies technology
copies communication copies life itself. Television, sonography, computer video display, and the telephone are all
apparatuses for the production of the nuclear family on
screen. Voice and touch are brought into life on screen.

   Kelly's cartoon works off the fact, which remains odd to
women of my menopausal generation, that in many
contemporary technologically mediated pregnancies, ex-
pectant mothers emotionally bond with their foetuses
through learning to see the developing child on screen
during a sonogram. And so do fathers, as well as members
of Parliament and Congress. The sonogram is literally a
pedagogy for learning to see who exists in the world.
Selves and subjects are produced in such 'lived experiences'. Quickening, or the mother's testimony to the movement of the unseen child-to-be in her womb, has here
neither the experiential nor the epistemological authority
it did, and does, under different historical modes of embodiment. In Kelly's version, the bonding produced by
computer-mediated visualisation also produces subjects
and selves; the touch at the keyboard is generative – emotionally, materially and epistemologically. But things work
both similarly and differently from the way they do on the
Sistine Chapel ceiling or in the Bell Telephone TV advertisement.

   In *Virtual Speculum* the greyish blobs of the television
sonogram have given place to the defined anatomical form
of the free-floating foetus. Kelly's on-screen foetus is more
like an in vivo movie, photograph or computer-graphic

reconstruction – all of which are received at least partly within the conventions of post-Renaissance visual realism, which the bloblike sonographic image has great difficulty invoking. The televised sonogram is more like a biological monster movie, which one still has to learn to view even in the late 20th century. By contrast, to those who learned how to see after the revolution in painting initiated in the 15th and 16th centuries in northern and southern Europe, the free-floating, anatomically sharp, perspectively registered foetal image appears self-evident at first viewing. Post-Renaissance anatomical realism and late-20th-century computer-generated corporeal realism still share many, although not all, viewing conventions and epistemological assumptions.

The foetus like the one in *Virtual Speculum* is the iconic form that has been made so familiar by the exquisite, internationally distributed images produced by the Swedish biomedical photographer Lennart Nilsson. Endoscopic intrauterine foetal visualisation began in the 1950s, well before sonograms were part of the cultural terrain. The visible foetus became a public object with the April 1965 *Life* magazine cover featuring Nilsson's photograph of an intrauterine eighteen-week-old developing human being encased in its bubblelike amniotic sac. The rest of the Nilsson photos in the *Life* story, 'The Drama of Life Before Birth', were of extrauterine abortuses, beautifully lit and photographed in colour to become the visual embodiment of life at its origin. Not seen as abortuses, these gorgeous foetuses and their descendants signified life itself, in its transcendent essence and immanent embodiment. The visual image of the foetus is like the DNA double helix – not just a signifier of life but also offered as the-thing-in-itself. The visual foetus, like the gene, is a technoscientific sacrament. The sign becomes the thing itself in ordinary magico-secular transubstantiation.

Nilsson's images have spiked the visual landscape for the past thirty years, each time with announcements of originary art and technology, originary personal and scientific experience, and unique revelations bringing what was hidden into the light. Nilsson's photographs are simultaneously high art, scientific illustration, research tool. and mass popular culture. 'The Drama of Life Before Birth' was followed by the popular coffee-table-format book, *A Child is Born*; the NOVA television special in 1983, 'The Miracle of Life'; the lavishly illustrated book on the immune system, including images of developing foetuses, *The Body Victorious*; and the August 1990 *Life* cover photo of a seven-week-old foetus, with the caption 'The First Pictures Ever of How Life Begins', and the accompanying story, 'The First Days of Creation'. Finally, moving from conception through breastfeeding, *A Child Is Born* was issued in 1994 as a compact-disk adaptation whose content-rich multimedia design offers interactive features as part of the visual foetal feast. Truly, we are in the realm of miracles, beginnings and promises. A secular terrain has never been more explicitly sacred, embedded in the narratives of God's first Creation, which is repeated in miniature with each new life. Secular, scientific visual culture is in the immediate service of the narratives of Christian realism. 'These are the days of miracle and wonder.' We are in both an echo chamber and a house of mirrors, where, in word and image, ricocheting mimesis structures the emergence of subjects and objects, It does not seem too much to claim that the biomedical, public foetus – given flesh by the high technology of visualisation – is a sacred-secular incarnation, the material realisation of the promise of life itself. Here is the fusion of art, science, and creation. No wonder we look.

Three Poems
for Reproductive Justice
Tracy Fuad
(2019-23)

Birth

You were born in a brutalist building.
Rising above a long body of water.
The body, a bypass canal.

You were born beneath six beaming spotlights.
Born of a sharpness, and set to music.
In the backroom, on a tablet, through a portal.

A glory, a watermark's scar.
And with a great whoosh, Orlando.
Orlando, known by the land.

And the unbowing was there.
And the ecstatic, a humming.
And a great sorrow was there.

Iraq Vag Panic

You could say it wrong, like my wracked
brain or with the wrong g
like gag or Garamond.
Some words are nearly in ruins.
       Yesterday the gynaecologist told me
       I spell my name wrong, should have an o between
                    the f and u.
       Am I trying to get pregnant?
In my country, he begins.
And then, between my parted legs, tells me that over there,
       they do everything that we do,
       just behind closed doors.
Am I anxious?
Well, someone is tweeting at me from a burner account,
       or my step-grandma's trying to troll me again.
But I've already gone quick-violet.
On the plane, beside me
is a healer who tells me about her interest
in belly dancing.
Belly good is what my grandpa says instead of *very*.
Not his accent, just his joke.
We approach the fertile crescent:
Hewlêr, Kirkuk, Baghdad – three neon shocks.
Across the aisle a woman opens up
a document that just says ART.
Then selects the text in baby blue
and makes it shrink.
Timing, says the healer. Such a powerful force in life.

Flowers

The week that I arrived there was an outbreak, which put us all on edge, and I woke up with jagged breath at each night's middle, wailing to my metal box which pinged my wails across the ocean.

The tide filled and emptied the basins around me twice daily.

The hourglass of sand I ordered on the internet arrived on time, and the days passed calendrically.

I read The Field Guide to Cape Cod and tread lightly on the lichen, which I knew my feet were capable of killing. One night, globs of algae washed up, pulsing with their own dim light.

I hadn't meant to let in the part of me that hated me, but there it was, hovering above my folded body in the attic that was, for a spell, my home.

I flew across the ocean, and when I came back, I could no longer sleep.

Something foreign had lodged in me and formed a cord, leeching from me what it needed.

A storm came and knocked out the power, then another. We all got sick, then recovered. An absence watched me as I lay in bed all day, rubbing my belly where I thought it might be.

Then sound, at frequencies too high to hear, was pulsed into my abdomen, reflecting back a mass that quivered in space with regular rhythm, a beating preceding an actual heart.

What is the point of flowers, a child had asked his mother last summer while I was bussing tables,
> lingering over smeary plates to eavesdrop on her answer.

The roses which proffer odd blossoms all winter here in the dunes of the Cape came as cargo, stashed on a passenger ship heading to Boston from England which foundered and wrecked in fair weather the first day of March in the middle of a century of revolution, empire and collapse. Driven ashore, the boat broke apart, discharging its cargo of nutmeg and linens and nursery stock, drowning some dozens, including the captain, who had conspired, it later came out, to sink the ship, doubly-insured, worth more sunk than afloat.

A man who'd lost all five of his daughters pulled the damning letters from a suitcase. Then gathered and planted the pear and plum seedlings cast up by the sea, a wrecker's garden.

The roses took root all on their own and spread along the cape's long arm, invasive.

The point of flowers, the mother had explained with a surgeon's precision, is to lure in bees, which pollinate the flowers so the flowers can make more flowers. Yes, the

child replied, but what's the point, and I saw the seeds of a
nihilism with which I was once well-acquainted.

It's foolish, I think, to think that you know what you want.

My Childhood under Northern Ireland's Abortion Ban
Rachel Connolly
(2022)

There is a leaflet I remember reading compulsively when I was in primary school. I would have been eight or nine years old and got it from one of the booths set up by anti-choice protesters who would often gather in town. The text was neon pink and printed on silky black paper, design choices that made the content seem sensational, even pornographic. Across one corner there was an image of a tiny human body blurred by a glowing outline. The religious imagery I grew up with was full of saints portrayed similarly.

That leaflet lived in my pocket for a while. I unfolded and refolded it until the shininess faded and it was quartered with thick, white veins. I only vaguely remember what it said, the usual gory myths about infertility and vacuums and the capacity a foetus has to feel pain, always using the word 'baby' instead of 'foetus'. The feelings it evoked I recall much more clearly: revulsion, shock and fascination.

That was in Belfast around 2001. You could not get an abortion and the entire concept was taboo, shrouded in secrecy and misinformation. Until 2019 – thanks mainly to the Democratic Unionist Party, which used the issue to appeal to its fundamentalist Presbyterian base – it was a criminal offence to have or perform an abortion in Northern Ireland unless the pregnancy was deemed to be life-threatening or to pose a risk of permanent damage to mental or physical health. I never knew of anyone who met that criteria. There were no exemptions for sexual crimes or fatal foetal abnormalities. The best you could do was order pills from the internet, for which you could be prosecuted, or travel to England. You had to pay for an abortion in England even though this procedure was free for English people on the NHS and we paid the same taxes as they did towards funding it.

The unfairness of that particular element – paying taxes towards health care from which you are barred – only struck me in my early twenties. Why only then? In theory, I have been pro-choice, just like my parents, for as long as I can remember. But growing up immersed in a culture with an abortion ban influences how you feel, if not how you think.

I could tell an uncomplicatedly sympathetic story about living as a teenage girl in a place where abortion was banned. One in which I lived in constant terror of getting pregnant, seething over the injustices of the patriarchy and taking plucky, practical measures to subvert it. A story where I had pocket money stowed fastidiously under a mattress and a sophisticated understanding of gender and power. But to do so would not only misrepresent my experience of the ban but also downplay its power and influence, stretching like a horizon over so many actions, words and thoughts. It's difficult to say exactly where its consequences end.

I didn't make resourceful contingency plans. Instead, I remember taking an ostrich-like approach to the possibility of getting pregnant. I tried to think about it as little as possible. This translated to being squeamish about anything to do with female reproductive health, never getting

STI tests, and using daft, counterproductive contraception methods that were rumoured to work doubly well. Wearing a condom and then also pulling out, for one. Or avoiding penetrative sex, which almost always meant performing acts oriented around male pleasure.

This didn't feel oppressive or terrifying, it was just life; a restrictive culture doesn't tend to appear as such except in a wider context. But I do remember being terrified of abortion itself. I thought of it as grizzly and maiming – something dangerous and illicit rather than a medical procedure. Another protester's booth I recall vividly had a selection of buckets that they claimed were used during abortions 'for the babies'. This fire-and-brimstone theatricality was a common tactic of anti-choice protests – or maybe 'celebrations' is a better word since the objective of the protest was already a reality.

It was ridiculous but effective. When I had an abortion a few years ago (a decision I made because I didn't want a child, and which I have rarely thought about since), I felt no emotional or moral reservations. I still fainted, twice, while the nurse was trying to talk me through the procedure, at the memory of those graphic leaflets. Afterwards, I was livid that the climate of my childhood could have that physical effect on me years later.

Abortion was made needlessly traumatic, even for women who could get around the ban. Someone I knew of, who flew to Manchester for an abortion, had to return home hours later, bleeding profusely on the plane and then at work the next day. She told me she was so terrified of being reported to the police she didn't tell her husband or any friends, let alone her boss or co-workers. Instead, she worked through the bleeding in a state of dread, praying that it wasn't suggestive of a complication, for almost two weeks with no medical attention. When it stopped, she had to hope for the best.

There are more diffuse societal impacts, too. Things that I can't say for sure were about the abortion ban but that I think in hindsight probably would have been different if there hadn't been one. The embarrassment around sex, the culture of large families with enormous child-care responsibilities for the woman only, the behaviour I now understand as virulent misogyny.

When I was at school, being a girl was akin to a form of punishment. The whole concept of sex and sexuality was shrouded in shame. The sex education we had was administered by Presbyterian groups who would come in and talk to an entire grade at once about the evils of sex before marriage while everyone giggled and blushed. Of course, they didn't talk about queer relationships. They didn't talk about STIs or contraception, either. Girls I knew who talked about being on contraception mostly said it was for their skin. When I went on the pill at sixteen, the doctor gave me a talk about appropriate behaviour and respectability.

I can remember feeling like some of the boys at my school really hated girls. Although I doubt I articulated it to myself as clearly as that at the time; it can be difficult to separate memories from the reflections you impose on them in hindsight. But I did have a gut instinct to avoid certain boys. I know I thought of some of them as scary. The boys everyone would hear stories about. When a girl would pass out drunk at a party, those boys would take her clothes off and take pictures of her. Or take turns sexually assaulting her, although we wouldn't have called it that. The point of these stories, as we usually saw them at the time, was that the girl involved had embarrassed herself.

Sometimes we would agree it was bad, and when we gossiped about it, we would say we felt sorry for her. I remember one story, about a boy in the year above me who would always feature in these kinds of stories and was in a secret relationship with a girl who was about thirteen. He was seventeen or eighteen. (I don't know who this relationship was a secret from; I barely knew him and I knew about it.) The way I heard it, her parents were away and she had people over to her house for drinks, including this boy and some of his friends. She passed out drunk, and he took all her clothes off and tied her up in Christmas tree lights, turned them on, and took pictures of her. Then he left, leaving the lights on. When she woke up in the morning, her body was covered in tiny burns and she had to go to the hospital.

Recently, I saw an old school friend of mine, Jake. We laughed about a party we had gone to when we were around sixteen, hosted by a boy in our school whose dad owned some pizza restaurants. Their family lived in a big house outside of Belfast surrounded by fields and patches of forest. They had a decked-out barn with bar stools and a mini-fridge. There was a bonfire and they had hired porta-potties. We told the story of that party to each other the way you retell well-worn stories with old friends, asking the other person if they remember details you know they will. Remember when that boy passed out in the porta-potty? Remember you tried to smoke weed but you could never inhale, right? Remember I drove you home?

During our conversation, I recalled something from that night I hadn't thought about in a long time. I was standing by the bonfire, flirting with this boy I'd fancied for a while, and he grabbed my bag and ran off into the forest with it. He wasn't one of the boys who tended to feature in those bad stories, although a lot of his friends did. I ran after him and found him hiding behind a tree, where we wrestled for the bag. We ended up on the ground, him sitting on top of me with one leg on either side of my torso. He grabbed my wrists, held them down by my sides, and laughed. I didn't know how to respond to that, so I laughed too.

He asked about my boyfriend, if it was true he was at the university in our city. I said he was. He looked down at me, raised his eyebrows, and then climbed off me slowly and we stood up. There was soil and leaves in my hair. I didn't bring that anecdote up to Jake, but I thought about it in the taxi home, trying to figure out, years later, what was going on there, if it was dangerous or a game.

For the rest of that taxi journey, I found myself replaying similar memories. I can never think of a single experience of misogyny without a whole chain of linked events unfolding before me. The time while travelling I snuck onto the private beach of a luxury hotel with a man staying in my hostel and ended up pinned on the floor like that again, wondering if he was joking or not. The time a man in a bar in Manchester came up behind me, separated my bum cheeks with his hands, pressed his crotch between them, and then spent the rest of the night badgering me while his friends watched and laughed. The time I was walking home and a car parked a little bit ahead of me so I hid in a stranger's garden, lying under a bush, while the man who had been in the car walked up and down the street looking for me. Times in nightclubs in London when I haven't wanted to talk to someone so he has shouted abuse at me or grabbed me. Being flashed on public transport – a gesture that seems, comparatively, so unthreatening I tend to joke about it with friends after. The chain unfolds and unfolds.

I look back on these events with detachment, trying to decide if a certain situation was dangerous, how dangerous it was, or how it started or ended up a certain way. Sometimes I think these are situations that, in hindsight, were bound to have taken a threatening turn and I must be the only person on earth who wouldn't have been able to see that (internalised misogyny, I know). Mostly I feel angry at the sense of constantly playing a rigged game.

Just as there is a palatable way to talk about abortion, there is a palatable way to talk about gendered violence and misogyny, using the language of trauma as it is sign-posted in movies. But real life is full of different kinds of people with different coping mechanisms. Misogyny is not only male violence but also a simplistic stereotype of female behaviour and emotions projected uniformly onto all of us. It is good-victim narratives and treating women with kindness and sympathy only if we cry and pretending that we only have abortions because we can't afford children.

Trying to get out from under this is the project of a life-time. Determining how you feel about the prospect of motherhood versus how you have been told to feel. Accepting that you have been a victim even though you don't behave the way they're supposed to. Reckoning with the times you have participated in misogyny instead of just being subjected to it. Wondering how much of the misogyny I remember from growing up was because of the abortion ban and how much was just the normal amount. Asking the impossible question: What level of hatred and violence towards women is normal?

Abortion for Beginners
T.L. Cowan
(2020)

Abortion has always been special to me. I was raised in a small town in Ontario, just a few hours' drive north of Toronto. Until Grade 6, I went to a local, rural public elementary school; during these years I was very aware that I was one of a few Catholic kids in the school and certainly the only kid I knew besides my own brothers and sisters whose parents were obsessed with abortion. I mean, they really hated abortion and really loved unborn foetuses and took us kids to all kinds of rallies. Our house was full of anti-abortion pamphlets, information packages and fund-raising swag. They held meetings. I read all of the materials, heard all of the speeches and memorised the gory details. I knew about suction abortions and saline abortions and D&Cs. I knew about a heartbeat at ten weeks or twelve weeks, and how big the feet were again at such-and-such week. But it was wasted learning. No one in my peer group cared a bit about abortion.

In the mid-1980s, our parents transferred us to the Catholic school, an hour-long bus ride away.* At first, I thought that perhaps in a Catholic school there would be kids like me with parents like mine and I expected abort-

* In 1984, Catholic schools became fully funded by the Province of Ontario.

73

ion would be something we'd talk about *all the time* and I was looking forward to it. Abortion was the thing I knew most about in the world and I was ready to be an expert. I was disappointed to discover that, even in Catholic School, none of the other kids wanted to talk about abortion unless a person was lucky enough to know someone whose older sister had had one. (This happened to me twice, and let me tell you, it was thrilling. I had so much specialised knowledge to share.) But I was still the only kid in my class for whom abortion was the only current event worth knowing about. At home, when we watched the news, it was to follow the Real Crime story of abortion clinic celebrity murderer Dr Henry Morgentaler. We even knew people who were in jail for various crimes against abortion, and sometimes there would be stories on TV about them, the heroes of the day.[†] We were the only family I knew for whom the primary destination in The City (Toronto) was the Morgentaler abortion clinic on Harbord Street. No Eaton Centre or *Cats* at the Elgin Theatre for us. Our big city family activity was meeting up with our parents' friends, and slowly walking back and forth on the sidewalk, carrying mangled foetus signs and singing church songs. From time to time someone would get carried away by the activist spirit and try to storm the door, or chain themselves to the door, or start yelling and charge the doctors and nurses or the people going in to get abortions. And sometimes there were large marches of thousands of adults and child-

[†] In 1983, Morgentaler opened an abortion clinic on Harbord Street in Toronto; until 1988 when he won *R v. Morgentaler* (his second constitutional challenge of Canada's federal abortion laws), this clinic operated illegally. From 1969 to 1988 federal abortion laws dictated that abortions could be performed only when a committee of doctors agreed that continuing the pregnancy would put the woman's life or health at risk. Even after 1988 the clinic remained an anti-choice protest destination; it was firebombed in 1992.

ren, which started at the Ontario Legislature, Queen's Park, and snaked around downtown Toronto. By the time I was a teenager, I was familiar with the route. At least once I coaxed some other teenagers into a speed-marching-while-carrying-a-mangled-foetus-sign race. Who cares that I was wearing a pink-cotton, drop-waisted, ankle-length sundress that I sewed myself? I won that march. But mostly our Toronto time was spent walking back and forth on a sidewalk to the tune of 'Peace Is Flowing Like a River.'

Unsurprisingly, perhaps, it was while slowly walking back and forth in front of the Harbord Street clinic that I saw lesbian feminists for the first time. This was early on, when I was somewhere around six or eight maybe. The lesbian feminists were marching on the other side of the street, in what I now know is called a counter-protest. They were carrying NO WIRE HANGERS signs. I learned much later that this was a motif borrowed from the famous scene in *Mommie Dearest* (1981). There were dozens or even hundreds of them, *all of those women together*, and I couldn't take my eyes off of them. They took my breath away. After that first time, I spent every hour of every day fantasising about them and hoping I would see them again. I looked forward to the next trip to Toronto and was always on the lookout for them. I imagined everything about them: how they all knew each other, what kind of food they ate, where they bought their clothes, where they got their hair cut, what their houses looked like and that perhaps they even lived together in *apartments*. I loved the idea of living in an apartment, I loved these women and I loved abortion for bringing them to me.

I guess I was eleven or so when the film *The Silent Scream* (1984) was released and began to make its way around the anti-abortion venue circuit of high schools, community centres and church basements, screened for the purpose of scaring teenagers and swaying popular opinion in the years leading up to the big Supreme Court abortion case in Canada. For some time, and I am not sure how long, my parents toured The Silent Scream and would leave our house in the evenings to give a screening (a screaming) and, I suppose, to lead a post-screening (post-screaming?) discussion. I'm sure I've seen The Silent Scream, probably projected onto our living room wall, but the only memories I have are of the voice of the narrator, the great anti-abortionist Barnard Nathanson, at once alarmist and patronising. I have a foggy memory that, a few years later, The Silent Scream may have been shown in my Grade 8 Catholic School sex-ed class, and that when I heard the rumour that this was going to happen, I casually bragged, 'Oh, I've already seen it.'

But I have earlier, vivid memories of the existence of the film because it opened a magical window for me – the window into babysitters. I don't know how often my parents screened this film. In my mind, it went on for months, or even years. Most keenly, I remember feeling with certainty and pride that they were doing something far more impressive and professional than usual: in the early evening, they both got dressed up in smart clothes for these nights out and practised their speeches. Watching them get ready to go out gave me a warm feeling of middle-class comfort, like this is what it would be like to have parents with money and education, with careers. I had always been ashamed of our family – the fact that we had very little money and that my mom stayed home. I desperately wanted her to stop having babies and to go back to school or at least to get a job. On Silent Scream nights, not only did my parents leave the house looking classy, they also hired babysitters to look after us. This was, without a doubt, the highlight of my childhood. It's likely that it was mostly older ladies from the church who would stay with

us, but I've grafted a better memory. I'm sure there were at
least a few *Silent Scream* nights in which we got an actual
teenage girl babysitter. I know it's not unusual for pre-teen
queers to fall in love with the gum-chewing volatility of
their babysitters. But how many of you can say that you
experienced the hot bliss of your first lez crushes while
your parents were out showing what is perhaps the most
obscene anti-abortion horror film of all time?

While I feel sorry for all the people who sat through
those screenings, all I care to remember are those hair-
sprayed and frosted goddesses sitting on our couch eating
chips and letting me stay up late as long as I had my pyjamas
on. Is it possible that their boyfriends came over? Did they
talk on the phone? Whatever did they say to me? I don't
remember any of these details. All I remember is that I was
ecstatic with their proximity – that they were in my house
and that their jeans were skin tight. These girls were in
high school and I loved them. They were magical creatures
of glossy disdain, and abortion brought them to me.

The years following the *Silent Scream* babysitter window
passed in a haze of misery. The only exception was a few
months of 1987, when I won several regional public
speaking competitions for my speech 'The Life of an Unborn Child'. It was written and performed from the point
of view of a cheerful foetus who does not get aborted.
With this public speaking success under my belt, I raked in
enough award money to buy myself a peach and white
floral knock-off Laura Ashley dress for Grade 8 graduation.
Once again, abortion was good to me.

Later that same year I turned thirteen and got a job as a
chambermaid and waitress at a nearby summer resort. I
was by far the youngest person working there. I forged an
exciting life for myself – arriving home by my curfew but
then sneaking out of my bedroom window to sprint back

to the party in the staff cabin. I made new friends. I found
alcohol and cigarettes. I could not believe my luck. If you
have ever had the good fortune to be the youngest person
in the secret world of small-town under-age party life, you
might appreciate how it felt like I was doing everything
right when, later that year, the movie Dirty Dancing (1987)
came out, and affirmed all of my life choices. Just as a reminder: Dirty Dancing is a sexy movie set in the staff cabin
of a summer resort, with an abortion at its narrative centre.
It would be impossible to overstate the importance of Dirty
Dancing for me. It truly was the most vital and happiest
thing in my life for years. Like everyone, I had the
soundtrack on cassette, and I listened to it millions of
times, dreaming of adversity and forbidden romance.
Come the summer of 1988, I was back working at the resort and we dirty danced our way through every night.
Grinding is still actually the only way I know how to dance.
Let's think about Dirty Dancing as an abortion movie. In the
opening scene, we learn that Baby is on vacation at a resort
with her educated, stylish parents and her clueless, vain
sister. Right away on the first night, Baby escapes the resort's boring scheduled guest activities and discovers the
staff cabin and the dirty dancing. That scene of discovery,
when the doors burst open and everyone is just all over
each other; it's what I had always hoped people would do,
if given the chance. But Baby is humiliatingly square –
she's easily shocked and bad at moving her hips. However,
very soon after this humiliation, the luckiest thing happens to Baby: she finds Penny crying in a heap and learns
that she needs an abortion but that it's impossible because
it can only happen on a night when Johnny and Penny
have a dancing gig at another resort and no one else can fill
in for her because everyone else has to work. But Baby can
do it because *she doesn't have to work*! Do you remember the

dance lesson scenes in the studio with Penny and Baby? Penny's bodysuit. Baby's knotted T-shirt and leotard. All of that steamy femme-on-femme screen time. Brought to us by abortion. The next fabulous thing to happen to Baby is that Penny's abortion goes *all wrong* and Baby has to be very brave and get her doctor father to come to help to save Penny's life. And then, as a reward for being so brave, Baby gets to lose her virginity! As it has been for me, abortion was so lucky for Baby. By the time I got to university, I upgraded my love-affair with abortion. In frosh week, I learned that a girl could ask for the morning-after pill in Student Health Services and I could not get my hands on it soon enough. My whole first year, I did nothing but take the morning-after pill. I was hooked on the smallest of abortions. I don't know if I was ever even pregnant, but I craved that crampy, decisive discharge for its own sake. While everyone else was into beer and hash, I was into vodka and morning-after pills. My addiction to the morning-after pill lasted only as long as my brief experiment in heterosexuality, and I am grateful to that period of my life for all of those sweet little abortions.

The morning-after pill was my gateway drug to becoming a lesbian, among other things. I am the cautionary tale. It's what patriarchal anti-abortionism (I know, they mean the same thing) has always feared: that if women could have abortions, they might not need men at all. The cultivation of heritage patriarchy – which keeps the old seeds alive, growing those ideas over and over again, year after year – produces a perverse fruit: a genetic obsession with outlawing queers and abortion. And, indeed, queers and abortions, we are the same thing. Living in a family that taught me to hate queers as much as abortion, I needed to become an abortion before I could become a queer. I imagined myself *never having been born, never having existed*, in order to make a life full of queer impossibilities. This is a little bit like what happens with my favourite abortion crush of all time, the flaky and ambitious Sally Bowles (famously played by Liza Minnelli) in *Cabaret* (1972). Released just a year before *Roe v. Wade* in the United States, *Cabaret* uses abortion procedurally, as a way to keep the movie interesting, innovative, both future-oriented and complicit. Narratively, it allows Sally to keep on living an unexpected life. Unlike *Dirty Dancing*, abortion doesn't drive the plot in *Cabaret*. Instead of screening abortion, *Cabaret* off-screens abortion. After a decadent and drawn-out three-way affair, Sally finds out she is pregnant. Instead of moving back to England with her gay boyfriend, Brian, to live out her days in a dinky little cottage in Cambridge with a playpen in the bedroom and diapers on the towel rack and a life of hating each other, she trades in her prized fur coat for an abortion. The abortion happens offstage and is marked only by Sally arriving back to the apartment without her fur.

As she walks away from Brian, Sally is thinking ahead to her next audition. Choosing to stay in Weimar-era Berlin with Nazism on the rise, Sally is thinking only of her own momentum. Without looking back, she gives a backwards wave, and flashes her shocking green fingernails one last time, saying, It may not amount to anything, but you never know. This line offers the gift of uncertainty, of Sally's tentative, capricious, immoral, and possibly reprehensible future. This is an abortion in pursuit of a future of stupid decisions, mistakes, risks, failures, great loss, and potential. There are many kinds of girls in this world and Sally Bowles is one of those kinds; for girls like me who identify with Sally – her desperation, her big dreams, her hustle – there's never been a better abortion.

'But then I wouldn't be here'
Denise Riley
(2005)

What kind of utterance is it that declares, I have the breath to make this noise only because your sort failed to stop me from ever drawing breath in the first place?

Such an assertion, springing from the very state of being alive, sounds irresistible when uttered in such a tone that to query it would mean wishing for its speaker's death. The clinching announcement by someone on an anti-abortion platform is that she herself would have been aborted (rather than adopted or fostered as she was) had a liberal law obtained at the period of her own conception. Her argument, issuing from the perverse privilege of a hypothetical almost-death, runs: 'If abortion had been readily come by then, as you want it to remain now, then I would not have lived to challenge you today.' In this vein, too, a speaker defending the rights of the disabled might point out that had prenatal diagnostic screening existed when her own mother was pregnant, she would never have been able to bear witness as a survivor of spina bifida. That's a different line of argument from reporting that the experience of living with a particular disability is far less debilitating than it looks from the outside and concluding that economic considerations, justified by claims about the sufferings of the disabled, shouldn't dictate abortion policy. Instead, those declarations founded on the sheer condition of being alive run, 'The law you propose in the name of choice, but which is effectively eugenics, would have seen to it that I was destroyed after conception. Disagree with me, and you want me dead. Or at least you want to erase me in retrospect; you want me never to have lived.' To which the usual response from those seated elsewhere on the platform is a politely murmured, 'I'm sure we're all very grateful that you are here with us today!' For the charge 'You lot really want me dead!' is more of a discharge from a verbal blunderbuss which knocks out its opponent – unless she is icy enough to reply, 'Quite right, I do.' Yet who would walk, eyes wide open, into this set trap and then retort to the trapper's astonished injured face, 'Actually yes, you'd have been aborted under any decently liberal law, had your mother so decided; and so what?' Knowing the implausibility of this cruel exchange, the formulaic 'I'd not be here now if you'd had your way!' rests on its power to stifle such a reply. Such linguistic domination, though, will exert its own strains on itself, and despite its public effectiveness. Unassailable speech must be always readying itself against the permanent threat of approaching assailants. Its rhetoric is also a make of character armour, which does have its advantages; except that to go around clanking in a burnished carapace is terribly hot and burdensome for the armoured ones.

There's humour in the not quite dead. Freud's 1905 paper on 'Jokes and Their Relation to the Unconscious' clipped this out of a satirical weekly: 'Never to be born would be the best thing for mortal men. But, adds the philosophical comment in Die Fliegenden Blätter, this happens to scarcely one person in a hundred thousand.' The witticism aims straight at the heart of any fantasied not-being. But it would surely wither under the stern rejoinder of the one imagining herself in retrospect as the never-born, the eliminated victim of social eugenics. Here a decorum of who speaks stifles any comment on the mode or style of what's said. If there is a moral authority of suffering, as often asserted, this can readily become an authoritarianism of suffering. Fiercely imperative, it knows: we have endured, so you will listen to us. It holds out the gravitas of speaking out of a lived position: the bodily situated demonstration whose power is its very standing as utterance on the lips of the ontologically qualified utterer. This conviction of entitlement to authoritative speaking is underscored by a strong sense of propriety. Rightful speech, it's implied or stated, dwells in the mouths of the afflicted only. And this dictates the admissibility of what's articulated. So, as many hold today about the word n———, it's permissible to use it only if you are it. Others, though, are adamant that no black speaker should ever say it; the word is too historically disgraced, too demeaning, too grotesquely racist to sully any mouth, however teasingly companionable the user's intent. But in this instance there's at least an animated public debate; whereas in the case of abortion legislation, the asserted moral authority emerging from the 'experience' of nearly being not alive rests on an unchallenged propriety which dampens dissent. The forceful appeal it makes from its supposedly fragile anchorage in this world can obscure any disagreement by others in the same boat. It allows scant room for similarly placed speakers to moderate that ringing 'speaking as a . . ., I know,' especially when the '. . .' represents a near abortion which was converted into the pure triumph of being. A modern decorum of utterance rules, in a delicate marriage of linguistic terrorism and etiquette. And by implication everyone who was more or less satisfactorily adopted must, just by virtue of their early history, share this common and illiberal opinion; yet evidently they do not. Nor do you hear it said by people miserably brought up in a children's home. Yet 'But I wouldn't be here now' is so arm-twisting a formulaic utterance that it subdues other private circumstances and conclusions. Were these heard, there'd be a permanent skirmish between contradictory stances, each based on differing personal experiences. For example, equally pitched at the claim from experience is that objection which tries to shake open the dominant form: 'Well, I'm adopted too, but that doesn't mean that I'm anti-abortion, or that I wanted my mother to have lived under such a restricted law that she had to go through the misery of having me in secret, handing me over to a children's home then going on with her life as if nothing had happened.' And, whatever the vexation for me of having to issue such a testimonial, it's only this kind of counter-witnessing from the ambivalent viewpoint of the insider which can crack the monolith of the deduction that all those who were once theoretically at risk of being aborted must axiomatically be opposed to a liberal abortion law.

But it's a hard task. By invoking the threatened extinction of their very lives, the negative privilege of the spokespersons for the near-aborted claims an unanswerability. These speakers' statements of their own retrospective vulnerability seems itself to be invulnerable. Yet from the standpoint of where it leads the argument, it isn't. The trajectory of this appeal to the condition of being alive isn't infallibly conservative, for 'But they wouldn't be here today if you lot had had your way!' is also occasionally proclaimed from the side of liberalism. Here 'they' refers instead to those existing children who were only born thanks to in vitro fertilisation technology, while the 'you lot' refers to those opposed to the process because it entails discarding some embryos along the way. Or if one were to deploy the same logic as that of someone objecting that she herself would have been aborted under any liberal law, there's an obvious reply: 'But then you wouldn't ever have been conscious to realise the fact of your own early destruction.' This, though, is far too cool an observation for that smouldering terrain of feeling where the '*you lot want me dead*' is pitched.

It's here that today's liberalism runs into difficulties. For the recording and listing of hurt have long been prominent in the linguistic armoury of bitterly recalled experiences: of the concentration camps, of diaspora, of poverty, of racist violence, of sexual hatred. And described experience has undeniably formed an effective polemic for many liberation movements, including feminism. So it's especially disconcerting for that strain of feminism which has itself drawn on the impassioned gravity of the 'I feel' to have to register an equally ardent 'I feel' from among the anti-abortion adopted, women and men determined to record their feelings of relief at being alive at all. For now the limits of the appeal to personal sensibilities as a ground for a liberal politics are suddenly and acutely in sight.

It is at the sharpest and thinnest point of the evidence drawn from the witnessing self – the point of this self's imagined near-vanishing from life at the abortionist's hands – that a listener can start to wonder whether too great a claim of entitlement consequent on the personal has been fed in. 'But then I wouldn't have lived' becomes a variant of that excessively personalised strain of questioning; the why me genre, such as 'Why do I have this incurable illness?' Or, to take a narrower example, the differently exaggerated personalising of those badges and T-shirts

85

which used to confront all eyes with 'How Dare You Assume I'm Heterosexual.' This slogan's drawback, formidable a provocation as it was, was its attribution to others of
their constant calculation about, and keenly interested
judging of, its utterer's sexual disposition. But to glimpse
such badges incited privately indignant or anxious rebut-
tals of 'I didn't assume . . .' Were you forcibly hailed by this
question on the lapel of the person sitting opposite you,
one silent reaction was 'But why should you so crossly
assume that I'm the proper target of your sense of offence,
that I'm remotely concerned with you and your sexuality,
or that everyone, whatever their own sexual inclination, is
busily assessing you – and then, worse, why should you
dare, as you say, to assume that I'm heterosexual myself,
anyway?' Another possible response to the brandished 'How
Dare You Assume I'm Heterosexual' was simply pragmatic:
'I assume it, only because statistically it's a reasonable as-
sumption; and this doesn't imply any antagonism on my
part towards homosexuality.' Whereas the decidedly an-
ti-erotic nagging of the slogan itself was no advertisement
for queer joy. Still, all onlookers realised that the badges'
point was to make explicit a broad social presumption in
favour of heterosexuality, rather than to take focused aim at
any individual opponent. Nevertheless, the very syntax of
'How Dare You Assume' did point its finger, if indiscrim-
inately, at each and any onlooker. So this pseudo-personal
accusation couldn't do otherwise than incite a myriad of
efforts at personal exculpation. The ironic upshot was that
its reliance on addressing individuals fetched up, not in
rendering the personal political, but instead in provok-
ing clusters of always personal but hidden rejoinders. In
this manner the sought-for critical erosion of the public-
private distinction instead ends up with a carping and
secretive defensiveness.

To return, though, to the case at hand: as I said, it's often taken as read that, having escaped elimination yourself, your escapee status entails that you must vigorously denounce abortion. It doesn't. Nor does it mean that I must be deemed 'self-hating' when I campaign for abortion rights. (Here, having just complained about the I tyranny, I am resorting to it, although in the minor key of not-I.) In a reworking of Kantian altruism, Wendy Brown in her 1995 book *States of Injury* proposes an idea of enlarging what one was born towards what one hopes for others: 'I want this for us.' This stance requires imaginative unselfishness; where that's lacking, then far too much of the personal, understood as gain, is fed into the argument. But 'I want this for us' could mean not 'I want all the potentially aborted ones, as I'd have been, to be preserved by means of a more restrictive abortion law' but instead 'I want other women to have the same freedom of choice under the law as I now have. And I don't want my own existence to be used to reinforce a claim which would burden existing lives.' For I'm not compelled to make a universal stance out of just one aspect of my own history, the accident of my unwanted conception, magnifying it until it overwhelms all other considerations.

Yet 'so you wish me dead!' does rest on an excess of self-reference, perhaps born of horror at the realisation that you'd have been discarded as grossly substandard had the technology existed to run a quality control on you before your delivery. Still, everyone's grip on life is, in some way, tenuous. Admittedly this common sense of our frail adherence to the surface of this world carries a very different resonance from that of specifically being a candidate for abortion due to disability screening as a national policy. But to pursue, for the moment, just the broader uncertainties: few people can be sure of having been un-ambivalently wanted by even one of their parents, while many realise or have good reason to suspect that they weren't. Yet surely such initial 'wantedness' is over-blown as a requirement for leading a life. That slogan of 'every child a wanted child,' which once rang out on 1970s pro-abortion marches, is as pious a eugenic sentiment as ever crossed the lips of a well-meaning but sheltered feminism. Not because of the burden of being terribly wanted and its cloying expectations – but because your subsequent life is not exhaustively determined by your initial desirability in the eyes of your progenitors. No doubt the conviction of having been wanted must be reassuring, especially in a modern setting thick with faith in the virtues (which lie so close to the old vanities) of self-esteem. But it's a conviction hardly essential to living and its inescapable trains of fortune and accident. You can be perfectly aware that to your mother, your conception came as a sickening blow, that your father angrily denied paternity and left for good, that inept amateur attempts to abort you were tried: still, you find yourself stoutly in the here and now. And despite that private history of yours, you can still regret that abortion had been so hard to get in the past, even though its earlier availability would have guaranteed your own extirpation. You don't have to let a phantasm of your own infancy dictate your espoused cause; instead you can prefer to preserve the present relatively liberal law. Not, though, because of your own death wish, although some will be quick to swear to you that this is the real reason lying below your apparent liberalism. But because you can, coherently, want advantages for others that you personally would not have profited from, or indeed would have died under.

The murderousness summoned up in my imagination by a reiterated 'Had easier abortion choices existed in

those days, then I wouldn't have lived' is really presuppos-
ing a choice made by my actual parent when faced with
the charming reality of me – as distinct from the plainer
scenario of an impersonal decision made by my potential
parent to abort. This retrospective dread of the killer mother
could and does hit many. We might all, the officially wanted and the illegitimate unwanted alike, cry out on occasion to our parents that they'd rather we hadn't been born.
This may be all too true. (Certainly it's likely to become
true for the duration of the moment that the parent hears
that irritatingly self-regarding plaint.) From the maternal
standpoint, your child may well have been no sought-after
conception, but an oversight, a lapse, or the outcome of a
merely halfhearted gesture at contraception; the decision
to continue with the pregnancy may have been hard won,
a slow resignation after the event, while pleasure in the
child's existence may come late, if at all; some may always
view its being with an inwardly cold eye; then the once
intensely-wanted child may disappoint, if its mother's
roseate imaginings are shattered by its presence. To such
common hazards of frank unwelcomeness, or the ordinary
ambiguities of wantedness, can be added the very long
odds against anyone's managing to exist at all. An endless
string of accidents has preceded any birth – which I'll see
if I envisage the contingency of, say, my great-great-grand-
mother's birth and her own lack of success subsequently
in preventing the conception of my great-grandfather,
and then I multiply that kind of chance a millionfold to
cover my own arrival. The world rustles with spirit ad-
herents who never made it, the lost prospective souls of
miscarriages, the near misses of unfrozen deselected embryos, discarded hopes. True that no such reminders of the
wholly arbitrary nature of any life at all would assuage the
misery of someone haunted by the prospect of her own

non-life, deliberately sought. But then there's advantage in taking that historical fact of your unwantedness hard on the nose – yet not staggering backwards bleeding heavily from the impact. For if you ought 'by rights' not to have made it into this world at all, yet you did so by a hair's breadth, then it's all the more quietly exhilarating to find yourself, against the odds, solidly alive. Yet at the same time, your full enjoyment of your own narrow squeak of an achieved life will arguably include your wish for others' liberty to enjoy theirs. And this wish for others runs more ways than one; it does not dictate which side you must fall on or whose liberty you must conjure. By no means must it automatically propel you to the defence of the imagined unborn.

The linguistic showstopper of 'But under your liberal abortion law, I wouldn't have existed' falls like a lead weight upon any exchange. It could only be bumped back into life (ultimately this will be the animation of comedy) if someone else who is similarly ontologically challenged also raises the retort 'Nor would I – and so?' The fact that your loyalties aren't, in fact, pre-assigned by the nature of your conception makes for a likely dash into infantile combat with others who will all too confidently speak for you. The old war of 'We are!' versus 'Well, I'm not!' starts up. Mutual sniping has its field day. The liberal dissenter who announces, 'Just because I'm adopted myself doesn't mean I'm going to join in with this anti-abortion line' can sound foot-stamping, naively egotistical in her renunciation. But this is because she's been forced to throw her own intensely personal claim against the universalised personal claim of 'Your pro-choice law would have destroyed all possibility of our existence.' Her seemingly idiosyncratic assertiveness in declaring that she, for one, wouldn't have wanted to live at the cost of the immiseration of her mother's generation is the only recourse she has, even while through it she ends up apparently willing her own destruction. Imagined orders of death clash here. To counter those who repudiate readily obtainable abortion on the grounds that the murder of their own unwanted kind would follow, she lays tacit claim instead to shelter other women, reluctantly pregnant, through her own imagined pre-birth noble suicide.

Yet her (my) stance is also latently humorous. Not because of its altruistic impulse, shot through though it may be with self-aggrandisement. But because an argument intended to contest the claimed sovereignty of experience of life has ended up by asserting the preferability of having no experience at all: 'Well, speaking for myself, I'd rather never have been born at such a cost to others . . .' Once uttered, this stance deflates itself. Straight towards comedy is where all aspects of the claim from being alive must logically and inexorably go. If the anti-abortionist sobs, keeping one eye open to gauge the effect of her rhetoric, 'But you'd have killed me!' then the pro-abortionist declares, 'Let me have died for you!' There's a fine example in the script of the 1979 movie, Monty Python's Life of Brian, of an apparent act of self-abnegation which has actually been dictated by the relentless grammar of its surroundings. It comes at a point when a crowd of followers are flocking after their putative messiah and saviour in the reluctant shape of Brian, who's exasperated by their subservient zeal:

> Brian: Look, you've got it all wrong! You don't need to follow me! You don't need to follow anybody! You've got to think for yourselves! You're all individuals!
> Crowd: Yes, we're all individuals!
> Brian: You're all different!
> Crowd: Yes, we are all different!
> Homogenous Man [in crowd]: I'm not.

A Defence of Abortion
Judith Jarvis Thomson
(1971)

Most opposition to abortion relies on the premise that the foetus is a human being, a person, from the moment of conception. The premise is argued for, but, as I think, not well. Take, for example, the most common argument. We are asked to notice that the development of a human being from conception through birth into child-hood is continuous; then it is said that to draw a line, to choose a point in this development and say 'before this point the thing is not a person, after this point it is a person' is to make an arbitrary choice, a choice for which in the nature of things no good reason can be given. It is concluded that the foetus is, or anyway that we had better say it is, a person from the moment of conception. But this conclusion does not follow. Similar things might be said about the development of an acorn into an oak trees, and it does not follow that acorns are oak trees, or that we had better say they are. Arguments of this form are sometimes called 'slippery slope arguments' – the phrase is perhaps self-explanatory – and it is dismaying that opponents of abortion rely on them so heavily and uncritically.

I am inclined to agree, however, that the prospects for 'drawing a line' in the development of the foetus look dim. I am inclined to think also that we shall probably have to agree that the foetus has already become a human person well before birth. Indeed, it comes as a surprise when one first learns how early in its life it begins to acquire human characteristics. By the tenth week, for example, it already has a face, arms and less, fingers and toes; it has internal organs, and brain activity is detectable. On the other hand, I think that the premise is false, that the foetus is not a person from the moment of conception. A newly fertilised ovum, a newly implanted clump of cells, is no more a person than an acorn is an oak tree. But I shall not discuss any of this. For it seems to me to be of great interest to ask what happens if, for the sake of argument, we allow the premise. How, precisely, are we supposed to get from there to the conclusion that abortion is morally impermissible? Opponents of abortion commonly spend most of their time establishing that the foetus is a person, and hardly any time explaining the step from there to the impermissibility of abortion. Perhaps they think the step too simple and obvious to require much comment. Or perhaps instead they are simply being economical in argument. Many of those who defend abortion rely on the premise that the foetus is not a person, but only a bit of tissue that will become a person at birth; and why pay out more arguments than you have to? Whatever the explanation, I suggest that the step they take is neither easy nor obvious, that it calls for closer examination than it is commonly given, and that when we do give it this closer examination we shall feel inclined to reject it.

I propose, then, that we grant that the foetus is a person from the moment of conception. How does the argument go from here? Something like this, I take it. Every person has a right to life. So the foetus has a right to life. No doubt the mother has a right to decide what shall happen in and to her body; everyone would grant that. But surely a person's right to life is stronger and more stringent than the mother's right to decide what happens in and to her body, and so outweighs it. So the foetus may not be killed; an abortion may not be performed.

It sounds plausible. But now let me ask you to imagine this. You wake up in the morning and find yourself back to back in bed with an unconscious violinist. A famous unconscious violinist. He has been found to have a fatal kidney ailment, and the Society of Music Lovers has canvassed all the available medical records and found that you alone have the right blood type to help. They have therefore kidnapped you, and last night the violinist's circulatory system was plugged into yours, so that your kidneys can be used to extract poisons from his blood as well as your own. The director of the hospital now tells you, 'Look, we're sorry the Society of Music Lovers did this to you – we would never have permitted it if we had known. But still, they did it, and the violinist is now plugged into you. To unplug you would be to kill him. But never mind, it's only for nine months. By then he will have recovered from his ailment, and can safely be unplugged from you.' Is it morally incumbent on you to accede to this situation? No doubt it would be very nice of you if you did, a great kindness. But do you have to accede to it? What if it were not nine months, but nine years? Or longer still? What if the director of the hospital says, 'Tough luck, I agree, but now you've got to stay in bed, with the violinist plugged into you, for the rest of your life. Because remember this. All persons have a right to life, and violinists are persons. Granted you have a right to decide what happens in and to your body, but a person's right to life outweighs your right to decide what happens in and to your body. So you cannot ever be unplugged from him.' I imagine you would regard this as outrageous, which suggests that something really is wrong with that plausible-sounding argument I mentioned a moment ago.

In this case, of course, you were kidnapped, you didn't volunteer for the operation that plugged the violinist into your kidneys. Can those who oppose abortion on the ground I mentioned make an exception for a pregnancy due to rape? Certainly. They can say that persons have a right to life only if they didn't come into existence because of rape; or they can say that all persons have a right to life, but that some have less of a right to life than others, in particular, that those who came into existence because of rape have less. But these statements have a rather unpleasant sound. Surely the question of whether you have a right to life at all, or how much of it you have, shouldn't turn on the question of whether or not you are a product of a rape. And in fact the people who oppose abortion on the ground I mentioned do not make this distinction, and hence do not make an exception in case of rape.

Nor do they make an exception for a case in which the mother has to spend the nine months of her pregnancy in bed. They would agree that would be a great pity, and hard on the mother; but all the same, all persons have a right to life, the foetus is a person, and so on. I suspect, in fact, that they would not make an exception for a case in which, miraculously enough, the pregnancy went on for nine years, or even the rest of the mother's life.

Some won't even make an exception for a case in which continuation of the pregnancy is likely to shorten the mother's life, they regard abortion as impermissible even to save the mother's life. Such cases are nowadays very rare, and many opponents of abortion do not accept this extreme view. All the same, it is a good place to begin: a number of points of interest come out in respect to it.

1. Let us call the view that abortion is impermissible even to save the mother's life 'the extreme view'. I want to suggest first that it does not issue from the argument I mentioned earlier without the addition of some fairly powerful premises. Suppose a woman has become pregnant, and now learns that she has a cardiac condition such that she will die if she carries the baby to term. What may be done for her? The foetus, being to life, but as the mother is a person too, so has she a right to life. Presumably they have an equal right to life. How is it supposed to come out that an abortion may not be performed? If mother and child have an equal right to life, shouldn't we perhaps flip a coin? Or should we add to the mother's right to life her right to decide what happens in and to her body, which everybody seems to be ready to grant – the sum of her rights now outweighing the foetus's right to life?

The most familiar argument here is the following. We are told that performing the abortion would be directly killing the child, whereas doing nothing would not be killing the mother, but only letting her die. Moreover, in killing the child, one would be killing an innocent person, for the child has committed no crime, and is not aiming at his mother's death. And then there are a variety of ways in which this might be continued. (1) But as directly killing an innocent person is always and absolutely impermissible, an abortion may not be performed. Or, (2) as directly killing an innocent person is murder, and murder is always and absolutely impermissible, an abortion may not be performed. Or, (3) as one's duty to refrain from directly killing an innocent person is more stringent than one's duty to keep a person from dying, an abortion may not be performed. Or, (4) if one's only options are directly killing an innocent person or letting a person die, one must prefer

97

letting the person die, and thus an abortion may not be performed.

Some people seem to have thought that these are not further premises which must be added if the conclusion is to be reached, but that they follow from the very fact that an innocent person has a right to life. But this seems to me to be a mistake, and perhaps the simplest way to show this is to bring out that while we must certainly grant that innocent persons have a right to life, the theses in (1) through (4) are all false. Take (2), for example. If directly killing an innocent person is murder, and thus is impermissible, then the mother's directly killing the innocent person inside her is murder, and thus is impermissible. But it cannot seriously be thought to be murder if the mother performs an abortion on herself to save her life. It cannot seriously be said that she must refrain, that she must sit passively by and wait for her death. Let us look again at the case of you and the violinist: There you are, in bed with the violinist, and the director of the hospital says to you, 'It's all most distressing, and I deeply sympathise, but you see this is putting an additional strain on your kidneys, and you'll be dead within the month. But you have to stay where you are all the same. Because unplugging you would be directly killing an innocent violinist, and that's murder, and that's impermissible.' If anything in the world is true, it is that you do not commit murder, you do not do what is impermissible, if you reach around to your back and unplug yourself from that violinist to save your life.

The main focus of attention in writings on abortion has been on what a third party may or may not do in answer to a request from a woman for an abortion. This is in a way understandable. Things being as they are, there isn't much a woman can safely do to abort herself. So the question asked is what a third party may do, and what the mother may do, if it is mentioned at all, if deduced, almost as an afterthought, from what it is concluded that third parties may do. But it seems to me that to treat the matter in this way is to refuse to grant to the mother that very status of person which is so firmly insisted on for the foetus. For we cannot simply read off what a person may do from what a third party may do. Suppose you find yourself trapped in a tiny house with a growing child. I mean a very tiny house, and a rapidly growing child – you are already up against the wall of the house and in a few minutes you'll be crushed to death. The child on the other hand won't be crushed to death; if nothing is done to stop him from growing he'll be hurt, but in the end he'll simply burst open the house and walk out a free man. Now I could well understand it if a bystander were to say: 'There's nothing we can do for you. We cannot choose between your life and his, we cannot be the ones to decide who is to live, we cannot intervene.' But it cannot be concluded that you too can do nothing, that you cannot attack it to save your life. However innocent the child may be, you do not have to wait passively while it crushes you to death. Perhaps a pregnant woman is vaguely felt to have the status of house, to which we don't allow the right of self-defence. But if the woman houses the child, it should be remembered that she is a person who houses it.

I should perhaps stop to say explicitly that I am not claiming that people have a right to do anything whatsoever to save their lives. I think, rather, that there are drastic limits to the right of self-defence. If someone threatens you with death unless you torture someone else to death, I think you have not the right, even to save your life, to do so. But the case under consideration here is very different. In our case there are only two people involved, one whose life is threatened, and one who threatens it. Both are innocent: the one who is threatened is not threatened because of any fault, the one who threatens does not threaten because of any fault. For this reason we may feel that we bystanders cannot interfere. But the person threatened can.

In sum, a woman surely can defend her life against the threat to it posed by the unborn child, even if doing so involves its death. And this shows not merely that the theses in (1) through (4) are false; it shows also that the extreme view of abortion is false, and so we need not canvas any other possible ways of arriving at it from the argument I mentioned at the outset.

2. The extreme view could of course be weakened to say that while abortion is permissible to save the mother's life, it may not be performed by a third party, but only by the mother herself. But this cannot be right either. For what we have to keep in mind is that the mother and the unborn child are not like two tenants in a small house which has, by an unfortunate mistake, been rented to both: the mother owns the house. The fact that she does adds to the offensiveness of deducing that the mother can do nothing from the supposition that third parties can do nothing. But it does more than this: it casts a bright light on the supposition that third parties can do nothing. Certainly it lets us see that a third party who says 'I cannot choose between you' is fooling himself if he thinks this is impartiality. If Jones has found and fastened on a certain coat, which he needs to keep him from freezing, but which Smith also needs to keep him from freezing, then it is not impartiality that says 'I cannot choose between you' when Smith owns the coat. Women have said again and again 'This body is my body!' and they have reason to feel angry, reason to feel that it has been like shouting into the wind. Smith, after all, is hardly likely to bless us if we say to him, 'Of course it's your coat, anybody would grant that it is. But no one

may choose between you and Jones who is to have it.'

We should really ask what it is that says 'no one may choose' in the face of the fact that the body that houses the child is the mother's body. It may be simply a failure to appreciate this fact. But it may be something more interesting, namely the sense that one has a right to refuse to lay hands on people, even where it would be just and fair to do so, even where justice seems to require that somebody do so. Thus justice might call for somebody to get Smith's coat back from Jones, and yet you have a right to refuse to be the one to lay hands on Jones, a right to refuse to do physical violence to him. This, I think, must be granted. But then what should be said is not 'no one may choose,' but only 'I cannot choose,' and indeed not even this, but 'I will not act,' leaving it open that somebody else can or should, and in particular that anyone in a position of authority, with the job of securing people's rights, both can and should. So this is no difficulty. I have not been arguing that any given third party must accede to the mother's request that he perform an abortion to save her life, but only that he may.

I suppose that in some views of human life the mother's body is only on loan to her, the loan not being one which gives her any prior claim to it. One who held this view might well think it impartiality to say 'I cannot choose.' But I shall simply ignore this possibility. My own view is that if a human being has any just, prior claim to anything at all, he has a just, prior claim to his own body. And perhaps this needn't be argued for here anyway, since, as I mentioned, the arguments against abortion we are looking at do grant that the woman has a right to decide what happens in and to her body.

But although they do grant it, I have tried to show that they do not take seriously what is done in granting it. I suggest the same thing will reappear even more clearly when we turn away from cases in which the mother's life is at stake, and attend, as I propose we now do, to the vastly more common cases in which a woman wants an abortion for some less weighty reason than preserving her own life.

3. Where the mother's life is not at stake, the argument I mentioned at the outset seems to have a much stronger pull. 'Everyone has a right to life, so the unborn person has a right to life.' And isn't the child's right to life weightier than anything other than the mother's own right to life, which she might put forward as ground for an abortion?

This argument treats the right to life as if it were unproblematic. It is not, and this seems to me to be precisely the source of the mistake.

For we should now, at long last, ask what it comes to, to have a right to life. In some views having a right to life includes having a right to be given at least the bare minimum one needs for continued life. But suppose that what in fact is the bare minimum a man needs for continued life is something he has no right at all to be given? If I am sick unto death, and the only thing that will save my life is the touch of Henry Fonda's cool hand on my fevered brow, then all the same, I have no right to be given the touch of Henry Fonda's cool hand on my fevered brow. It would be frightfully nice of him to fly in from the West Coast to provide it. It would be less nice, though no doubt well meant, if my friends flew out to the West Coast and brought Henry Fonda back with them. But I have no right at all against anybody that he should do this for me. Or again, to return to the story I told earlier, the fact that for continued life the violinist needs the continued use of your kidneys does not establish that he has a right to be given the continued use of your kidneys. He certainly has no right against you that you should give him continued use of your kidneys. For nobody has any right to use your kidneys unless you give him this right – if you do allow him to go on using your kidneys, this is a kindness on your part, and not something he can claim from you as his due. Nor has he any right against anybody else that they should give him continued use of your kidneys. Certainly he had no right against the Society of Music Lovers that they should plug him into you in the first place. And if you now start to unplug yourself, having learned that you will otherwise have to spend nine years in bed with him, there is nobody in the world who must try to prevent you, in order to see to it that he is given something he has a right to be given.

Some people are rather stricter about the right to life. In their view, it does not include the right to be given anything, but amounts to, and only to, the right not to be killed by anybody. But here a related difficulty arises. If everybody is to refrain from killing that violinist, then everybody must refrain from doing a great many different sorts of things. Everybody must refrain from slitting his throat, everybody must refrain from shooting him – and everybody must refrain from unplugging you from him. But does he have a right against everybody that they shall refrain from unplugging you from him? To refrain from doing this is to allow him to continue to use your kidneys. It could be argued that he has a right against us that we should allow him to continue to use your kidneys. That is, while he had no right against us that we should give him the use of your kidneys, it might be argued that he anyway has a right against us that we shall not now intervene and deprive him of the use of your kidneys. I shall come back to third-party interventions later. But certainly the violinist has no right against you that you shall allow him to continue to use your kidneys. As I said, if you do allow him to use them, it is a kindness on your part, and not something you owe him.

The difficulty I point to here is not peculiar to the right of life. It reappears in connection with all the other natural rights, and it is something which an adequate account of rights must deal with. For present purposes it is enough just to draw attention to it. But I would stress that I am not arguing that people do not have a right to life – quite to the contrary, it seems to me that the primary control we must place on the acceptability of an account of rights is that it should turn out in that account to be a truth that all persons have a right to life. I am arguing only that having a right to life does not guarantee having either a right to be given the use of or a right to be allowed continued use of another person's body – even if one needs it for life itself. So the right to life will not serve the opponents of abortion in the very simple and clear way in which they seem to have thought it would.

4. There is another way to bring out the difficulty. In the most ordinary sort of case, to deprive someone of what he has a right to is to treat him unjustly. Suppose a boy and his small brother are jointly given a box of chocolates for Christmas. If the older boy takes the box and refuses to give his brother any of the chocolates, he is unjust to him, for the brother has been given a right to half of them. But suppose that, having learned that otherwise it means nine years in bed with that violinist, you unplug yourself from him. You surely are not being unjust to him, for you gave him no right to use your kidneys, and no one else can have given him any such right. But we have to notice that in unplugging yourself, you are killing him; and violinists, like everybody else, have a right to life, and thus in the view we were considering just now, the right not to be

killed. So here you do what he supposedly has a right you shall not do, but you do not act unjustly to him in doing it.

The emendation which may be made at this point is this: the right to life consists not in the right not to be killed, but rather in the right not to be killed unjustly. This runs a risk of circularity, but never mind: it would enable us to square the fact that the violinist has a right to life with the fact that you do not act unjustly towards him in unplugging yourself, thereby killing him. For if you do not kill him unjustly, you do not violate his right to life, and so it is no wonder you do him no injustice.

But if this emendation is accepted, the gap in the argument against abortion stares us plainly in the face: it is by no means enough to show that the foetus is a person, and to remind us that all persons have a right to life – we need to be shown also that killing the foetus violates its right to life, i.e., that abortion is unjust killing. And is it?

I suppose we may take it as a datum that in a case of pregnancy due to rape the mother has not given the unborn person a right to the use of her body for food and shelter. Indeed, in what pregnancy could it be supposed that the mother has given the unborn person such a right? It is not as if there are unborn persons drifting about the world, to whom a woman who wants a child says 'I invite you in.'

But it might be argued that there are other ways one can have acquired a right to the use of another person's body than by having been invited to use it by that person. Suppose a woman voluntarily indulges in intercourse, knowing of the chance it will issue in pregnancy, and then she does become pregnant; is she not in part responsible for the presence, in fact the very existence, of the unborn person inside? No doubt she did not invite it in. But doesn't her partial responsibility for its being there itself give it a right to the use of her body? If so, then her aborting it would be more like the boys taking away the chocolates, and less like your unplugging yourself from the violinist – doing so would be depriving it of what it does have a right to, and thus would be doing it an injustice.

And then, too, it might be asked whether or not she can kill it even to save her own life: If she voluntarily called it into existence, how can she now kill it, even in self-defence?

The first thing to be said about this is that it is something new. Opponents of abortion have been so concerned to make out the independence of the foetus, in order to establish that it has a right to life, just as its mother does, that they have tended to overlook the possible support they might gain from making out that the foetus is dependent on the mother, in order to establish that she has a special kind of responsibility for it, a responsibility that gives it rights against her which are not possessed by any independent person – such as an ailing violinist who is a stranger to her.

On the other hand, this argument would give the unborn person a right to its mother's body only if her pregnancy resulted from a voluntary act, undertaken in full knowledge of the chance a pregnancy might result from it. It would leave out entirely the unborn person whose existence is due to rape. Pending the availability of some further argument, then, we would be left with the conclusion that unborn persons whose existence is due to rape have no right to the use of their mothers' bodies, and thus that aborting them is not depriving them of anything they have a right to and hence is not unjust killing.

And we should also notice that it is not at all plain that

this argument really does go even as far as it purports to. For there are cases and cases, and the details make a difference. If the room is stuffy, and I therefore open a window to air it, and a burglar climbs in, it would be absurd to say, 'Ah, now he can stay, she's given him a right to the use of her house – for she is partially responsible for his presence there, having voluntarily done what enabled him to get in, in full knowledge that there are such things as burglars, and that burglars burgle.' It would be still more absurd to say this if I had had bars installed outside my windows, precisely to prevent burglars from getting in, and a burglar got in only because of a defect in the bars. It remains equally absurd if we imagine it is not a burglar who climbs in, but an innocent person who blunders or falls in. Again, suppose it were like this: people-seeds drift about in the air like pollen, and if you open your windows, one may drift in and take root in your carpets or upholstery. You don't want children, so you fix up your windows with fine mesh screens, the very best you can buy. As can happen, however, and on very, very rare occasions does happen, one of the screens is defective, and a seed drifts in and takes root. Does the person-plant who now develops have a right to the use of your house? Surely not – despite the fact that you voluntarily opened your windows, you knowingly kept carpets and upholstered furniture, and you knew that screens were sometimes defective. Someone may argue that you are responsible for its rooting, that it does have a right to your house, because after all you could have lived out your life with bare floors and furniture, or with sealed windows and doors. But this won't do – for by the same token anyone can avoid a pregnancy due to rape by having a hysterectomy, or anyway by never leaving home without a (reliable!) army.

It seems to me that the argument we are looking at can

establish at most that there are some cases in which the unborn person has a right to the use of its mother's body, and therefore some cases in which abortion is unjust killing. There is room for much discussion and argument as to precisely which, if any. But I think we should sidestep this issue and leave it open, for at any rate the argument certainly does not establish that all abortion is unjust killing.

5. There is room for yet another argument here, however. We surely must all grant that there may be cases in which it would be morally indecent to detach a person from your body at the cost of his life. Suppose you learn that what the violinist needs is not nine years of your life, but only one hour: all you need to do to save his life is to spend one hour in that bed with him. Suppose also that letting him use your kidneys for that one hour would not affect your health in the slightest. Admittedly you were kidnapped. Admittedly you did not give anyone permission to plug him into you. Nevertheless it seems to me plain you ought to allow him to use your kidneys for that hour – it would be indecent to refuse.

Again, suppose pregnancy lasted only an hour, and constituted no threat to life or health. And suppose that a woman becomes pregnant as a result of rape. Admittedly she did not voluntarily do anything to bring about the existence of a child. Admittedly she did nothing at all which would give the unborn person a right to the use of her body. All the same it might well be said, as in the newly amended violinist story, that she ought to allow it to remain for that hour – that it would be indecent of her to refuse.

Now some people are inclined to use the term 'right' in such a way that it follows from the fact that you ought to allow a person to use your body for the hour he needs, that he has a right to use your body for the hour he needs, even though he has not been given that right by any person or act. They may say that it follows also that if you refuse, you act unjustly towards him. This use of the term is perhaps so common that it cannot be called wrong; nevertheless it seems to me to be an unfortunate loosening of what we would do better to keep a tight rein on. Suppose that box of chocolates I mentioned earlier had not been given to both boys jointly, but was given only to the older boy. There he sits stolidly eating his way through the box, his small brother watching enviously. Here we are likely to say, 'You ought not to be so mean. You ought to give your brother some of those chocolates.' My own view is that it just does not follow from the truth of this that the brother has any right to any of the chocolates. If the boy refuses to give his brother any he is greedy, stingy, callous – but not unjust. I suppose that the people I have in mind will say it does follow that the brother has a right to some of the chocolates, and thus that the boy does act unjustly if he refuses to give his brother any. But the effect of saying, this is to obscure what we should keep distinct, namely the difference between the boy's refusal in this case and the boy's refusal in the earlier case, in which the box was given to both boys jointly, and in which the small brother thus had what was from any point of view clear title to half.

A further objection to so using the term 'right' that from the fact that A ought to do a thing for B it follows that R has a right against A that A do it for him, is that it is going to make the question of whether or not a man has a right to a thing turn on how easy it is to provide him with it; and this seems not merely unfortunate, but morally unaccept-able. Take the case of Henry Fonda again. I said earlier that I had no right to the touch of his cool hand on my fevered brow even though I needed it to save my life. I said it would be frightfully nice of him to fly in from the West

Coast to provide me with it, but that I had no right against him that he should do so. But suppose he isn't on the West Coast. Suppose he has only to walk across the room, place a hand briefly on my brow – and lo, my life is saved.

Then surely he ought to do it – it would be indecent to refuse. Is it to be said, 'Ah, well, it follows that in this case she has a right to the touch of his hand on her brow, and so it would be an injustice in him to refuse'? So that I have a right to it when it is easy for him to provide it, though no right when it's hard? It's rather a shocking idea that anyone's rights should fade away and disappear as it gets harder and harder to accord them to him.

So my own view is that even though you ought to let the violinist use your kidneys for the one hour he needs, we should not conclude that he has a right to do so – we should say that if you refuse, you are, like the boy who owns all the chocolates and will give none away, self-centred and callous, indecent in fact, but not unjust. And similarly, that even supposing a case in which a woman pregnant due to rape ought to allow the unborn person to use her body for the hour he needs, we should not conclude that he has a right to do so; we should say that she is self-centred, callous, indecent, but not unjust, if she refuses. The complaints are no less grave; they are just different. However, there is no need to insist on this point. If anyone does wish to deduce 'he has a right' from 'you ought,' then all the same he must surely grant that there are cases in which it is not morally required of you that you allow that violinist to use your kidneys, and in which he does not have a right to use them, and in which you do not do him an injustice if you refuse. And so also for mother and unborn child. Except in such cases as the unborn person has a right to demand it – and we were leaving open the possibility that there may be such cases — nobody is morally required to make large sacrifices, of health, of all other interests and concerns, of all other duties and commitments, for nine years, or even for nine months, in order to keep another person alive.

6. We have in fact to distinguish between two kinds of Samaritan: the Good Samaritan and what we might call the Minimally Decent Samaritan. The story of the Good Samaritan, you will remember, goes like this:

> A certain man went down from Jerusalem to Jericho, and fell among thieves, which stripped him of his raiment, and wounded him, and departed, leaving him half dead.
>
> And by chance there came down a certain priest that way: and when he saw him, he passed by on the other side.
>
> And likewise a Levite, when he was at the place, came and looked on him, and passed by on the other side.
>
> But a certain Samaritan, as he journeyed, came where he was, and when he saw him he had compassion on him.
>
> And went to him, and bound up his wounds, pouring in oil and wine, and set him on his own beast, and brought him to an inn, and took care of him.
>
> And on the morrow, when he departed, he took out two pence, and gave them to the host, and said unto him, 'Take care of him; and whatsoever thou spendest more, when I come again, I will repay thee.' (Luke 10:30-35)

The Good Samaritan went out of his way, at some cost to himself, to help one in need of it. We are not told what the options were, that is, whether or not the priest and the Levite could have helped by doing less than the Good Samaritan did, but assuming they could have, then the fact they did nothing at all shows they were not even Minimally Decent Samaritans, not because they were not Samaritans, but because they were not even minimally decent.

111

These things are a matter of degree, of course, but there is a difference, and it comes out perhaps most clearly in the story of Kitty Genovese, who, as you will remember, was murdered while 38 people watched or listened and did nothing at all to help her. A Good Samaritan would have rushed out to give direct assistance against the murderer. Or perhaps we had better allow that it would have been a Splendid Samaritan who did this, on the ground that it would have involved a risk of death for himself. But the 38 not only did not do this, they did not even trouble to pick up a phone to call the police. Minimally Decent Samaritanism would call for doing at least that, and their not having done it was monstrous.

After telling the story of the Good Samaritan, Jesus said, 'Go, and do thou likewise.' Perhaps he meant that we are morally required to act as the Good Samaritan did. Perhaps he was urging people to do more than is morally required of them. At all events it seems plain that it was not morally required of any of the 38 that he rush out to give direct assistance at the risk of his own life, and that it is not morally required of anyone that he give long stretches of his life – nine years or nine months – to sustaining the life of a person who has no special right (we were leaving open the possibility of this) to demand it.

Indeed, with one rather striking class of exceptions, no one in any country in the world is legally required to do anywhere near as much as this for anyone else. The class of exceptions is obvious. My main concern here is not the state of the law in respect to abortion, but it is worth drawing attention to the fact that in no state in this country is any man compelled by law to be even a Minimally Decent Samaritan to any person; there is no law under which charges could be brought against the 38 who stood by while Kitty Genovese died. By contrast, in most states in this country women are compelled by law to be not merely Minimally Decent Samaritans, but Good Samaritans to unborn persons inside them. This doesn't by itself settle anything one way or the other, because it may well be argued that there should be laws in this country as there are in many European countries – compelling at least Minimally Decent Samaritanism. But it does show that there is a gross injustice in the existing state of the law. And it shows also that the groups currently working against liberalisation of abortion laws, in fact working towards having it declared unconstitutional for a state to permit abortion, had better start working for the adoption of Good Samaritan laws generally, or earn the charge that they are acting in bad faith.

I should think, myself, that Minimally Decent Samaritan laws would be one thing, Good Samaritan laws quite another, and in fact highly improper. But we are not here concerned with the law. What we should ask is not whether anybody should be compelled by law to be a Good Samaritan, but whether we must accede to a situation in which somebody is being compelled – by nature, perhaps – to be a Good Samaritan. We have, in other words, to look now at third-party interventions. I have been arguing that no person is morally required to make large sacrifices to sustain the life of another who has no right to demand them, and this even where the sacrifices do not include life itself; we are not morally required to be Good Samaritans or anyway Very Good Samaritans to one another. But what if a man cannot extricate himself from such a situation? What if he appeals to us to extricate him? It seems to me plain that there are cases in which we can, cases in which a Good Samaritan would extricate him. There you are, you were kidnapped, and nine years in bed with that violinist lie ahead of you. You have your own life to lead. You are sorry, but you simply cannot see giving up so much of your life to the sustaining of his. You cannot extricate yourself, and ask us to do so. I should have thought that – in light of his having no right to the use of your body – it was obvious that we do not have to accede to your being forced to give up so much. We can do what you ask. There is no injustice to the violinist in our doing so.

7. Following the lead of the opponents of abortion, I have throughout been speaking of the foetus merely as a person, and what I have been asking is whether or not the argument we began with, which proceeds only from the foetus's being a person, really does establish its conclusion. I have argued that it does not.

But of course there are arguments and arguments, and it may be said that I have simply fastened on the wrong one. It may be said that what is important is not merely the fact that the foetus is a person, but that it is a person for whom the woman has a special kind of responsibility issuing from the fact that she is its mother. And it might be argued that all my analogies are therefore irrelevant – for you do not have that special kind of responsibility for that violinist; Henry Fonda does not have that special kind of responsibility for me. And our attention might be drawn to the fact that men and women both are compelled by law to provide support for their children.

I have in effect dealt (briefly) with this argument in section 4 above; but a (still briefer) recapitulation now may be in order. Surely we do not have any such 'special responsibility' for a person unless we have assumed it, explicitly or implicitly. If a set of parents do not try to prevent pregnancy, do not obtain an abortion, but rather take it home with them, then they have assumed responsibility for it, they have given it rights, and they cannot now withdraw support from it at the cost of its life because they now find it difficult to go on providing for it. But if they have taken all reasonable precautions against having a child, they do not simply by virtue of their biological relationship to the child who comes into existence have a special responsibility for it. They may wish to assume responsibility for it, or they may not wish to. And I am suggesting that if assuming responsibility for it would require large sacrifices, then they may refuse. A Good Samaritan would not refuse – or anyway, a Splendid Samaritan, if the sacrifices that had to be made were enormous. But then so would a Good Samaritan assume responsibility for that violinist; so would Henry Fonda, if he is a Good Samaritan, fly in from the West Coast and assume responsibility for me.

8. My argument will be found unsatisfactory on two counts by many of those who want to regard abortion as morally permissible. First, while I do argue that abortion is not impermissible, I do not argue that it is always permissible. There may well be cases in which carrying the child to term requires only Minimally Decent Samaritanism of the mother, and this is a standard we must not fall below. I am inclined to think it a merit of my account precisely that it does not give a general yes or a general no. It allows for and supports our sense that, for example, a sick and desperately frightened fourteen-year-old schoolgirl, pregnant due to rape, may of course choose abortion, and that any law which rules this out is an insane law. And it also allows for and supports our sense that in other cases resort to abortion is even positively indecent. It would be indecent in the woman to request an abortion, and indecent in a doctor to perform it, if she is in her seventh month, and wants the abortion just to avoid the nuisance of postponing a trip abroad. The very fact that the arguments I have been drawing attention to treat all cases of abortion,

or even all cases of abortion in which the mother's life is not at stake, as morally on a par ought to have made them suspect at the outset.

Second, while I am arguing for the permissibility of abortion in some cases, I am not arguing for the right to secure the death of the unborn child. It is easy to confuse these two things in that up to a certain point in the life of the foetus it is not able to survive outside the mother's body; hence removing it from her body guarantees its death. But they are importantly different. I have argued that you are not morally required to spend nine months in bed, sustaining the life of that violinist, but to say this is by no means to say that if, when you unplug yourself, there is a miracle and he survives, you then have a right to turn round and slit his throat. You may detach yourself even if this costs him his life; you have no right to be guaranteed his death, by some other means, if unplugging yourself does not kill him. There are some people who will feel dissatisfied by this feature of my argument. A woman may be utterly devastated by the thought of a child, a bit of herself, put out for adoption and never seen or heard of again. She may therefore want not merely that the child be detached from her, but more, that it die. Some opponents of abortion are inclined to regard this as beneath contempt – thereby showing insensitivity to what is surely a powerful source of despair. All the same, I agree that the desire for the child's death is not one which anybody may gratify, should it turn out to be possible to detach the child alive.

At this place, however, it should be remembered that we have only been pretending throughout that the foetus is a human being from the moment of conception. A very early abortion is surely not the killing of a person, and so is not dealt with by anything I have said here.

Girl
Jamaica Kincaid
(1978)

Wash the white clothes on Monday and put them on the stone heap; wash the colour clothes on Tuesday and put them on the clothesline to dry; don't walk barehead in the hot sun; cook pumpkin fritters in very hot sweet oil; soak your little cloths right after you take them off; when buying cotton to make yourself a nice blouse, be sure that it doesn't have gum in it, because that way it won't hold up well after a wash; soak salt fish overnight before you cook it; is it true that you sing benna in Sunday school?; always eat your food in such a way that it won't turn someone else's stomach; on Sundays try to walk like a lady and not like the slut you are so bent on becoming; don't sing benna in Sunday school; you mustn't speak to wharf-rat boys, not even to give directions; don't eat fruits on the street – flies will follow you; but I don't sing benna on Sundays at all and never in Sunday school; this is how to sew on a button; this is how to make a buttonhole for the button you have just sewed on; this is how to hem a dress when you see the hem coming down and so to prevent yourself from looking like the slut I know you are so bent on becoming; this is how you iron your father's khaki shirt so that it doesn't have a crease; this is how you iron your father's khaki pants so that they don't have a crease; this is how you grow okra – far from the house, because okra tree harbours red ants; when you are grow-ing dasheen, make sure it gets plenty of water or else it makes your throat itch when you are eating it; this is how you sweep a corner; this is how you sweep a whole house; this is how you sweep a yard; this is how you smile to someone you don't like too much; this is how you smile to someone you don't like at all; this is how you smile to someone you like completely; this is how you set a table for tea; this is how you set a table for dinner; this is how you set a table for dinner with an important guest; this is how you set a table for lunch; this is how you set a table for breakfast; this is how to behave in the presence of men who don't know you very well, and this way they won't recognise immediately the slut I have warned you against becoming; be sure to wash every day, even if it is with your own spit; don't squat down to play marbles – you are not a boy, you know; don't pick people's flowers – you might catch something; don't throw stones at blackbirds, because it might not be a blackbird at all; this is how to make a bread pudding; this is how to make doukona; this is how to make pepper pot; this is how to make a good medicine for a cold; this is how to make a good medicine to throw away a child before it even becomes a child; this is how to catch a fish; this is how to throw back a fish you don't like, and that way something bad won't fall on you; this is how to bully a man; this is how a man bullies you; this is how to love a man, and if this doesn't work there are other ways, and if they don't work don't feel too bad about giving up; this is how to spit up in the air if you feel like it, and this is how to move quick so that it doesn't fall on you; this is how to make ends meet; always squeeze bread to make sure it's fresh; but what if the baker won't let me feel the bread?; you mean to say that after all you

are really going to be the kind of woman who the baker
won't let near the bread?

On 'A Defence of Abortion'
Amia Srinivasan
(2022)

The most famous philosophical treatment of abortion is an essay by Judith Jarvis Thomson published in 1971, two years before *Roe v. Wade* was decided, in the inaugural issue of the journal *Philosophy and Public Affairs*. 'A Defence of Abortion' opens by dispensing with the standard pro-choice premise that the foetus is not a person. A 'newly implanted clump of cells', Thomson writes, is 'no more a person than an acorn is an oak tree', but 'we shall probably have to agree that the foetus has already become a human person well before birth.' But is that what matters? Imagine, Thomson says, that you wake up to find that the Society of Music Lovers has hooked your circulatory system up to a famous violinist with a life-threatening kidney ailment. Unless you stay in bed, attached to him for nine months (you are the only one with the right blood type), he will die. Are you morally permitted to unplug the violinist? The hospital director explains why not:

> Tough luck, I agree, but you've now got to stay in bed, with the violinist plugged into you . . . Because remember this. All persons have a right to life, and violinists are persons. Granted you have a right to decide what happens in and to your body, but a person's right to life outweighs your right to decide what happens in and to your body.

Thomson suggests that most readers will find the doctor's logic 'outrageous'. Yes, the violinist is a person; but no, obviously, his right to life does not trump your right to bodily autonomy. Similarly with the foetus: it might be a person, but even so don't you have the right to abort it?

The intuitive power of Thomson's thought experiment is undeniable. But its intuitiveness rests on a liberal individualism that feminists, including those who were fighting for access to abortion at the time Thomson was writing, have long wanted to resist. For social conservatives, the foetus – better yet, 'the unborn baby' – is an object of hysterical devotion (giving rise to what Lee Edelman has called 'the fascism of the baby's face'), just as a famous violinist might be to his fans. But foetuses – not the idea, but the creatures themselves – exist at the borders of life, on the margins of humanity. And it is at the borders and margins of 'the human', 'personhood', 'consciousness' and 'life' that feminists have identified those most in need of protection and liberation: women, disabled people, queer people, people of colour, immigrants, children, non-human animals, nature. To assimilate a foetus not only to an adult, but to a famous, high-status adult (an adult with a fan club!) is to distract from the vulnerability of certain forms and stages of human life. This vulnerability, the fact that none of us is a perfectly independent and autonomous self, means that, like it or not, we need each other. We are all the violinist; and we are all his host. This is, yes, an outrage: but it is the outrage of human existence. To elevate that outrage to an ethical principle, as Thomson encourages us to do, is to indulge the destructive fantasy that we can simply unplug and be free.

What would it be to have a pro-abortion politics that did not flee from vulnerability and dependency – that did not take as its implicit starting point the perspective of the sovereign, perfectly autonomous individual? It would be an abortion politics that, as feminists of colour have long been urging, shifted its focus from 'choice' to 'justice', drawing a connection, for example, between anti-abortion politics, campaigns of forced sterilisation of Black and poor women, and the demonisation of 'welfare mothers', 'benefits scroungers' and the 'hyper-fecund' women of the global south. It would be a politics that made safe and free abortion part of a much broader package of social provision that recognised human need as a public rather than a private concern: universal healthcare, childcare, housing, basic income and so on. It would be an abortion politics, not unironically, that would advance the aim conservatives claim they care so much about: the reduction of foetal killing.

But there's the rub of anti-abortion politics: it does not, on the whole, meaningfully reduce the rate of abortion. What anti-abortion laws do guarantee is an increase in the suffering of those with unwanted pregnancies, and in the state's ability to punish those people – especially poor women – who seek or facilitate abortion. This is a feature, not a bug, of anti-abortion politics. Anti-abortion laws are designed not to reduce foetal deaths, but to punish those who resist the prevailing reproductive order. They are a reminder that it is the function of women to devote themselves, psychically and bodily, to the maintenance of social and economic life, and the prerogative of the state to ensure that they do so.

The word 'sex' is not used in 'A Defence of Abortion'; the word 'intercourse' appears just once. For Thomson, the fact that human foetuses are produced by sexual activity was ethically irrelevant to the question at hand. But for most 'pro-lifers', sex – in both its senses – is the fundamental issue: playing non-voluntary host to a parasitical

123

violinist may be an outrage against individual liberty, but playing host to a foetus is, for a woman who chooses to have sex, the appropriate outcome. What's more, for the woman who chooses to have sex for reasons other than reproduction – for pleasure, for money, for the hell of it – carrying a foetus to term is her just desert. This is why Thomson's thought experiment, for all its power, exercises little grip on the patriarchal worldview. At the slightest incursion on men's liberty, patriarchy bridles wildly. But the unspoken condition of men's freedom is women's unfreedom. Every abortion wanted, sought and completed is an offence against the social order. In this, at least, the anti-abortionists are right.

Abortion is about Freedom,
not just Privacy
Keeanga-Yamahtta Taylor
(2022)

It wasn't a protest, but a defence against a protest. For much of 1989, the year I turned seventeen, I would wake up on Saturdays, at around 6 a.m., and head to a local abortion clinic. The clinics in Buffalo, New York, where I lived, had recently become ground zero in the battle over abortion. Each day, anti-abortion protesters showed up, armed with signs showing images of what they claimed were aborted foetuses, and tried to blockade the clinic doors to prevent clients from entering. Our counter-protest aimed to get there first, and to form a moving picket that kept the protesters away and allowed clients to pass through.

By the end of the 1980s, the war against abortion was in full swing. It had been revitalised by Reagan's rise and the platform that his presidency provided for a growing evangelical right. Gaudy televangelists decried 'feminazis' and argued that abortion threatened women's traditional roles as caretakers and mothers. A street movement of anti-abortion activists engaged in intimidation tactics, attempting to stop women from entering clinics. In upstate New York, the most prominent activist group was called Operation Rescue. Randall Terry, a former used-car salesman who became a born-again Christian in the 1970s, led it.

Terry likened his crusade to the civil-rights movement and welcomed comparisons between himself and Martin Luther King. In an interview in 1989, he remarked, 'The blacks were demonstrating for their own rights, and we are rescuing other people and standing up for babies' rights . . . There can be absolutely no compromise on this, any more than there was compromise on whether white southerners should have slaves.'

Failing to persuade women through conventional forms of protest, the anti-abortion right adopted increasingly violent tactics. In 1989, Terry said, 'I believe in the use of force.' He added, adopting a more moderate tone, 'I think to destroy abortion facilities at this time is counterproductive because the American public has an adverse reaction to what it sees as violence.' But the inflammatory rhetoric of Terry and the right in describing foetal tissue as 'unborn babies' justified in the minds of protesters the growing use of force. According to Susan Faludi's classic book *Backlash*, 'between 1977 and 1989, 77 family planning clinics were torched or bombed (in at least seven cases during working hours, with employees and patients inside), 117 were targets of arson, 250 received bomb threats, 231 were invaded and 224 vandalised.' According to the *Times*, men opposed to abortion killed at least eleven people, including abortion providers, at clinics between 1993 and 2015.

A few months before my seventeenth birthday, my mother bought me a subscription to *Seventeen* magazine. It seemed an odd choice, given its conventional make-up ads and utterly normative portraits of white girls. I was in the midst of coming out as a lesbian and found the whole thing jarring. But, in the mix of ads and grooming tips, there were articles that captured my attention, including one about the erosion of rights for teenagers. A small sidebar noted, as an example, that teenagers were required to get parental consent before receiving an abortion. The issue struck me viscerally. I had been fighting constantly with my father and stepmother about curfews, smoking and the socialists I was hanging out with. The idea that they might decide whether or not I had a baby was enraging, obliterating any notion of self-determination.

I had never thought much about abortion before, but I had thought often about pregnancy; my mother had said, almost in a whisper, that her grandmother had told her that, as soon as girls have their periods, they can't let boys touch them. In Texas, where I had spent junior high, everyone knew that when some girls suddenly disappeared from school they were probably pregnant. During my freshman year of high school, a friend wore a coat every day until she, too, eventually disappeared. She had hidden her pregnancy for months before finally delivering a baby. It seemed to be only women and girls who suffered any consequence for pregnancy. Girls, not boys, disappeared from school. Girls, not boys, carried the weight of social stigma. Girls, not boys, had their entire lives turned upside down if they carried the pregnancy to term. It was terrifying; it was also radicalising.

On those mornings in Buffalo, anti-abortion protesters trickled out of their cars wielding their grotesque signs. The protesters – white men accompanied by women and, in some cases, even children – yelled at patients who showed up for their appointments, saying that they were killing their babies. We chanted back, 'Pro-life, your name's a lie, you don't care if women die.' The clinic defenders, as we counter-protesters called ourselves, were a combination of campus activists, socialists, lesbians and feminists – a motley crew of the Buffalo left. We had some inevitable tension with the owners of the clinic, who worried that our counter-protests might alienate patients, too. But, as the right escalated its tactics to shut clinics down, we came to feel that we were keeping the clinics open and allowing women to exercise a constitutional right.

The Supreme Court's decision to overturn *Roe v. Wade* has brought old feelings of astonishment and disgust back to the surface. The court's utter disregard for the rights of women and of trans and nonbinary people who have the capacity to become pregnant is shocking in the 21st century. In the text of the majority opinion – as, indeed, in the original 1973 *Roe* opinion – the rights of women as full citizens hardly seem to register.

Justice Harry Blackmun, who wrote for the *Roe*-affirming majority in 1973, included a brief list of the potential detriments of forcing women to carry pregnancies to term:

> Maternity, or additional offspring, may force upon the woman a distressful life and future. Psychological harm may be imminent. Mental and physical health may be taxed by childcare. There is also the distress, for all concerned, associated with the unwanted child, and there is the problem of bringing a child into a family already unable, psychologically and otherwise, to care for it. In other cases, as in this one, the additional difficulties and continuing stigma of unwed motherhood may be involved.

In the recent majority opinion overturning *Roe*, Justice Samuel Alito makes the fantastical claim that a world hostile to pregnant women no longer exists. Alito contends that, in 'many' cases, women now have access to maternity leave. (He doesn't bother to mention that it is often unpaid.) He claims that medical care associated with pregnancy is covered by private insurance or government assistance. (He neglects to mention that many women must still pay large out-of-pocket expenses.)

Yet women should have the right to control their reproduction, not only because of the potential emotional or
financial hardship but because it is a pre-condition to their
full and free participation in our society. If women cannot
dictate this most basic aspect of their being, then the Supreme Court has effectively consigned them to a secondary
tier of citizenship. Alito rationalises that the late arrival of
civil rights for women makes those rights less real than if
they had arrived earlier. He argues that the right to abortion, because it was enshrined only in the 1970s, is not
'deeply rooted in the nation's history and tradition'. He
seems unworried that this might actually only serve to emphasise the profound misogyny endemic throughout
American history; women did not even gain the right to
vote until well into the 20th century.

The original rationale for *Roe* relied on arguments about
privacy. Blackmun, arguing that abortion should be permitted in the first trimester, wrote that at this stage 'the
abortion decision in all its aspects is inherently, and primarily, a medical decision, and basic responsibility for it
must rest with the physician.' Of course, the right to privacy is crucial in mitigating the power of the state to interfere with personal decisions. But, beyond any notion of
privacy, it is also important to protect the more fundamental freedom of women to control their own bodies.
Even in the 1973 decision, women's bodily autonomy
goes largely unremarked upon. J.D. Vance, who is running
to become a Republican senator in Ohio, recently argued,
'It's not whether a woman should be forced to bring a
child to term; it's whether a child should be allowed to
live.' But the hard truth about the reversal of *Roe* is that
women will be forced to bring a child to term. As Betty
Friedan, author of *The Feminine Mystique*, wrote, in 1969,
'There is no freedom, no equality, no full human dignity

129

and personhood possible for women until we assert and demand the control over our own bodies, over our own reproductive process.'

But Friedan's vision of freedom was incomplete. Access to abortion was the bare minimum necessary for women to achieve equality in America. Real self-determination and equality could only be achieved by ending the socially and economically subordinate role of women in our society – a burden that fell heaviest on poor and working-class women of colour. Women cannot be free so long as society perpetuates the expectation that they are the unpaid stewards of household labour: cooking, cleaning, child rearing and keeping their husbands sexually satisfied. Working-class women, especially Black and brown women, were expected not only to perform this work inside their homes but to work outside their homes, too, to financially support their families. Freedom and equality could only be realised through fair and equal pay – for work at home and as part of the workforce. This also meant that society had to take seriously the provision of safe, sound, subsidised childcare. Women's rejection of their role as the central pivot in the reproduction of society put them in conflict with the rising religious right, and also with elected officials who rejected the growth of the state agencies and institutions necessary to relieve women from caretaking roles. The rising expectations of young women, fuelled by their participation in the civil-rights movement in the 1960s, erupted in the years that followed. Women demanded birth control, freedom from sterilisation, and freedom to abort unwanted pregnancies. Those who seek to roll back the clock not only intend to strip women of the right to abortion but to undermine their efforts to be independent of men and the nuclear family as well.

In the 21st century, it is easy to be deluded that the increased presence of women, including women of colour, in politics and business is evidence that women have achieved equality. The Mississippi attorney general, in arguing this year that *Roe* should be struck down, noted, 'Sweeping policy advances now promote women's full pursuit of both career and family.' In fact, women make up the majority of those who live in poverty in the US. Women make only 83 cents on the dollar that men earn. Broken down along lines of race and gender, the wage gap widens dramatically: Black women make 64 cents for every dollar made by a white man; Latinas make 57 cents. Forcing women to carry unwanted pregnancies to term only adds to their economic burden. But the Supreme Court's ruling, by ushering in a regime of forced births, will be devastating even among those who have some financial means. No woman can escape the cloud of inferiority that is necessarily attached to having no say over when and whether to be pregnant. Moreover, pregnancy itself is a physical and emotional burden that sometimes has deadly consequences. The US has a higher rate of maternal mortality than Canada, the UK and eight other European nations. There is no equivalent medical condition imposed on men. This creates a disparity of experience and consequence in the law that is a perfect example of basic discrimination.

Life-altering poverty and potential death are, of course, the most extreme examples of what can go wrong when unintended and unwanted pregnancy is forced upon women. But the right to abortion should not only be tied to the most tragic outcomes. Newscasters trying to get anti-abortion elected officials to affirm their support of draconian restrictions even in extreme cases – such as when a thirteen-year-old in Arkansas is raped by a relative,' an example presented to that state's governor, Asa Hutchinson – miss the point that abortion is a human right. The bans on abortion even in the event of rape or incest, or when the health of the mother is threatened, certainly betray the extraordinary misogyny that animates opposition to the procedure. But the right to abortion is an affirmation that women and girls have the right to control their own destiny. Without the ability to control when, where, how and if one chooses to become pregnant or give birth, no other freedom can be achieved.

In 1992, the abortion wars came to a head in Buffalo. For months, Operation Rescue had been planning to lay siege to Buffalo abortion clinics during what they called the Spring of Life. The mayor, Jimmy Griffin, had invited them to do so, saying, 'I want to see them in this city. If they can shut down one abortion mill, they've done their job.' It seemed like a clear indication that the police would not interfere with their efforts. Counter-protesters from around the country mobilised in the beleaguered Rust Belt city. In the end, we stopped Operation Rescue. Arrests of anti-abortion activists helped to publicise their cause, but we were able to keep the clinics in Buffalo open.

Eight years later, after I had moved to Chicago, I once again experienced the fear involved in being at an abortion clinic. This time, I was not a clinic defender but a client. In the spring of 2000, I became pregnant, after having sex with a male friend after a party at my apartment. I knew within a week that something was happening to my body: I was exhausted, and the spicy food that I usually liked to eat made me nauseated. A pregnancy test confirmed my fears. My friend and I decided to split the cost of an abortion, and my girlfriend at the time drove me to a Planned Parenthood office in Chicago. A year earlier, the office had received a letter oozing a mysterious liquid and had been evacuated. I worried about going to the facility and being accosted by bigots and fanatics.

But, on a cold and rainy day in the middle of the week, only people working at the facility were there. The procedure was quick, not entirely painless, and then over. Driving home, I threw up on the side of the road. There was nothing tragic or extraordinary about my experience. I had unprotected sex with a friend and became pregnant. Neither of us intended to be in a relationship, let alone have a child together. I was gay and in my own relationship, and he was straight and single. We were both broke but not poor, and we were able to scrape together the $300 necessary. But, if I had been forced to carry that pregnancy to term, my life would have been forever changed. A key strategy in the fight for reproductive freedom has involved 'abortion speak-outs' or 'shouting out your abortion' – an attempt to fight against the right's contention that abortion is harmful, tragic and always regretted. We should trust women, and others, to know what to do with their own bodies.

The Supreme Court's reversal of the right to abortion has usurped the rights and freedom of people who have the capacity to become pregnant. But anyone – including lesbians, gays, bisexuals, and transgender people – whose freedoms are not directly enshrined in the constitution could see their rights threatened. Justice Clarence Thomas minced no words when he argued, in an opinion he wrote concurring with the majority, that precedent-setting cases that used the right to privacy and due process to guarantee the legality of contraception, gay sex, and gay marriage should be next in the firing line. There is no doubt that, if Republicans gain a congressional majority and win the White House, they will try to impose a national ban on abortion. The recent flurry of attacks on trans youths' access to prescriptions and medical care has helped to legitimise the power of the state to control the bodies of women and girls when it comes to pregnancy. The right wants to assert control over an array of non-normative sexualities, family units and ways of being in the world. And in allowing for some discrimination, largely against trans youth and athletes, the door to rank bias has now been kicked in, legitimising all of it. Today we reap the whirlwind.

A generation ago in Buffalo, a wide range of ordinary people came together to protect access to abortion clinics. In that instance, it was clear to us how the right's broad goals were knotted together. We understood that, if they were successful in shutting down Buffalo's clinics through brute force, it would generate momentum for the rest of their agenda, which included attacking gays, Black women on welfare, single mothers, undocumented immigrants and anyone else that did not fit in or conform to their narrow 'family values' world view. This is a frightening new world, but we can learn from earlier eras. We can also use these renewed attacks to form the solidarity necessary to rebuild the movements that can and will challenge the right's growing momentum.

It's Morning (Sickness)
in America
Lauren Berlant
(1994)

The conditions of American citizenship are always changing. But these transformations of pregnancy and foetality have had extreme cultural effects. The emergence of foetal personhood as a legal and medical category, and as a site of cultural fantasy, has been a major stimulus for thinking anew about what citizenship means as an identity category and what it implies for the theory and practice of national identity. These changes have happened in a number of domains, and the combined effects of these changes have created a crisis, the responsibility for which pregnant women and their foetuses are bearing.

How to explain the concentration of complex citizenship issues on the fate and status of a bare minimum unit of human material? Let us start at a beginning. By merging the American counter-discourse of minority rights with a revitalised Providential nationalist rhetoric, the pro-life movement has composed a magical and horrifying spectacle of amazing vulnerability: the unprotected person, the citizen without a country or a future, the foetus unjustly imprisoned in its mother's hostile gulag. This movement has fundamentally altered the aggregate meaning of nature, identity and the body in the construction of American nationality. Its transformations are of a scale unmatched in

American history since the enfranchisement of African Americans in 1868, which not only added a new group of 'persons' to 'the people' but had two other effects relevant to this investigation: it changed fundamentally the relative meanings and rules of federal and state citizenship, and it called into crisis the norms and principles of national embodiment. Clearly, however, unlike the African American subject, the foetus has no autonomous body. And unlike the African American subject, the foetus has no voice and thus cannot partake of the kinds of agency recognised in the protocols of the political public sphere. The success of the concept of foetal personhood depends on establishing a mode of 'representation' that merges the word's political and aesthetic senses, imputing a voice, a consciousness, and a self-identity to the foetus that can neither speak its name nor vote. This strategy of non-diegetic voicing has two goals: (1) to establish the autonomy of the foetal individual; and paradoxically, (2) to show that the foetus is a contingent being, dependent on the capacity of Americans to hear *as citizens* its cries *as a citizen* for dignity of the body, its complaints at national injustice.

Most Anglo-American feminist work on the politics of foetus personhood has focused on its theft of the meaning of gender, maternity and childbirth from women. Rosalind Petchesky, Paula Treichler, Faye Ginsburg, Emily Martin, Rayna Rapp, Zillah Eisenstein, Barbara Duden, Marilyn Strathern and many others have performed critical analyses crucial to this. They have explicated the ways in which new technologies and new modes of representation, such as foetal imaging, have created a nationwide competition between the mother and the foetus that the foetus, framed as a helpless, choiceless victim, will always lose – at least without the installation of surrogate legal and technological systems to substitute for the mother's dangerous body and fallen will. And they have established a powerful argument for redefining the conditions of gendered identity in America according to the difference that the capacity to reproduce makes in the woman's access to sociality, power and value.

In addition to witnessing the politics of woman's discipline to the norms of proper motherhood, it is important to recount this moment as a case study in the process of nation-formation and its reliance on manipulations of the identity form to occlude the centrality of reproduction to the processes by which the nation rejuvenates itself. In this light, the pregnant woman is the main legitimate space in which the category *female* converts into a national category and changes the meaning of citizenship – not just citizenship as a juridical category but also as a horizon of social practice and aspiration.

One reason the revitalisation of this category is so crucial now is that pro-life rhetoric has seen the relation between nature and nation as central to its sacred logics. Citizenship is the category in which these two formations are supposed to merge, but the arguments for their relation differ in different contexts. First, the narrative of natural development from gendered womanhood to pregnancy and motherhood has provided one of the few transformational lexicons of the body and identity we have. It has framed womanhood in a natural narrative movement of the body, starting at the moment a child is sexed female and moving to her inscription in public heterosexuality, her ascension to reproduction and her commitment to performing the abstract values of instrumental empathy and service that have characterised norms of female fulfilment. Some anti-feminist anti-abortion activists view the modern woman as no longer trained in or committed to the rigours of natural femininity; pregnancy appears not only to threaten rupture in a traditional notion of the continuity between feminine value and motherhood but to threaten the nat ional future as well.

Anxieties around the relation between proper womanhood and proper motherhood have long been evident in middle-class-identified women's reform movements. In so recasting the pregnant body as, at its best, a vehicle for the state's 'compelling interest' in its citizens, the pro-life nation that currently exists sanctions the pregnant woman as American only insofar as she becomes impersonal and public, committed to submitting her agency to the 'compelling interests' of any number of higher powers. She is juridically and morally compelled to exchange the privacy protections of gender for a kinder, gentler state. Claudia Koonz has documented a similar conversion of gender to nationality in the conscription of German women to reproduce citizens for the Third Reich. At this time in America, however, the reproducing woman is no longer cast as a potentially productive citizen, except insofar as she procreates: her capacity for other kinds of creative agency has become an obstacle to national reproduction.

This is the logic by which the pregnant woman sutures femininity, nature and nation. The emergence of pregnancy into ordinary representation makes this suture vulnerable to unravelling, and as it threatens to do so, so many of the hard-won political transformations in notions of women's authority over reproduction have unravelled as well. But if one effect of the discourse on foetal personhood is a crisis in the capacity of a maternalised gender to organise a discursive field that links women's private activity to national history and the future, from the point of view of foetality, counter claims for female authority over the foetus seem to block or distort the narrative of natural development.

Thus, in pro-life discourse, the aim of national reproduction merges with the claim that foetuses, like all persons, ought to have a politically protected right to natural
development. This version of the 'costructuration' of nature
and nation is behind the pro-life appropriation of tactics
from feminist and other minority-American 'identity'
movements: asserting that the 'silence' and 'invisibility' of
the foetal person will be redressed by its imputed speech
and visibility; assuming the point of view of victimised
citizenship by redefining radically the meaning, the history, and the dimensionality of the body; challenging and
transforming stereotypes that define identity in the public
sphere, emphasising the claim pure protection of the identity form that American national membership is supposed
to provide.

The movement for foetal rights is thus also a development in the history of national sentimentality, where complex political conditions are reduced or refined into the
discourses of dignity and of the authority of feeling. It suggests strongly that the subject position of the national victim, the 'minority subject', has become a cultural dominant
in America: in this moment of mass nationality and global
politics, power appears always to be elsewhere, and political authenticity depends on the individual's humiliating
exile from somebody else's norm. A nationwide estrange-
ment from an imagined hegemonic centre seems now to
dignify every citizen's complaint.

As the ways in which norms of representing privilege
in the political public sphere shift, such that people seek
minority status in order to trump other forms of national
demand; as the mass media produces further transformations of the scale of political experience in America; as
pro-life and aligned forces incite the law to renaturalise
national identity; and as everyone seems to experience

nationality as a species of trauma, it seems necessary to rethink relations between identity and embodiment in the national public sphere. My aim is to be able to understand slogans such as 'Support Our Future Troops!'

What kinds of anxiety and theory of personhood are expressed by such a slogan? How can we make sense of recent alliances between imperialism and pro-life patriotism, or between anti-choice, pro-natalist, anti-drug propagandas and pedagogy, which have produced collectively the anti-madonna, the mother who poisons or aborts her child, as a new traumatised national icon? To understand how the pregnant woman and the foetus have become so broken up and fetishised, both in their fracture and in the fantasy of their reunification, we must think about how national norms of corporeality work, and about the nation-making function of the minority stereotype. This critical project would not be possible without the unsettling redescriptive efforts of postcolonial and sex-radical intellectual activists – for example, Gilles Deleuze and Félix Guattari's 'What Is a Minor Literature?', Gayatri Spivak's work with Mahasweta Devi's 'Draupadi, Breast-Giver' and 'Douloti the beautiful', Eve Sedgwick's *Epistemology* and Gayle Rubin's epistemologically rigorous activism against sexual taxonomies that dominate identity in the United States. Situated in very different national and international struggles for cultural and political legitimation, this work imagines ways of using a culture's caste-making gestures towards the body to produce resistance and interference. Minority identity is often experienced as corporeal discomfort: the mouth, the anus, the cancerous breast, and 'perverted' sex, for example, not only serve as evidence of the places where cultures install symbolic truths on the body at the expense of the subject's dignity and authority but also serve as inspiration that a radical counter-use of metonymy might be executed to turn dominant cultures from imperial into contingent – even phantasmatic – entities, into totalities lost in the shadow of the resistant, the perverse, the self-destructive member.

When the meaning of a person is reduced to a body part, the identity fragment figures as a sign of incomplete personhood; its dialectical other, the stereotype, masks this violence in images of self-unity, of the body's natural adequacy to the identity that names it violently. Homi Bhabha has argued that the stereotype is an essential mental ligament of modern national culture, as the common possession of aesthetic and discursive 'national' objects provides an affective intimacy among citizens that no commonly memorised political genealogy or mass experience of democracy has yet successfully effected. I have called the archive of these hieroglyphic images the 'National Symbolic', and have suggested that the collective possession of its official texts – the flag, Uncle Sam, Mount Rushmore, the Pledge of Allegiance, even now, perhaps, JFK and Dr Martin Luther King – creates a national 'public' that constantly repudiates political knowledge where it exceeds performatively mythic national codes.

But the colonial spectacle or national stereotype serves more than to create national amnesia. Bhabha provides a 'positive' explanation of the stereotype's ambivalent function in mass cultural politics. To repeat and to elaborate on his argument: The colonial spectacle or the national stereotype is a hybrid form, a form of feeling, of alienation and of sociality. The stereotype circulates between subjects who have power as a kind of cultural property they control; it circulates among minority subjects as a site of masochistic identification (the minority/colonial subject as cultural property recognises itself in the objective circulation of its own form); it is additionally a site of social power, of apparent magical embodiment, and of collective authority. When the national hieroglyph is an object, its capacity to con dense and displace cultural stress is made possible by its muteness as a thing. But when the national stereotype represents a 'minority' person, the ambivalences of the culture that circulates the form are brought to the fore, for the national minority stereotype makes exceptional the very person whose marginality, whose individual experience of collective cultural discrimination or difference, is the motive for his/her circulation as a collective icon in the first place. This is how it happens, for example, that a homophobic culture loves its Liberace, and a racist culture its Eddie Murphy. In moments of intensified racism, homophobia, misogyny, and phobias about poverty, these 'positive' icons of national minority represent both the minimum and the maximum of what the dominating cultures will sanction for circulation, exchange, and consumption. As iconic minority subjects, they prove the potentialities of the marginal mass population to the hegemonic public; as minority exceptions, they represent heroic autonomy from their very identity; as 'impersonations' of stereotyped minority identity, they embody the very ordinary conditions of subjective distortion that characterise marginality.

Because it appears to be personhood in its natural completeness, prior to the fractures of history and identity, the foetus is supposed to be a solution, from the origin of human existence, to the corporeal violence that plagues America today. It has become an index of natural/national rights with respect to which adult citizens must derive their legitimation. Thomas Laqueur has shown brilliantly how manipulations of scale function to consolidate 'sex' as an identity category, a hieroglyph of unbroken development; I want to suggest how shifts of scale function, in mass national culture, to reroute social access to the body and to the body politic. Let me begin again, not by tracing the trajectory of the foetus but by looking at its intimate opposite, the pregnant woman's body. The changing social dimensionality of the new pregnant hybrid American form will enable us to think pregnancy itself not as a scene for the production of children, nature, or the future, but as a scene for the production of the adult, its forms and norms of intelligible life.

Abortion Spoken Word:
Choose Your Side
Storm Cecile
(2022)

FIRST SPEAKER: Isn't it funny how people make decisions that don't affect them? A woman's womb isn't public property nor a man's prerogative; it takes two to create life but only one must burden it. Women take one step forward and then five back – what the heck is this? Woman and mother are not synonymous.

[Stands up to walk]

She is her own being, autonomous and, see, part of reproductive freedom is the liberation to be erogenous. Men are just as sexual but then women bear the consequence.

So what . . . Abortion gets abolished then one must have confidence in this government, no childcare, no formula. We're sick and tired of the politics.

[Sits down]

Your morality, it doesn't bother me. Sometimes abortion is necessary, sometimes it looks like shame, other times it looks like the face of abuse, guilt, rage.

What if a child's right to life is a woman's death plight? Must she, what, carry our own coffin and pray to God that she survives?

Abortion has allowed women to build economies and businesses without pregnancy holding her back and yet we want to go back to a time when she was enslaved to a man. Nah, we've come too far for this. Life is only a gift if you actually want it.

You may not like this, but this is a fact, motherhood should be a choice and not a trap.

[Pause]

SECOND SPEAKER: So, if it is about women's rights then what about children's rights?

And if a heartbeat beats in week six then who gives you the right to beat life out of a foetus?

Is your body an asylum that you must seek freedom from nature's season? Has the woman's womb become a warzone, an embellished graveyard? What about your agendas? Your Margaret Sanger eugenics?

Since Black Lives Matter does that change at conception? Police with guns were protests but doctors with knives get acceptance.

Wombs wombed with war. Guess there's no place for rest, bodies brutally bulleted in life and abortion celebrated for death. Ectopics. Rape. We sympathise and understand, but ectopic pregnancies actually need healthcare; you decide to use abortion as a contraceptive plan. You say men are not involved but you choose them. You say anyone is a woman who claims it. So which one is it? Which one are you saying? We're not pushing on your rights, we're pushing for life.

Reproductive freedom should not come at the cost of foetal genocide, or children having –

[Stands up]

– the right to thrive. You can't expect to have sex and not be exempt from nature's conquest.

So before you defend abortion, first know what you are defending. The child's feet are ripped from its legs, and you call that healthcare. I guess it's fair for you to assume that everything is about you.

Or like it or not –

[Sits down]

You were created to care for another too. You've wounded in wisdom so answer me this: if a foetus isn't human then why is there a procedure to kill it?

Bacteria is considered life on Mars, but a heartbeat is insignificant. You can have your choices, but know that every action has a precipitant.

Criminalising
a Constitutional Right
Madeleine Schwartz
(2020)

National discussions of abortion – of any services that
might end a pregnancy, make contraception available,
or provide other means of regulating one's capacity to bear
children – usually focus on the Supreme Court. But for
many Americans, *Roe v. Wade* might as well have been overturned already. Whether Ruth Bader Ginsburg or Amy
Coney Barrett, five conservative justices or six, many American women live in counties without clinics, or cannot
afford to pay for an abortion, or do not know how to slip
under the limbo bars to get one. Many Americans cannot
access basic medical care no matter what decisions they
make, but state-level legislation makes abortion in particular nearly impossible to procure in much of the country.
Almost four hundred state-level restrictions were proposed
in the first half of 2019 alone. This week in Louisiana, voters
amended the state constitution to make clear that there is
no right to abortion or to abortion funding.

These restrictions have led to clinic closures. At least 275
clinics providing abortion services have shut down since
2013, according to The New York Times. Abortions are not
performed in many hospitals and cannot be paid for by
federal Medicaid in most cases, further imperilling clinics.
An abortion clinic is a money-losing venture. And anti-

abortion forces have money on their side.

Four years ago, in what was widely seen as a victory for the abortion rights movement, the Supreme Court in *Whole Woman's Health v. Hellerstedt* overturned a law that made running a clinic in Texas prohibitively expensive by requiring clinics to make costly and unnecessary updates. Yet a year later, Amy Hagstrom Miller, who runs Whole Woman's Health, had to shut down her clinic in Austin. An anti-abortion organisation outbid her for its offices and set up a crisis pregnancy centre in its stead. (She was later able to reopen it.) Since then, states have introduced new laws that impose additional restrictions on access to abortion; narrow Supreme Court victories are unlikely to lead to expanded care.

Most troubling of all is a wider criminalisation of women's choices regarding their reproductive health. Our country's approach to women's health is marked by a lack of support and an appetite for punishment; jail time over medical care, prosecution over diagnosis. According to Michele Goodwin's masterful recent study, *Policing the Womb: Invisible Women and the Criminalisation of Motherhood*:

> Robust legislating that chips away at reproductive rights and encroaches on women's reproductive healthcare is about more than abortion. Rather, it is about . . . the humanity, dignity, and citizenship of girls and women.

The National Advocates for Pregnant Women (NAPW), a small non-profit that has led the research and defence of such cases, tabulates that some eight hundred 'arrests and equivalent deprivations of liberty' of pregnant women have been made since 2005, for crimes including murder, manslaughter, and feticide. This, they note, is likely a gross underestimate. (In Alabama alone almost five hundred women have been prosecuted for foetal endangerment since 2006, according to an investigation by ProPublica.)

What do such cases look like? For some months now, I've been tracking these stories. Take, for example, the case of Anne Bynum, in Monticello, Arkansas. In 2015 Bynum was a single mother with a four-year-old-son. She was arrested upon bringing a stillborn baby to the hospital, after attempting to induce labour at about 33 weeks, which she believed would be safe, for a child she hoped to put up for adoption. The local press covered the case extensively. The sheriff suggested the possibility of murder charges.

The timing of the trial is what caught my interest. In the summer of 2016, I had taken a three-week break from working as an assistant at this magazine to fly to El Salvador and report on its mistreatment of women who had had miscarriages. El Salvador is one of six countries in the world where abortion is outlawed. But the country had become so aggressive in what it called the protection of life that much of its legal energy was spent on going after women: either those who had broken the law by aborting their pregnancies or those who had simply, for reasons beyond their control, had miscarriages or stillbirths.

I now realise I could have stayed home: the United States goes after women, too. Our legal system is more and more predisposed against them. As maternal deaths have increased, often due to a combination of poverty and a broken health system – and already maternal mortality here is much higher than in most developed countries, especially among Black women – politicians have enshrined legal protections for foetuses. Nearly a dozen such laws are put forth every year. In Washington State, legislation proposed providing 'to unborn children the equal protection of the laws of this state'; in Iowa, bill SF 259 would amend the 'definition of person from the moment of conception until natural death under the criminal code.' The government is more and more zealous in its prosecution of women – for having or facilitating access to abortions or simply having a pregnancy loss that deviates from how prosecutors imagine pregnancy to be.

In Anne Bynum's case, the police became involved after she arrived at the hospital with her stillborn daughter. One nurse testified that alarm bells rang for her because Bynum did not seem emotional, at least not in the way the nurse would have expected. Bynum was questioned at the hospital by a lieutenant from the sheriff's office and arrested five days later. Two months later, felony charges were filed against her for 'concealing a birth' and 'abuse of a corpse' – because she had hidden her pregnancy from her mother, who had threatened to kick her and her son out of the trailer in which they lived if she got pregnant and because, in the confusion and exhaustion after delivery, she put her stillborn daughter in a bag and had fallen asleep before getting her son to school and going to the hospital. (The charge of 'abuse of a corpse' was dropped after the indictment.) She was tried in the state courthouse in Drew County, Arkansas.

Based on the abstract of the trial submitted to the appellate court, the rules for evidence seemed oddly relaxed; in one instance a Wikipedia page was cited. Expertise seemed politicised: one witness was recognised as having become 'a doctor without an ounce of taxpayer money . . . a doctor with five children in tow.'

Then there was the fact that both the lawyer for the prosecution and the lawyer for the defence regularly mentioned that Bynum had had prior abortions. Bynum's defence lawyer said, according to an abstract of the trial, that he had vetted his jurors to find out who was 'pro-life.' He told them, 'That's the kind of jurors I want cause I think they're the best. People that value life take the time to determine, look into things, make judgments.'

The jury retired to deliberate at 6.01 p.m. At 6.04 p.m., they found Bynum guilty and then sentenced her to up to six years in jail. Two years later, represented by NAPW lawyers, her case was overturned on appeal. By that time she had lost custody of her son. She was charged with the cost of his foster care. When she could not pay, her driver's licence was revoked, meaning that she could no longer drive to work.

For many women who are pregnant, any problem or loss that occurs is potentially a criminal act. The targets of foetal endangerment laws were, for decades, Black and brown women; these cases received relatively little press attention. Now, according to Lynn Paltrow, NAPW's founder and lead lawyer, it is white women who have used drugs who are more likely to be arrested. 'Since 2005, the majority arrested have been low-income women, rural white women,' she says, though she adds that Black and brown mothers remain disproportionately targeted in the overall criminal law system.

The standards for these cases often seem subjective and odd, as is the scientific evidence on which they are based. In the case of Latice Fisher, a Black, 32-year-old mother of three who was arrested in Mississippi after having a still-birth at home in 2017, an autopsy report determined that her baby had been born alive and had died of asphyxiation. The examiner came to this conclusion thanks to a test in which a piece of lung tissue is dropped into water and seen to float or not. If the baby had breathed outside the womb, the tissue would weigh less than that of an unborn child, whose lungs are not yet full of oxygen.

The idea of using floating lungs to test oxygen levels was described in 140 AD by the Roman physician Galen and first used in the United States in 1881 in Texas against a

Black woman named Sallie Wallace, who was charged with strangling her son. Even then, as the North-eastern law professor Aziza Ahmed has shown, it was seen as unreliable. In Fisher's case, the autopsy was delayed for 81 hours, possibly changing the structure of the tissue being tested.

State prosecutors charged Fisher with murder – in the words of one court document, with 'killing her infant child while in the commission of an act eminently dangerous and evincing a depraved heart'. During the arrest, her cell phone had been taken from her. Prosecutors found that she had researched abortion pills ('Buy abortion pills, mifepristone online, misoprostol online').

The crux of the case centred on whether the baby had been born alive or not. The case was dismissed last year, and earlier this year a new grand jury voted not to reindict her, but by then Fisher's face had appeared repeatedly on the local news in connection with the murder charge. She lost her job as a police dispatcher, and with it, her health insurance.

State prosecutors take cues from one another. Currently, a 26-year-old woman named Chelsea Becker is in jail in California. Last September, Becker experienced a stillbirth. The state of California charged her with murder because she had used methamphetamine at some point during her pregnancy. Her defence attorneys made the argument that citing drug use alone ignores all the other reasons why a pregnancy might not come to term. 'Increasingly,' wrote Dr Mishka Terplan of the Friends Research Institute in Baltimore and Dr Tricia Wright, a practitioner affiliated with the University of California San Francisco School of Medicine, in material submitted to the court, research shows that pregnancy outcomes have far more to do with economic, social and environmental conditions experienced in the course of one's life, rather than anything one does or does not do while pregnant.

Drug use can cause birth defects, but so can alcohol use (which is not criminally prosecuted in the same way), and so can poverty. So can living in a country that allots so few of its resources to ensuring healthy pregnancies. It does not seem a coincidence that so many of these cases involve women who might not appear 'sympathetic' in the eyes of the general public, who might easily be painted as bad mothers, and who lack the resources – both of money and of education – to defend themselves in a legal system predisposed to finding them guilty. 'The road to arresting women for having abortions is being paved by the cases involving pregnant women and drug use,' says Paltrow.

Prosecutors cited California penal code 187: 'Murder is the unlawful killing of a human being, or a foetus, with malice aforethought.' But Paltrow points out that subsection 3 specifically says that the law 'may not be used against the mother of the foetus for anything she solicits or consents to.' The prosecutors in Becker's case argued, she explained, that this law only applies for those 'consenting to a legal abortion.' The implication is that Becker, who took drugs, is a murderer, and so would be any woman in California who had a self-abortion.

Becker's bail was originally set at $5 million and later reduced to $2 million. (By way of comparison, the bail for Derek Chauvin, the police officer accused of fatally choking George Floyd, was set at $1 million.) She has been held in jail throughout the Covid-19 pandemic. When I talked with her in July, she had just gotten out of 'the hole,' as she called it, the solitary cell she was moved to when her case hit the news. The guards, she said, were not wearing masks. She had only a vague sense of the pandemic. 'They've done a pretty good job of keeping all of that secret.' She is one of the first two women to face murder charges in Kings County, California, for the stillbirths of their foetuses. (The other, Adora Perez, a 29-year-old woman in Hanford, California, is currently serving eleven years in prison.)

Why California, that liberal paradise? The prosecutor's brief seems to suggest that one reason to prosecute women is that other states are doing so. It cites South Carolina's history of criminalising the use of drugs and notes that 'the United States Supreme Court declined to review the South Carolina Supreme Court's decision.' The implication is that California could do the same. (California's attorney general recently filed an amicus brief supporting Becker's appeal, claiming that the law was misapplied and misrepresented.)

The last eight months of contagion, illness, and death have forced a public reckoning about the inequalities of health care in this country. Anyone who has spent any time looking at women's health in the United States would not be surprised. The men who make the laws – and in the cases described, the prosecutors and judges are primarily male – seem to see punishment as their profession and purpose. Punishment for women who have taken control of their bodies, I almost wrote. But were any of these women really in full control of their situations?

In the absence of clinics, or in view of the cost of the procedure, more and more women administer their abortions themselves. Calculating the exact number of women who do so is difficult, but researchers have tracked both an increase in the number of women who say they have induced their own abortions and an uptick in Google searches for abortion pills. The right to abortion is legally protected, but in much of the country pursuing this right on one's own is not allowed by law. As of 2019, six states have criminalised self-induced abortions; there are nine states in which foetal harm laws 'fail to adequately protect pregnant people from criminalisation', according to the abortion-rights advocacy group If/When/How. Fourteen more have laws that can be applied to women who induce their own abortions. Most of these laws are initiated at the state level with majority-Republican legislatures. While Republican lawmakers may say their aim is not to punish women, court records prove the opposite. If/When/How calculates that there have been at least 21 arrests of individuals for ending a pregnancy or helping a loved one do so since 2000.

One such woman is Ursula Wing, a Web developer living in New York City. In 2012 Wing described taking an abortion pill. She wrote about it on her blog, 'The Macrobiotic Stoner.' In more normal circumstances, she wrote, someone could follow 'the typical, recommended, approved, tested, documented blahblahblah method of chemical abortion in the United States': go to a clinic, get two drugs, and pay $500 for the experience. '$500,' she wrote. 'Are you NUTS? I've got a mortgage and a kid to take care of.'

'It seems to me that the FDA is making what COULD be an easy, private, inexpensive process, a royal pain in the neck,' she continued. 'A woman knows when it's a good time to have a baby, and when it's not. And this is of greatest consequence to the ultimate health and happiness of our society, and planet.'

From about 2016, according to an indictment, she started to provide pills to others. 'I believe in action, and civil disobedience,' she wrote in a blog post. She set up a site called 'My Secret Bodega.' She pretended she was selling jewellery. 'Gold electroplate twisted multi-rope collar necklace' was code for 'MTP Kit of one mifepristone 200 mg pill and four misoprostol 200 mg pills.' She imported the drugs from India and sent them around the world, disguising the packages as shipments of jewellery. The pills were hidden in a small panel taped inside a larger envelope. In 2018 a man named Jeffrey Smith in Wisconsin slipped two abortion pills – ordered by him from Wing's website – into the drink of a woman he had impregnated. He was charged with an attempted first-degree intentional homicide of an unborn child and delivery of unprescribed prescription drugs in Wisconsin.

In February 2019, Wing posted on her blog that FDA agents wearing bullet-proof vests came to the apartment where she lived with her young daughter, her roommate, and her roommate's son. 'I got up and walked through the kids' room to see a beige and black clad man with a crew-cut coming down the stairs,' she continued. 'In the movies, people scream at the monsters,' she continued, 'but in real life, we get quiet in the face of terror.' As described in the blog post, her roommate took her daughter to school. Wing went to her workplace and told her colleagues she would need to take the rest of the day off. When she returned, she noted that the officers had found 'everything they were looking for . . . the boxes of medication under my desk, and the priority mail envelopes ready to go out, sitting in a tote bag hanging off an open drawer.'

She wondered what her neighbours would think. The FDA agents said they'd been told they were there to investigate a rat infestation. Her daughter asked if she was going to jail. 'Agent P told me he didn't think I was the "kingpin,"' she later wrote. 'What the hell is that supposed to mean?' She continued:

It's nearly 2 a.m. as I write this, and I'm getting five to ten emails per day from pregnant women begging me for help. Is this the First World? . . . What happens when the demands of the few eclipse the needs of the many, in a system that damns more than it saves? Such a system requires lots of enforcement. Surveillance requires enormous manpower, and a police state in which the majority are not in agreement with the rule of law that a few privileged beneficiaries hold dear, consumes too many resources to be sustainable. Can you believe they flew these assholes out from Wisconsin to raid little old me? And put them up in the finest Manhattan hotels, I'm sure.

In March, Wing pled guilty to 'conspiracy to defraud the United States,' a charge that carries a fine of up to $250,000 and imprisonment of up to five years. She was sentenced in July to two years of probation, a $10,000 fine, as well as $61,753, the sum of the proceeds found to have been illegally obtained, in civil forfeiture. (My reporting on her case comes from court documents. She declined to be interviewed for this article.)

It's no stretch to imagine a future in which access to abortion is even more limited, and maternal health care so scarce that any miscarriage would invite suspicion of actions made newly criminal. Yet the hardships already affecting American women are disturbing enough, and increasingly commonplace. For every person unjustly arrested in connection with childbirth, there are countless numbers who see their lives otherwise ruined or stolen from them by a legal system that favours the potential of the unborn over the reality of life. As recently as this summer, as states tried to further restrict access to abortion by pointing to the pandemic as a pretext to restrict care, women were still asking for help on Ursula Wing's eight-year-old blog post about abortion pills:

> Can someone email me If they information [sic] on how to get the pill from the states. I Already ordered from a website . . . however covid might mean I'll never receive the package in time.

Or as another said, 'Does anyone have any extra?? Please I'm desperate!!!!'

From Kind to Women
Jayne Kavanagh, Lisa Hallgarten and Angela Poulter
(2017)

Wendy Savage
Retired obstetrician and gynaecologist
The first woman I ever saw who'd had an unsafe abortion
was when I was doing my obstetrics second month at
Forest Gate Hospital in East London. She was a married
woman of 35 or so. She'd had three children and then
she'd found herself pregnant again, and she'd syringed
herself. Ahe came in with renal failure and her husband
used to visit her, and the love between them was obvious
and it was just terrible seeing her die. Because in 1957, or
1958 it might have been, there wasn't the treatment for
renal failure that there is today. I really didn't know much
about contraceptives in those days.

I went to Africa. My housemaid, she came to me, she
was seventeen. She told me she was pregnant. And I said,
well go and tell your parents. I'm sure they will understand. So she went off home and she came back to Inugu.
She hadn't told her parents. She had gone to a native doctor. and she started to vomit blood. And I took her down
to the hospital in the car. And half an hour later, they rang
me and said she was dead. It was then that I learned that
women would do anything to get rid of an unwanted
pregnancy.

Thelma Hobbs

I became pregnant, was really terrified and didn't know what to do but the boy that had got me pregnant knew a woman who would possibly help me and that was the beginning of me having this illegal abortion, which was not a very nice thing because I didn't know where I was going to go for this and I didn't know the person.

I can remember getting a bus. I think it was Thornton Heath where I went, and I got on the bus and nobody came with me which made things really scary.

The woman opened the door and she was looking round to see if anybody was looking to see who was going to the house. And when we went inside it was all dark and I really was scared because she didn't explain anything of what she was going to do but she took me into the kitchen and still didn't put the light on.

I think possibly she didn't want the neighbours to know that I was in the kitchen. And eventually she made me kneel down and took my dress and knickers off and I don't know what she did really but she inserted something and I was absolutely trembling.

It was such an awful experience that it has stayed with me all my life because of the fear that I might get found out, somebody might know and I've never really forgotten it.

Diane Munday
Abortion Law Reform Association (ALRA) Vice Chair, 1967

It was a convent of nuns who ran a midwifery service throughout the east end of London and in fact my husband's cousin thought she wanted to be a nun and when she'd qualified at Middlesex went and worked there. And I

remember the phrase now, she said, every Peabody building has its Knitting Needle Nora, and she decided that
legal abortion was preferable. There was a network everywhere and women knew about it. They never spoke about
it.

Unlike today, when abortion is really part of everybody's
vocabulary, it was a word in the early 1950s and before
that, there was never ever, ever mentioned. I first came
across it when I was in my early twenties, when somebody
I knew, a young mother with three young children, actually died following a backstreet abortion. Her mother
told my mother, and my mother told me. And I was utterly
shocked. Maybe I'd led a sheltered existence, but I don't
think so. And I was doing research at one of the London
teaching hospitals and mentioned it over lunch to a group
of doctors I was working with. And one of them said, you
stay behind on Friday evening and we'll show you the
reality of abortion, which is a common occurrence. I then
discovered that all the London teaching hospitals, and I
guess the big provincial ones, though I don't know, put
wards aside on Friday and Saturday evenings to treat the
work of the backstreet abortionists with women admitted,
septic bleeding, some of them dying. And this was what
happened before abortion became legal.

Later, I became pregnant for the fourth time in four
years. This was in the days before the pill. And I knew, I just
knew that in fact I would not have another child at that
time. I bought my abortion in Harley Street and when I
came round from the anaesthetic, I remember remembering the young woman who died and realising that because
I had a chequebook to wave in Harley Street I was safe, I
was well. My husband had a wife, my three young sons
had a mother, whereas this other woman who didn't have
money, in fact, left behind a grieving widow and three

motherless children. And that was really the start of my campaigning.

I felt passionate about women who didn't have money, being able to have what I saw then and see now as the privilege of a safe legal termination of an intolerable pregnancy.

I had already asked around and I had the phone number of a gynaecologist in London who I was told did abortions for quite large sums of money. And I phoned him in an old red telephone box, no mobile phones at all.

And he said, come and see me this evening. I later discovered, when I went to him for money for the campaigns, that he had been converted, as it were, to doing abortions when as a very young gynaecological registrar, he refused a young woman an abortion, telling her, as was the custom at that time, go home, have the baby, and when it arrives, you'll love it.

And she killed herself that night. And he said he felt that he had killed her, as surely as if he'd taken a gun and shot her with it. And from that time on, he provided this service.

When I was campaigning, I had already decided that it had to be made respectable to have had an abortion, acceptable, because that was what people, ordinary, normal, psychiatrically healthy women were doing and had done from time immemorial, regardless of what the law said about it, regardless of what their church and their priest said about it. So it needed, if the law was to be changed, to be recognised that this was part of human female experience.

The Abortion Act was a compromise, concessions all the way. I can't count how many hours I spent sitting in rooms in the House of Commons, almost trading. We had the Royal College of GPs. We had the Archbishop of Canterbury's representatives. And it was if you let so and so go through, we will not stop so and so. It was a balance. It was a compromise. But it was the best we could get. It was that Act or nothing. And quite clearly, it was much, much better than nothing.

Malcolm Potts
Retired Obstetrician and Gynaecologist and ALRA member, 1967
I remember sitting opposite a woman in Marie Stopes's clinic in Whitfield when I was a young doctor and the woman was a bit older than me and you say how many children have you had and she's had three. Have you had any abortions? Thirteen!

And she could see I was a bit surprised. So she said, it's my neighbour down the road doctor what syringes me out. So she had had thirteen induced abortions with an enema syringe, which was the common way of inducing abortion. You took an enema syringe, put soapy water in it, pushed it through the cervix and squeezed it.

She had survived that. You could also get emboli and die while it's happening. It's not a good way to do an abortion. But it was the sort of matter of factness of it. Don't all women do this? Don't all women have thirteen abortions?

Hilda Matthews
In 1963, I got pregnant and I had a very supportive boy-friend. We didn't have much money. I don't know if he knew an abortionist or not, because obviously there would have always been this undercurrent of who you know somewhere along the line. And how he knew about it, be-cause I didn't think I knew about it, but the solution was

165

to have a coat-hanger insertion. Well, we were all desperate. We just knew we had to do something to get rid of it.

And so my flatmate and my boyfriend had me out there with a coat hanger. And I really cannot remember actually having pain. I was so embarrassed about the whole thing that she had to be part of this dreadful thing that we were going through.

But it was never more than just something you have to do. You never thought of it as a life or anything like that. It was just, you know, you're pregnant, so you have to get rid of it. And I must have started bleeding after that, but not too much. I can't imagine being overcome by a lot of bleeding. I must have gone to the doctor. I cannot remember that. And they gave me a D&C [dilation and curettage] and I remember after the operation, lying in bed, and this very beautiful young doctor came to me.

She was lovely. And she just very gently said to me, what did you do? Oh, how did it happen?' And I just looked at her and I didn't tell her anything. And I realised she was trying to get information from me and I wasn't going to say anything, I wasn't going to involve my boyfriend or anybody else.

So I just kind of said no, and I didn't tell her. And she never came back again and nobody ever pushed me again for that information, which I thought was very interesting.

John Guillebaud
Emeritus Professor of Reproductive Health, UCL
An awful lot of things didn't work, and one of the things that one used to hear was that somebody would get themselves unwantedly pregnant and then would have heard somewhere around that potassium permanganate was good.

And they would take crystals of potassium permanganate

or the boyfriend would say, oh, don't worry, we'll have sex, it doesn't matter because I can give you this stuff and you'll lose the baby. But the trouble with potassium permanganate was you put it in the vagina and you bled.

And so the boyfriend would say, oh good, you're miscarrying, now I can go away, bye-bye, you're sorted. And then she'd go to hospital. And of course, absolutely no effect on the pregnancy, she was bleeding from a horrible ulcer of her vagina.

And so there she was left with the unplanned pregnancy, which of course is a catastrophe in the 1960s, if you didn't have a partner, and a horrible situation with the bleeding caused by the potassium permanganate.

Annette Spence
Retired Clinical Nurse Specialist in Contraception
A patient had just been brought up from casualty, so she was lying on a canvas with just a blanket over her. And sister said to me, wash her and get her ready for theatre.

And she gave me a theatre gown and some socks. And I went and got the screens. We didn't have curtains in those days. And I saw this poor girl lying there, white-faced. And I said, I'm just going to wash you. You're going down to theatre for a little operation. And I thought, God, what am I saying? I didn't know what to say to her. So I started to undress her and all her underwear was terribly stained with blood.

She was wearing a pink satin slip, I remember, and that was soaked with blood. I undressed her and I washed her. I tried to talk to her but she was shaking with fear and I was too young, I didn't know what to say.

And then she asked me for a bedpan and I brought the bedpan, helped her to sit on it. I had to hold onto her, in

167

case she fell off. And she, oh, she just leaned her head against me. I felt like putting my arms around her.

And when she had finished and I took the bedpan away, it was filled with blood. It was heavy as I carried it to the sluice. And I was horrified. I'd never seen so much blood.

Sister told us about abortion and what happened and how they dilated the cervix and sometimes tore the cervix because of the instruments they used.

And then as soon as the woman started to bleed, they took her out and either left her, put her in a phone box and phoned the ambulance or the hospital. We were horrified. Absolutely horrified.

Anne Ward

In 1965, I was sixteen years old at school and I became pregnant. My father's intention was to get me an illegal abortion. He had no qualms about it. This very moral man who was so ashamed at his daughter's falling from grace would get me an illegal abortion.

I fought him and he was a very dominant man but I was quite feisty really and I fought him. I wanted this baby. I was stupid, I was sixteen, I had no idea how I could have a life or any of those things. I didn't think about that. I just thought I am not losing this baby. I will have this baby.

He had to accept the fact that I wasn't going to have this abortion, at which point he cut off all contact with me. I lived in the house, but he wouldn't speak to me, and it was arranged for me to go into an unmarried mother's home in the January, when I must have been about five and a half, six months pregnant. In the meantime, I had to stay at home and stay in most of the time, and it was horrible and he was horrible. My mother was horrible, it was horrible.

I went into this unmarried mother's home. It was a cruel

place. You had no respect, no dignity. You weren't really allowed to leave. There were a group of I think six or seven girls, and I can remember them today, I know all their names, and the babies they had, and their stories. But once we left, that was the end of our contact, we just left.

I stayed there until Nic as born. I went into the hospital and Nic was induced early the next morning and she was born at six o'clock on the Wednesday evening. I had got my lovely daughter. But I remained there, my parents used to come and see me.

I had many fights with them because I wouldn't accept that Nicola was going to be adopted. I can remember on one occasion having a really unpleasant fight and the matron came down and said to my parents, you leave. If she carries on like this we will be putting her in a remand home and that baby will have to be fostered so she won't have the baby anyway so you just leave her to me. And that was it. There was no support or no one that said you might be able to do something different.

So when Nic was six weeks old she went in the morning. And I went home. There's so much pain and mess that doesn't stop with an adoption. It goes on forever.

David Paintin
Retired Obstetrician and Gynaecologist
ALRA member in 1967
One of the obstetrics and gynaecology consultants had a reputation for being kind to women. I didn't quite understand at first that what this meant was that he was sometimes willing to terminate a pregnancy, something his colleagues would have frowned upon and would not have been willing to do themselves.

Before abortion became legal in 1967, many gynaecolog-

169

ists were opposed to terminating pregnancy and those of us who did it were regarded as in a sense being traitors to the profession. I never faced any very serious criticism from colleagues, but in my early years at St Mary's it was clear that the older consultants would prefer me not to be providing legal abortions. They felt it was letting down the hospital. But as time went on and they became aware that I did no private practice, I wasn't gaining personally from providing abortion, it was done because I really felt it was the right thing to do, they slowly began to support me without necessarily doing abortions themselves, although I think some of them may have done rather more as time went on.

It did seem to me that women didn't have control, complete control, over their sexuality, that the male partner was very important and he could largely control whether or not contraception was used well. And I saw the women as victims of this, victims deserving help, particularly if the pregnancy would disrupt her life, as of course, in many cases, it would.

It was really to save the women from the problem of handling a child at a time in their life when they didn't really want to have such responsibility, plus the fact that women have difficulty in negotiating a sexual relationship that includes effective contraception. These two things really motivated me to provide a service.

David Steel
Liberal MP and sponsor of the Medical Termination of Pregnancy Bill, 1966
I think the thing that really motivated me was the fact that there were so many illegal abortions, either self-induced or criminal, something like thirty to fifty women a year

died from illegal abortion. And the wards of all our major hospitals had patients with so-called septic and incomplete abortion – something that's been abolished since the abortion act was passed. So these two things were very important. Also the support of the Royal College.

I remember going to see an abortion carried out by the secretary of the Royal College of Obstetricians and Gynaecologists. And he showed me the notes and I said, this person seems to me to have been highly educated, able to argue a case, but I'm not sure that it's actually within the law. And he said, that's the problem, the law is so vague that we have to say, well, this person has been able to argue a good case as to why she needs an abortion. Therefore we agreed to do it. But I thought, that's really not satisfactory at all.

There was obviously quite strong opposition from the Catholic Church. And I had a Catholic seminary in my constituency and they asked me to go and speak to them at least twice. And they were always extremely courteous, I have to say, and we had quite severe arguments. But I used an aid, the Church of England report, which was very important, produced by the Bishop of Durham, called Abortion and Ethical Discussion, and they argued very convincingly against the Catholic case.

But as a result of my conversations with them I introduced what was called the conscience clause in the bill during the committee stage to say that no nurse, no doctor should be required to take part in a procedure if it was against their conscience. And that was very important. And they welcomed that and they accepted that otherwise we disagreed.

Elphis Christopher
Retired consultant in family planning and reproductive care

I had worked at the Elizabeth Garrett Anderson hospital as a house physician and obstetrics as well. And I knew several of the consultants there and I knew one or two who would actually perform abortions, provided the woman satisfied the act requirement.

I remember vividly referring a woman there. She was an Afro-Caribbean woman. She had four children and she had a new partner. And she got pregnant again, not wanting to be pregnant. And she didn't want to be looking after another child.

I referred her to Elizabeth Garrett Anderson and she saw the consultant there. The consultant was not anti-abortion. She would do abortions, but she in her wisdom thought that this woman would regret having an abortion because it was a new partner and it was his first child.

I only later heard that that woman met someone from the Birmingham train, some relative, I don't know who it was exactly, who did a backstreet abortion on her. And she was taken to Guy's Hospital and died.

And that left me with an absolute determination that no woman that I ever met who wanted an abortion wouldn't be helped by me.

Abortion in Northern Ireland
Joanna Biggs
(2017)

There is one abortion clinic in Northern Ireland: a Marie Stopes clinic on Great Victoria Street. Great Victoria joins the two-up two-down red brick terraces of the Lisburn Road, where Ulster banners fly from the lamp-posts, to the City Hall with its eau-de-nil dome and pale stone statue of Queen Victoria. The clinic isn't easy to find: the signs beside the door at No 14 are for BioKinetic Europe, which runs clinical trials, MKB Law, and Bupa; next door there's a Tesco Express and Boojum, a 'Mexican Burrito bar'. Danielle Roberts, an abortion rights activist with Alliance for Choice, says that on the days the clinic is open – Thursdays and Fridays from 9 a.m. until 6 p.m. – you can't miss it: members of the pressure group Precious Life are always outside. ('We are saving babies, mothers, and indeed this country from the silent holocaust that is brutally destroying fifty million lives worldwide every year.') Danielle acts as an escort for women with appoint-ments on the eighth floor: two activists for every woman, one wearing a 'body cam, as there have been assaults and harassment'.

Abortion, or assisting abortion, is a crime in the UK. The 1967 Abortion Act that applies in England, Wales and Scotland gets round this with provisos that allow abortion to be lawfully performed: if the pregnancy is still under 24 weeks and two doctors agree that there would be 'grave permanent injury' to the 'physical or mental health of the pregnant woman', or serious danger to the child. In Northern Ireland, which never adopted the 1967 act, the 1861 Offences against the Person Act substitutes for it. Any pregnant woman 'with intent to procure her own miscarriage . . . shall be guilty of felony . . . and being convicted thereof shall be liable . . . to be kept in penal servitude for life' (this remains the maximum penalty). There have been amendments over the years – case law shows that abortion is lawful in Northern Ireland in exceptional circumstances – but nothing to make abortion legal in cases of rape, for instance, has ever been put on the statute book, and successive iterations of medical guidelines haven't made it clear under what conditions doctors would be acting legally (or illegally) when performing an abortion. And there seems to be no political will to make the situation clear: only the Green Party and the People Before Profit Alliance support decriminalisation; Sinn Fein wants 'limited reform'; but the Alliance Party claim abortion is a matter of individual conscience and the DUP are openly pro-life. To make things worse, there has been no government in Stormont since March, and the DUP now has a 'confidence and supply' arrangement with the Conservative government. Westminster ignored the situation for years before this summer. On 29 June, after Stella Creasy put forward an amendment to the Queen's Speech, the chancellor announced that Northern Irish women who travelled to England for an abortion could for the first time have that abortion paid for by the NHS, like every other citizen and taxpayer of the UK.

Sixteen 'terminations of pregnancy' officially took place in Northern Ireland in 2014-15. In 2012, the Department of Health produced a set of guidelines for doctors in Northern Ireland: a psychiatrist had to be consulted if a woman's mental health was thought grounds for termination, but there was no mention of the required rank of the psychiatrist or the need for a second opinion (the guidelines have since been superseded, but the requirement for a psychiatric opinion remains). It amounted to saying that a woman 'doesn't know what she wants', said Samina Dornan, a consultant obstetrician and gynaecologist at the Royal Maternity Hospital in Belfast, where the abortions took place. Samina was brought up in Pakistan, and has worked in India: she remembers a husband bringing his pregnant wife to see her, and when she advised him that the woman needed a caesarean section, and the cost of it, he turned out his pockets to reveal a fraction of the money – all he had. His wife didn't get the operation. For Samina, the UK is supposed to be a beacon, so 'why is there a darkness under the beacon?' Her husband, James Dornan, is an emeritus professor of Foetal Medicine at Queen's Belfast. 'It's very hard to have grey-haired men telling you you're a criminal,' James, grey-haired himself, put it. As a junior doctor, he remembers going to the fathers of women in trouble and telling them that their daughters wanted, indeed needed, their help. Samina said she found her work 'very very lonely' at times. It was as if her colleagues were saying to her: 'Have you not learned yet?'

As well as 16 official abortions, 833 women were recorded as having come to England from Northern Ireland in 2015 to have an abortion, and at least 1438 women bought abortion pills online. Women on Web, an international collective of women who've had abortions, doctors, researchers and other abortion rights supporters, will send a woman who appeals for help on their website a dose of mifepristone and misoprostol after a consultation with a

175

doctor and a donation of 70 to 90 euros depending on circumstances. (Abortion using pills when less than nine weeks pregnant is safer than taking antibiotics, and the British Pregnancy Advisory Service runs an aftercare line for those who have taken the pills at home.) The pills arrive in the post, and women take them at home over a day or so; Women on Web has instructions in many languages (as well as a simplified version for people who can't read easily) on how to take them. In April 2016, a 21-year-old woman was given a three-month suspended sentence at Belfast Crown Court for taking abortion pills when she was 19. Her two housemates, both women, had reported her to the police. 'She called the baby 'the pest' and kept saying she just wanted rid of it,' one of the housemates, who was 38, told the *Belfast Telegraph* anonymously. 'She came down carrying a plastic bag. I couldn't bring myself to ask what she had done with the baby. After my own miscarriage, my mind wasn't in a good place.' She found the foetus in the bin: 'He had fingers, little toes. Even now I have a picture in my mind of it. Its wee foot was perfect.' When she found she couldn't put the bin out on collection day, she called the police. 'This isn't anything to do with the rights and wrongs of abortion. I'm not anti-abortion. I believe there are circumstances, like rape, where it should be a woman's choice. This is about her attitude. It was as if she was getting rid of a piece of clothing.' In another case going through the UK courts a mother is being prosecuted for buying and giving abortion pills to her fifteen-year-old daughter, who was pregnant by a boyfriend she was scared of. The mother went to their GP after her daughter had had the abortion, worried about her daughter's emotional wellbeing, and mentioned what had happened. Two months later a doctor at the practice reported them to the police.*

If you can't buy the pills – say, you're more than nine

weeks pregnant, or you have a complicating condition, or you can't face it – you'll have to travel. On average, two women from Northern Ireland travel to England every day. Most are married, most are having their first abortion, most are between 20 and 34. Clinics in England have 'Irish prices', set slightly lower than private prices, but even so the cheapest available abortion with pills costs £274, and the average costs £410. Then there is a consultation fee of between £65 and £80. Then there are the travel costs: a round trip booked a week in advance on Ryanair in high summer – leaving at 6.55 a.m. and returning at 11.10 p.m. – costs £134.98. Then there's the journey to the airport: if you are in Belfast, a taxi will cost £16 from the Lisburn Road, but you'd have to spend much more if you need a night in Belfast before flying out. Then there's travel from the airport to the clinic – a day return on the Gatwick Express is £24.30 – and travel within London. There's the cost of a visa or a passport, childcare if you have children, and an overnight stay in London should you need it.

'I keep talking to our clients about planning their unplanned abortions,' said Mara Clarke of the Abortion Support Network, an independent charity in England that advises women who need an abortion as well as helping them financially and practically with travel and accommodation. Clarke told me of a fourteen-year-old girl who phoned for help – they sent a volunteer to accompany her from start to finish. 'We are dealing with human beings,' she said, and laughed at herself when she found herself saying she provides a 'bespoke' service, as if she were a Savile Row tailor. Clarke set up the Abortion Support Network when she moved to the UK from America, where she

* In 2019, the court dropped all charges: 'I am so thankful that the change in the law will allow other women and girls to deal with matters like this privately within their own family circle,' she said.

had put up women who'd come to New York for an abortion in her studio apartment, and found that women from Northern Ireland, the Republic of Ireland, the Isle of Man and the Channel Islands needed the same thing here. 'There's no typical client,' she said. When volunteers have completed their first shift for the helpline they often say to her: 'I didn't expect there to be so much laughter.' She knows that ASN has helped trans men travel for an abortion; she knows there are also women she hadn't been able to help. One woman rang for advice when she became pregnant despite having an IUD fitted. She couldn't travel and wanted to take the pills but had to have the IUD removed first, for safety. When she went to her doctor, they couldn't find the IUD's strings, so gave her an ultrasound scan to locate the device, and found the pregnancy at the same time. The doctors wouldn't remove the IUD in case it caused a miscarriage. She couldn't tell them that's what she wanted to happen. 'What can she do?' Clarke asked.

Financial and practical difficulties can be quantified, but the emotional costs of doing something your culture can't talk about, won't legislate for, and thinks is a sin aren't measurable. In 1971, Simone de Beauvoir, Catherine Deneuve, Delphine Seyrig, Jeanne Moreau and Agnès Varda, among others, signed the Manifeste des 343, declaring they'd had an abortion – who knows if they had or not – in an attempt to break the silence. The stunt was part, and a not insignificant part, of a movement that culminated four years later in the loi Veil (named after Simone Veil, then minister of health) and the decriminalisation of abortion in France. We can make conditions better for women who have to have an abortion – it is and has always been an emergency measure – but how do we change the way it is thought about? Talking about abortion was hard then, and it is hard now: I found no one who would talk to me about it in the time I was preparing this piece. There are, however, many accounts in print, some angry and sad, some regretful and calm and grateful, and women can tell their stories in their own way and in their own words online. Women on Web's site has many accounts by women of their abortions: the numbers of clots, the pain or lack of it, the seriousness or not of the encounter that led them to that point. The X-ile Project, based in the Republic of Ireland, collects pictures of women who've had abortions and posts them online, with no names, no details: a woman with a short black fringe and an off the shoulder top stands in front of a bookcase, a blonde in coral lipstick rests her chin in her hand, a woman kneels in fallen leaves with a dog lead in one hand and her other around her spaniel. On 20 August last year, @twowomen-travel live-tweeted a trip to London for an abortion, from the 'chilly' 6 a.m. flight out, to a blurred grey wall seen from the window of the black cab, to the pistachio green chairs in the clinic waiting room, where they met two women who'd travelled from Munster in the south-west of Ireland. Abortion has been illegal for so long that there are many historical accounts of cases: I found five in a transcript of an international tribunal on abortion held in 1989 to gather evidence in support of the 1967 act being extended to Northern Ireland. Witness C was 22 at the time – 'I found that everyone had someone with them and I had my knitting' – and remembers going under while having her hand stroked by a nurse who 'had her eyes made up fantastically; they were gorgeous.' Witness D, pregnant at 18 and just about to sit her A Levels, had tried hot baths, soap and throwing herself down the stairs before her mother phoned a minister. A process of consultations with psychiatrists, gynaecologists and ministers to establish her sanity began and nearly ended with a hysterectomy. 'I don't think I was being particularly irrational. I didn't want to have a baby. I hadn't planned to have a baby and I was asking for the right not to have to bring a child into the world that I didn't want.' Hearing these stories I kept thinking of the ones we don't get to hear: the women who considered, and even wanted an abortion, but who went ahead with their pregnancies after all; the women who took the pills without guilt and who don't think of their abortion any more because it doesn't trouble them; the women who died and may still be dying.

I haven't had an abortion but my mother did, after the 1967 act came into force in England. She has Alzheimer's now and can't speak much any longer, so I can't ask her about it. It's a silence I can't break, and I'm not even sure my mother would speak to me about it if I could break it. The arguments in favour of a humane abortion law don't require you to love someone who has had one: the idea that women should have control over their own bodies by having access to a safe abortion; that you don't eliminate abortion by making it harder to get, you just make it more dangerous; that a woman with friends and parents and a job and a life, is worth more to the world than a foetus that can't yet survive outside the womb, seems so logical, so kind, so practical and honest that it shouldn't be necessary for women to unfold their sexual and emotional history to get one. On the other hand, it does seem that changes in abortion law have historically been a result of the details of individual cases becoming known. The 1967 act was preceded by the Bourne case of 1938, when a gynaecologist turned himself in having performed an abortion at St Mary's Paddington on a fourteen-year-old girl who had been raped by several soldiers. (She had been turned away by St Thomas's on the grounds she might be carrying a future prime minister.) I only know about my mother's

abortion because my father told me how she had told
him: he remembers that they were travelling on the Tube
together not long after they met and he had a sense that
there was something she wasn't telling him. He pushed
her to say; she wouldn't. My father grew up in the Home
Counties in the late 1950s and early 1960s – 'sheltered', as
he might put it – and my mother knew he was against
abortion on principle. That time on the Tube, he kept asking her, and she gave in. And on hearing her story, he
changed his mind. What will happen next? It is not yet
clear how the abortions of women who have to travel over
to England from Northern Ireland will be paid for, and
whether travel costs will be reimbursed. Northern Irish
feminists can't rely on Westminster: many people re-
minded me of the moment in 2008 when Harriet Harman
blocked a move to extend the 1967 act to Northern Ireland
in order to gain votes from the DUP for 42-day detention
of terrorism suspects. If it makes travel to England harder,
Brexit will make access to abortion harder too. Although
opinion poll after opinion poll shows that there is support
in Northern Ireland for a better law on abortion, people
there, I was told, vote according to affiliation, and for ever
more extreme parties, as they know any measure will get
watered down under the power-sharing arrangement put
in place following the Good Friday Agreement. Even so,
there is energy around the various campaigns. In 1967
Britain was one of the first countries in Europe to improve
access to abortion, and although the law serves, I could
still go to jail if I bought pills for a friend and gave them to
her. I don't know quite how a modern abortion law would
go – perhaps it would start by ditching the 1861 act, having
no time limit and allowing abortion at a woman's request
– but I know that the threat of jail shouldn't be part of it.

Three Poems
Holly Pester
(2021)

Comic Timing

I went to Ilford on my own
walked up a dual carriageway
to McDonalds for a cup of tea and a think then
went back to the clinic with half a blueberry muffin
in my pocket
I was handed a white laminated
square with a number on it
I will be called by the number not
by my name I lied
on the form that asked if there was anyone
at home my Uber arrived
as the cramps started
I was told to be home within one hour the journey time was
45 minutes
I felt nauseous
breathed slowly
the driver talked about ratings
he liked chatty and punctual passengers he once gave a married
couple no stars when the man hit the woman
I felt dizzy we drove past his house that's my house
he looked up my ratings and said I was above average

you must be a nice person maybe normally more chatty
I tried to sound lovely
said I was unwell in a weak
voice he joked I would get no stars
if I was sick
I go through my to-do list
to clean an Airbnb
do it for money
I am a bad maid to capital's heart muscle there was one
night between guests
I had a plan to lie down
with the tv on
eat a Marks & Spencer cottage pie
sleep on the sofa wake up
change the bedding
go back to the big cold house I live in and feel treated
I knew
what to expect from
the last time the pain got
acute on a two-hour arc
I had had a hot bath
I had sat by the bath like a bird
and held
a bundle in my hand
poked about for a god or a plan
what survives a day?
but this time there was no build
up there was no flight
the pain stayed still from the clinic
to the brown
and honourable sofa
not getting easier or worse
I did not
feel anything passing through me

but the room was dark and
around me
I woke up at 7 a.m.
took some painkillers and finished cleaning I left the key
and got the bus
still bleeding a
bit still on the brink
of a big pain but going nowhere
my housemate was having a party
I was very tired but she
is out of sync and soulful
I needed to be dressed and nice
I made a bowl of beetroot
puree and hummus
I made a simple butter pastry grated cheese
into it twisted the dough into sticks they snapped in the
oven but smelt delicious for the people
I greeted them alone
didn't know any of them
the pain stayed still I smelt real leaned on the counter and
decided to drink
some of my friends arrived
I behaved normally
my good friend quietly asked me to stop being cruel to her
I was very disturbed
told her I didn't feel well
I followed smokers worried about my good friend's feelings until
I found her in the middle
of some laughing doing
an impression of a cat scratching a pole

her movements in a black
and white skirt

were comedic
and expert
she moved like a clown she
swung the lower half of her body
left-to-right she upped her arms
stopped to look at the room
through her hair then carried
on clowns invent new grace
for limbs out of ungraceful
lines in the room
I think I was mid verb
like my friend I said to my head
I am mid verb
maybe I have become the verb
I am not having
l am
abortive was the last thing I
thought before falling onto
the purple and habited bed
face down we have to feel
everything in our stomach
ache is tempo
I have seen millions of films
I get it
or there is no story only comedy
but my friend has clowned time
her skirt was so stripy
I am reading it now
a difference between being
scanned for a future
or past material
for latency or tendency
I am very interested in this and I
am interested in the catch of the bed

which idea is homeless?
what is surplus connection to poetry what is the
rushed little examinations on a screen out of view
screened from me the nurse
confirms she can see a vaguer noun
something like a burn
there is not a thing but time read
translated where there might be form
it is there or a picture of noise
not like a construct
of the noise like a head it's this
way up
he is waving
creatively
at the elaborate
so it is just legibility or esoteric
reading styles
the matter
is not interpreted it is agile
easily switches between verb and noun
I could be creative but
I am beginning
to think stuck linguistically
awkward to material or reality
cannot have
have to be
timely nothing has changed
I need to find my friend
the cat the clown so
she can tell me the time
she has animation to give
I went to Ilford alone
was handed a pink laminated square
a staff was inserted I felt

hungry time was coming out slowly
I shouldn't have expected it to happen all at once
but I was told to expect it to happen all at once
they held up the staff
red for someone
I feel like a comedy
that's probably a lot of it there
it's still going on

Aborted

Like history this sliced up worm carries on in both directions
I know thee, I have found thee, & I will not let thee go

They dug and buried
arrests were made

Giving birth by a hedgerow I ask the hedgerow what it feels
like to be broken into

It was verses we should've sung
bring back my
I doubled up

Is there a dead bird in you?
– no
        You're a strike-through line
dived over your sitter to the next incur

Ask me. Do lend here. I fail. I drink a foot. I ask the wall
What plot did you sneak
to improve the noun for staff?
to slur a rebel's speech

livers split   out pours solution
– a worm
        ask it

The Work and Its Record

You can't separate the work of cutting and glueing the
newspaper clippings and organising the meetings and
chairing and note taking and making the tea and catalog-
uing and nursing and protesting and caring and nurtur-
ing and washing the cups and booking the busses and de-
centralising and dismantling power and educating and
making the badges and tying the string and folding the
box and sending the letters and filing the files and fixing
the index and drawing the pamphlets and drawing the
logos and listing the agendas and doing the administrative
tasks and holding the door open and writing the songs
and singing the songs and singing the words bring back
my body bring back my body bring back my body to me
to the tune of 'My Bonnie Lies Over the Ocean'

and photocopying the songs and saving them and standing
in the picket line at Armagh Jail and refusing to strip and
refusing to wash and sweeping the floors and linking arms
and booking rooms and booking halls and booking meals
from the antifascist work from the trade union work from
the work of solidarity from the work of working making
money to eat from stopping the BNP campaigning outside
train stations from blocking Enoch Powell's Unborn Child
Protection Bill from licking the stamps and posting the
letters and lobbying MPs from making love notes on the
back of the envelope from signing on from wishing you
well and saying Merry Christmas and writing please call
me I cannot pay the telephone from supporting the miners'
strike from supporting the steelworkers' struggle from
blocking Alton's Bill and blocking the Embryo Bill and
blocking Corrie's Bill and the Infant Life Preservation Bill
and the Lord Bishop of Birmingham's Embryo Protection

Bill from writing the newsletter that says
dear Sisters from booking the May Day stall
from singing
Schoolgirls and Secretaries
Schoolgirls and Secretaries working women
and wives
Schoolgirls and Secretaries
Schoolgirls and Secretaries working women
and wives
from leaving a note that says look at page 14
it's horrendous
and reclaiming
the measure of 'survival' from the work of
survival
and resisting someone else saying when it is
the time of possible
survival and what is the time of possible
survival and whose survival
is possible and perceived and
what week of a body of its own weeks does
survival start at
from fighting the details of 14 weeks 18
weeks 20 weeks 24 weeks 28
weeks 28 weeks 28 weeks back to 24 weeks
from knowing
to survive means what lives next is different
and contains the fight
what survives will not be apart from what was conceived
as she conceived it what was lived is in what is conceived
as
survival
what survives is what is prolonged
continued-remade from what was lived
after and before

life beyond life
is not
made from outside it
the making point of survival can only be
attributed to + by she who
has lived
what survives? the work and the tradition of
living in the worker
in the records of their songs
the determination is produced from the
work done + sung and
cannot be separated from the work of the
fight from the work of
asking in the given and perceived moment who has the
right to life?
or from the work of hearing
one song sung to the tune of another's older song

Who's got the right to life?
Money buys it
Who's got the right to life?
War denies it
Who's got the right to life?
Those that live it
Who's got the right to life?
We that give it

From *Up the Junction*
Nell Dunn
(1963)

W^e went in.
    'Hello, darling. Hello, love.' Winny was about 45. She wore a red dress above her knees showing her varicose-vein legs, ankle socks and gym shoes.

'I had that Harry here again last night. He didn't go till six this morning. I made him sleep in the bath. He's bringing me 50 gals of paint tomorrer – free sample. "Well," I says to him, "you've had my free sample, now what about yours?"' She had delicate arms and huge bony hands with long red fingers which she waved around.

'Well, what have we here, Annie?'

'I've come, I've come . . .' said Rube, nervous.

'I know why you've come – there's only one reason good-looking girls come to see Winny. Here, Annie, pop across the off-licence and get me a quarter-bottle whisky.'

She gave her a ten-shilling note and Rube and I were left alone with Winny.

'How far are you gone, love?'

'About three months.'

Winny poked Rube in the stomach.

'Oh, then you've only got a small problem in there.'

'You see I can't keep it . . .' Rube began.

'Don't try and explain, love. How can you ever explain

anything? It's the most bloody impossible thing in the world. How much money have you got?'

'Four pounds.'

'Give it over. You don't look more than seventeen.'

'I'm eighteen next month.'

'Come on upstairs, then your friend can wait for you down here.'

But that wasn't the last time Rube and I trailed up to Wimbledon. She had to go seven times before anything happened. Often we'd go into the kitchen and Winny would be sitting on some man's knee. As Rube said, 'She wouldn't care if you was watching her – teasin' em, sloppin' over em.' Winny didn't eat anything all day. She was always on the bottle.

Later I'd cart Rube home weak-kneed and trembling on the bus. 'Terry came down for me last night – the first time in six weeks. He said, "Don't you go up there no more, I don't want no kid of mine to go down the drain." But Sylvie said, "Now she's started she's gotta keep on or it'll be born a monster." So Terry walks out, but not before he shouted so half the street can hear: "Anyway she was nothing but a cheap thrill."'

We rode past the park. The water lilies are opening red mouths. The birds hop in the flower garden and the crazy music streams from the fairground.

'When she does the syringe you feel a sort of weakening pain shoot up in yer . . .'

It was about six on a Sunday morning. There was a banging on my door. I looked out of the window and saw Johnny Macarthy below. I knew it must be serious because Johnny deserted from the army fifteen years ago and hadn't been outside his own house since in case they caught up with him – so far they hadn't.

I let him in out of the dark mist, 'It's Rube. She's ever so

194

bad. I want to phone up Winny.' Johnny phoned Winny. It rang a long time and when she finally answered it she said she couldn't come.

I went back over with Johnny. Rube was lying back against her mum's knees, a green eiderdown covering her, white and heaving.

'Let me get the doctor.'

'No, they might try and save the baby. I don't want no kids from that gink – we've enough kids in this house as it is without no more.'

'I told her, didn't I, to keep away from him?' said her mum.

A few hours later Rube started to shriek. Her jet-black hair stuck to her face and tiny rivulets of blue rinse coursed down her white cheeks. She was semi-delirious.

The smell of Sunday dinner cooking floated up the stairs. Rube bent up tight with pain.

'It's lucky I ain't got me health and strength no more else I'd do him, do him right up I would,' said her mum. Sylvie came in. 'I'll hold her now, Mum, if you want to go and have yer dinner. Ray says he'd hit him sky-high if it wasn't that he might get nicked for it.'

The voice of Johnny, sailed up from the kitchen: 'He'd better watch it from me, too – I shan't always be stayin' in, will I?'

Rube shrieked again.

'Let me ring the doctor.'

'Oh, all right then.'

In the kitchen everyone was eating. The light was full on. Ben E. King sang:

Oh yes, she said, yes,
And she opened her arms.
Oh yes, she said, yes and
She closed her eyes.

When I came back from ringing, Rube was shrieking, a long, high, animal shriek. The baby was born alive, five months old. It moved, it breathed, its heart beat.

Rube lay back, white and relieved, across the bed. Sylvie and her mum lifted the eiderdown and peered at the tiny baby still joined by the cord. 'You can see it breathing, look!'

Rube smiled. 'It's nothing – I've had a look meself.'

'I reckon she had some pluck going seven times,' said her mum.

Finally the ambulance arrived. They took Rube away, but they left behind the baby, which had now grown cold. Later Sylvie took him, wrapped in the *Daily Mirror* and threw him down the toilet.

From 'Abortion'
Andrea Dworkin
(1983)

Before the 1973 Supreme Court decision legalising abortion in the United States, abortion was a crime. Some abortions were medically licensed, but they were a minute percentage of the abortions actually undergone by women. This meant that there were no records of the illegal abortions performed (each abortion was a crime, each abortion was clandestine), no medical histories or records, no statistics. Information on illegal abortions came from these sources: (1) the testimonies of women who had had such abortions and survived; (2) the physical evidence of the botched abortions, evidence that showed up in hospital emergency rooms all over the country every single day-perforated uteruses, infections including gangrene, severe haemorrhaging, incomplete abortions (in which foetal tissue is left in the womb, always fatal if not removed); (3) the physical evidence of the dead bodies (for instance, nearly one half of the maternal deaths in New York State resulted from illegal abortions); (4) the anecdotal reminiscences of doctors who were asked for 'help' by desperate women. These sources provide a profile of the average woman who wanted and got an illegal abortion. Indisputably, she was married and had children: 'It has been repeatedly demonstrated that most criminal abort-

ions today are obtained by married women with children,'
wrote Jerome E. Bates and Edward S. Zawadzki in *Criminal
Abortion*, published in 1964. An estimated two thirds of the
women who got criminal abortions were married. This
means that up to two thirds of the botched abortions were
done on married women; up to two thirds of the dead
were married women; perhaps two thirds of the survivors
are married women. This means that most of the women
who risked death or maiming so as not to bear a child
were married – perhaps one million married women each
year. They were not shameless sluts, unless all women by
definition are. They were not immoral in traditional terms
though, even then, they were thought of as promiscuous
and single. Nevertheless, they were not women from the
streets, but women from homes; they were not daughters
in the homes of fathers, but wives in the homes of husbands. They were, quite simply, the good and respectable
women of Amerika. The absolute equation of abortion
with sexual promiscuity is a bizarre distortion of the real
history of women and abortion – too distorted to be acceptable even in the United States, where historical memory reaches back one decade. Abortion has been legalised
just under one decade. The facts should not be obliterated
yet. Millions of respectable, God-fearing, married women
have had illegal abortions. They thank their God that they
survived; and they keep quiet.

Their reasons for keeping quiet are women's reasons.
Because they are women, their sexuality or even percept-
ions of it can discredit or hurt or destroy them – inexplic-
ably shame them; provoke rage, rape, and ridicule in men.
Dissociation from other women is always the safest course.
They are not sluttish, but other women who have had
abortions probably are. They tried not to get pregnant
(birth control being illegal in many parts of the country

before 1973), but other women who had abortions probably did not. They love their children, but other women who have had abortions may well be the cold mothers, the cruel mothers, the vicious women. They are individuals of worth and good morals who had compelling reasons for aborting, but the other women who had abortions must have done something wrong, were wrong, are somehow indistinct (not emerged from the primal female slime as individuals), were sex not persons. In keeping the secret they cut themselves off from other women to escape the shame of other women, the shame of being the same as other women, the shame of being female. They are ashamed of having had this bloody experience, of having this female body that gets torn into again and again and bleeds and can die from the tearing and the bleeding, the pain and the mess, of having this body that was violated again, this time by abortion. Admitting to an illegal abortion is like admitting to having been raped: whoever you tell can see you, undress you, spread your legs, see the thing go in, see the blood, watch the pain, almost touch the fear, almost taste the desperation. The woman who admits to having had an illegal abortion allows whoever hears her to picture her – her as an individual in that wretched body – in unbearable vulnerability, as close to being punished purely for being female as anyone ever comes. It is the picture of a woman being tortured for having had sex.

There is the fear of having murdered: not someone, not real murder, but of having done something hauntingly wrong. She has learned (learned is a poor word for what has happened to her) that every life is more valuable than her own; her life gets value through motherhood, a kind of benign contamination. She has been having children in her mind, and getting her value through them, since she herself was a baby. Little girls believe that dolls are real babies. Little girls put dolls to sleep, feed them, bathe them, diaper them, nurse them through illnesses, teach them how to walk and how to talk and how to dress – love them. Abortion turns a woman into a murderer all right: she kills that child pregnant in her since her own childhood; she kills her allegiance to Motherhood First. This is a crime. She is guilty: of not wanting a baby.

There is the fear of having murdered because so many men believe so passionately that she has. To many men, each aborted pregnancy is the killing of a son – and he is the son killed. His mother would have killed him if she had had the choice. These men have a peculiarly retroactive and abstract sense of murder if she had had a choice, I would not have been born – which is murder. The male ego, which refuses to believe in its own death, now pushes backwards, before birth. I was once a fertilised egg; therefore to abort a fertilised egg is to kill me. Women keep abortions secret because they are afraid of the hysteria of men confronted with what they regard as the spectre of their own extinction. If you had your way, men say to feminists, my mother would have aborted me. Killed me. 'I was born out of wedlock (and against the advice that my mother received from her doctor),' Jesse Jackson writes in fervent opposition to abortion, 'and therefore abortion is a personal issue for me.' The woman's responsibility to the fertilised egg is imaginatively and with great conviction construed to be her relation to the adult male. At the very least, she must not murder him; nor should she outrage his existence by an assertion of her separateness from him, her distinctness, her importance as a person independent of him. The adult male's identification with the fertilised egg as being fully himself can even be conceptualised in terms of power. his rightful power over an impersonal

200

female (all females being the same in terms of function). 'The power I had as one cell to affect my environment I shall never have again,' R.D. Laing laments in an andro-centric meditation on pre-birth ego. 'My environment' is a woman; the adult male, even as a fertilised egg, one cell, has the right of occupation with respect to her – he has the right to be inside her and the rightful power to change her body for his sake. This relation to gestation is specifically male. Women do not think of themselves in utero when they think either of being pregnant or of aborting, men think of pregnancy and abortion primarily in terms of themselves, including what happened or might have happened to them back in the womb when, as one cell, they were themselves.

Women keep quiet about abortions they have had, illegal abortions, because they are humiliated by the memory of those abortions; they are humiliated by the memory of their desperation, the panic, finding the money, finding the abortionist, the dirt, the danger, the secrecy. Women are humiliated when they remember asking for help, beg-ging for help, when they remember those who turned away, left them out in the cold. Women are humiliated by the memory of the fear. Women are humiliated by the memory of the physical intrusion, the penetration, the pain, the violation; countless women were sexually as-saulted by the abortionist before or after the abortion; they hate remembering. Women are humiliated because they hated themselves, their sex, their female bodies, they hated being female. Women hate remembering illegal abortions because they almost died, they could have died, they want-ed to die, they hoped they would not die, they made promises to God begging him not to let them die, they were afraid of dying before and during and after, they have never again been so afraid of death or so alone; they had never before been so afraid of death or so alone. And women hate remembering illegal abortions because their husbands experienced none of this: which no woman forgives.

Women also keep quiet about illegal abortions precisely because they had married sex: their husbands mounted them, fucked them, impregnated them; their husbands determined the time and the place and the act; desire, pleasure or orgasm were not necessarily experienced by the women, yet the women ended up on the butcher's block. The abortionist finished the job the husband had started. No one wants to remember this.

Women also keep quiet about abortions they have had because they wanted the child, but the man did not; because they wanted other children and could not have them; because they never regretted the abortion and did regret subsequent children; because they had more than one abortion, which, like more than one rape, fixes the woman's guilt. Women keep quiet about abortions because abortion inside marriage is selfish, ruthless, marks the woman as heartless, loveless – yet she did it anyway. Women also keep quiet about abortions they have had, illegal abortions, because the woman who has had one, or tried to induce one in herself, is never really trusted again: if she will do that to herself – hurt herself, tear up her own insides rather than have a child – she must be the frenzied female, the female gone mad, the lunatic female, the female in rebellion against her own body and therefore against man and God, the female who is most feared and abhorred, the Medea underneath the devoted wife and mother, the wild woman, the woman enraged with the sorrow between her legs, the woman grief-stricken by the way men use her uterus, the woman who has finally refused to be forced and so she must be punished by the pain and the blood, the tearing and the terror.

The law gives a married woman to her husband to be fucked at will, his will; the law forced the woman to bear any child that might result. Illegal abortion was a desperate, dangerous, last-ditch, secret, awful way of saying no. It is no wonder that so many respectable, married, God-fearing women hate abortion.

the lost baby poem
Lucille Clifton
(1972)

the time i dropped your almost body down
down to meet the waters under the city
and run one with the sewage to the sea
what did i know about waters rushing back
what did i know about drowning
or being drowned

you would have been born into winter
in the year of the disconnected gas
and no car   we would have made the thin
walk over genesee hill into the canada wind
to watch you slip like ice into strangers' hands
you would have fallen naked as snow into winter
if you were here i could tell you these
and some other things

if i am ever less than a mountain
for your definite brothers and sisters
let the rivers pour over my head
let the sea take me for a spiller
of seas   let black men call me stranger
always   for your never named sake

From *The Heart of the Race*
Beverley Bryan, Stella Dadzie
Suzanne Scafe
(1985)

As Black women, our experiences as patients are not only determined by our economic status. As women, we have inherited a long medical tradition of male neglect. Historically, the control and manipulation of women's bodies by an all-male medical profession has meant that we have been consistently denied access to essential knowledge about ourselves. We have been fed myths, distortions and lies, so much so that the majority of women today still adhere to male-defined concepts of our physical, sexual and emotional identities. As sex objects, as long-suffering bearers of children or as menstrual beings, many women, Black and white, continue to accept roles which white men have chosen for us. Where our health is concerned, this has meant a consistent failure by male doctors to prioritise the health issues which most concern us. It is for this reason that we still allow ourselves to be wired up, legs akimbo, pumped with harmful drugs, peered into and subjected to inductions and interference we never asked for when giving birth. It's for this reason that our gynaecological and other needs as women have been consistently ignored or trivialised. And it's for this reason that we've allowed ourselves to be permanently damaged in the interests of 'family planning', the main purpose of which is to preserve at all costs the sexual enjoyment of men, regardless of the actual or potential effects on our health.

In family planning clinics, doctors rarely spend time with us to explain the various contraceptives available. The pill is often presented to us as the best method simply because it is easiest to prescribe.

I was first prescribed the pill after I'd had my baby. I was breastfeeding, though, and they made me feel sick so I stopped taking them. The doctor at the hospital advised me to go along to the family planning clinic. There I was given another type of pill, but these brought me up in lumps and rashes. I went back to the clinic and told them, and they gave me yet another brand. This one gave me migraines and it got so bad that I could hardly open my eyes with the pain I was in. So I went back again, and got my fourth packet. This time, whenever I had a period I felt as if my stomach was going to burst. My stomach swelled up and I was in excruciating pain. Eventually I went to the doctor about it, and he phoned an ambulance and sent me to the hospital for an examination. But they weren't too concerned about me in casualty even though I was crying, I was in so much pain. They left me on a trolley in the corridor for hours and when I couldn't take it any longer I got up and discharged myself. This meant I had to go back to the clinic. They suggested fitting an IUD. That was fine – no irregular periods, no pain – but it kept slipping so they had to take it out. It got stuck in the neck of my womb, and they spent half an hour at the clinic trying to get it out. At this point I felt that I'd had enough and I told them I wasn't prepared to try any more of their contraceptives. The woman started trying to patronise me and I left there very upset. I went home worrying about what I would use and I really started fretting, because the baby was still young and I didn't want another one so soon. Then my friend introduced me to one of the low oestrogen pills, and I went back to the clinic and asked if I could try it out. I really had to put up a fight to get them to prescribe it for me. You know why? Because it was a low dosage pill and they didn't think I was responsible enough to take it regularly at the same time every day.

Because we are considered a 'high promiscuity risk', Black and white working-class women are often encouraged to accept contraceptives involving less 'risk' – but the reduced risk of pregnancy is invariably considered more important than the increased risk to our health. And so we are prescribed coils, which can infect our fallopian tubes and cause sterility; or Depo Provera, which can have dangerous, long-term side-effects. When a Black woman enters a doctor's surgery, there is another dimension to this experience, particularly if the doctor is a white, middle-class man, as he usually is. In addition to the alienation arising out of our different sex and class we also have to face false assumptions about our lives and a host of communication barriers determined by race and culture. All these factors combine to make us feel even more vulnerable and exposed and even less confident to question doctors' prescriptions or make demands about what is best for us. And our vulnerability is compounded by the fact that doctors frequently ask their most important questions when we are lying flat on our backs on the couch in the surgery, when there is little dignity left to salvage and little hope of challenging, on the spot, any of their sexist and racist assumptions about us.

Our abuse at the hands of the family planning service is intensified even further by the many popular racist myths and stereotypes which abound about Black women's sexuality, enshrined within medical science. Black women's ability to reproduce has come to be viewed as a moral flaw,

209

to be frowned upon and controlled, so much so that doctors frequently take it upon themselves to exercise control over our fertility in the interests of (white) society. The consequences of this are evident in the numerous cases of Black women who receive unwanted sterilisations or terminations, or the damaging long-term contraceptive DP (Depo Provera), all in the interests of controlling the numbers of 'unwanted' Black babies. The fact that we may not view our unplanned children in this way within our own culture is of no consequence in a society where we are expected to conform to indigenous attitudes. Many paternal and apparently sympathetic doctors have persuaded Black women to accept an abortion or contraceptive she did not really want, out of a concern to control our fertility. And such attitudes are reflected not only through our experiences here in Britain, but in our countries of origin, where myths about the need for population control are used as an excuse for the unleashing of mass sterilisation and birth control programmes on Black and Third World women, often as part of the West's 'aid' package:

> If you're talking about Black women and fertility controls, you have to look first at the whole myth about the Third World being overpopulated. Even if you look at the land occupancy of our countries, you can see that this is a myth. Take Zimbabwe, for example – the population there is about seven million, which is roughly the size of the population of London alone, yet up until a few years ago they had mobile units going around the country every three months, pumping the women with Depo Provera and often not telling them what the injection was for or what the side effects could be. And that was before independence, when they were still trying to encourage whites to emigrate there. Now, how else are we to interpret this kind of policy? It's true that they use all these arguments about how there are

too many of us to feed and how we breed too much, but the fact of the matter is that the world has more than enough food to feed every man, woman and child. It's the way those resources are distributed which is the root of the problem.

And in a context where your children are your wealth and the only guarantee that you'll be looked after in your old age, you're talking about genocide. There's no other word for it. So you have to take that into account when looking at what happens to us here in Britain. You only have to talk to Black women – the number of us who suffer the consequences of bad birth techniques, for example, where the afterbirth is left in and becomes infected; or the number of us who get sterilised against our wishes, because some doctor persuades us to have it done when we go into hospital for something completely different. Or the number of young Black girls who are persuaded to have an abortion that they don't want and their mothers don't want them to have either. I'm not saying that every case is like this, of course these things happen sometimes for sound medical reasons.

But seeing and talking to a lot of Black women, as I do in my job, I've found there are far too many cases where there aren't any justifiable medical grounds. If you just looked at things and didn't check what is happening to Black women everywhere else in the world, you'd probably put it down to the production-line techniques in the hospitals we go to. Or you'd say, well, that's just because we tend to go to the run-down hospitals where there are no resources and not enough staff. But it's not as simple as that. If they don't take any care, that neglect is deliberate. There are a lot of doctors who don't even bother to make a secret of the fact that they go along with the idea that we are sapping this country's resources, and see it as their professional duty to keep our numbers down. They say things like, 'Well, you've already got two children, so why do you need to have any more? You might as well get your tubes tied when you come in for that D&C.' It's only when you hear Black women talking and realise how many of us this is happening to that you see things in perspective. And you begin to realise that it's not just about bad resources or neglect. It's about racism. They don't want us here anymore and they don't need our kids to work for them, so it's easier just to quietly kill us off.

It's for reasons such as these that, when the Women's Liberation Movement took up the issue of 'Abortion on Demand' in the early 1970s, Black women had to point out that we have always been given abortions more readily than white women and are indeed often encouraged to have terminations we didn't ask for. It's for this reason, too, that when the women's movement demanded 'free, safe and available contraception for all women', we had to remind them that for Black women this often means being used as guinea-pigs in mass birth control programmes, or as objects of 'research' when new forms of birth control need to be tested. And when the same women talked about 'A Woman's Right to Choose', we responded that for Black women, this must also mean having the right to choose to have our children, planned or unplanned. For us, the politics of women's health have always had that added racist dimension – a dimension which has been overlooked far too often by the white, middle-class women who constitute the majority in the women's movement.

Abortion
Audre Lorde
(1981)

Half-remembered information garnered from other people's friends who had been 'in trouble'. The doctor in Pennsylvania who did good clean abortions very cheaply because his daughter had died on a kitchen table after he had refused to abort her. But sometimes the police grew suspicious, so he wasn't always working. A call through the grapevine found out that he wasn't.

Trapped. Something – anything – had to be done. No one else can take care of this. What am I going to do?

The doctor who gave me the results of my positive rabbit test was a friend of Jean's aunt, who had said he might 'help'. This doctor's help meant offering to get me into a home for unwed mothers out of the city run by a friend of his. 'Anything else,' he said, piously, 'is illegal.' I was terrified by the stories I had heard in school and from my friends about the butchers and the abortion mills of the *Daily News*: cheap kitchen table abortions. Jean's friend Francie had died on the way to the hospital just last year after trying to do it with the handle of a #1 paint brush.

These horrors were not just stories, nor infrequent. I had seen too many of the results of botched abortions on the bloody gurneys lining the hallways outside the Emergency Room.

Besides, I had no real contacts.

Through winter-dim streets, I walked to the subway from the doctor's office, knowing I could not have a baby and knowing it with a certainty that galvanised me far beyond anything I knew to do.

The girl in the Labor Youth League who had introduced me to Peter had had an abortion, but it had cost $300. The guy had paid for it. I did not have $300, and I had no way of getting $300, and I swore her to secrecy telling her it wasn't Peter's. Whatever was going to be done I had to do. And fast.

Castor oil and a dozen Bromo-Quinine pills didn't help.

Mustard baths gave me a rash, but didn't help, either.

Neither did jumping off a table in an empty classroom at Hunter, and I almost broke my glasses.

Ann was a Licensed Practical Nurse I knew from working the evening shift at Beth David Hospital. We used to flirt in the nurses' pantry after midnight when the head nurse was sneaking a doze in some vacant private room on the floor. Ann's husband was in Korea. She was beautiful and friendly, small, sturdy and deeply black. One night, while we were warming the alcohol and talcum for P.M. Care backrubs, she pulled out her right breast to show me the dark mole which grew at the very line where her deep-purple aureola met the slightly lighter chocolate brown of her skin, and which, she told me with a mellow laugh, 'drove all the doctors crazy'.

Ann had introduced me to amphetamine samples on those long sleepy night shifts, and we crashed afterwards at her bright kitchenette apartment on Cathedral Parkway, drinking black coffee and gossiping until dawn about the strange habits of head nurses, among other things. I called Ann at the hospital and met her after work one night. I told her I was pregnant.

'I thought you was gay!'

I let that one pass. I asked her to get me some ergotrate from the pharmacy, a drug which I had heard from nurses' talk could be used to encourage bleeding.

'Are you crazy?' she said in horror, 'you can't mess around with that stuff, girl, it could kill you. It causes haemorrhaging. Let me see what I can find out for you.'

Everybody knows somebody, Ann said. For her, it was the mother of another nurse in Surgery. Very safe and clean, fool-proof and cheap, she said. An induced miscarriage by Foley catheter. A homemade abortion.

The narrow hard-rubber tube, used in post-operative cases to keep various body canals open, softened when sterilised. When passed through the cervix into the uterus while soft, it coiled, all fifteen inches, neatly into the womb. Once hardened, its angular turns ruptured the bloody lining and began the uterine contractions that eventually expelled the implanted foetus, along with the membrane. If it wasn't expelled too soon. If it did not also puncture the uterus.

The process took about fifteen hours and cost $40, which was a week and a half's pay.

I walked over to Mrs Munoz's apartment after I had finished work at Dr Sutter's office that afternoon. The January thaw was past, and even though it was only 1 p.m., the sun had no warmth. The winter grey of mid-February and the darker patches of dirty Upper East-Side snow. Against my peacoat in the wind I carried a bag containing the fresh pair of rubber gloves and the new bright-red catheter Ann had taken from the hospital for me, and a sanitary pad. I had most of the contents of my last pay envelope, plus the $5 Ann had lent me.

'Darling, take off your skirt and panties now while I boil this.' Mrs Munoz took the catheter from the bag and poured boiling water from a kettle over it and into a shallow basin. I sat curled around myself on the edge of her broad bed, embarrassed by my half-nakedness before this stranger. She pulled on the thin rubber gloves, and setting the basin upon the table, she looked over to where I was perched in the corner of the neat and shabby room.

'Lie down, lie down. You scared, huh?' She eyed me from under the clean white kerchief that completely covered her small head. I could not see her hair, and could not tell from her sharp-featured, bright-eyed face how old she was, but she looked so young that it surprised me that she could have a daughter old enough to be a nurse.

'You scared? Don't be scared, sweetheart,' she said, picking up the basin with the edge of a towel and moving it onto the other edge of the bed.

'Now just lie back and put your legs up. Nothing to be afraid of. Nothing to it – I would do it on my own daughter. Now if you was three, four months, say, it would be harder because it would take longer, see. But you not far gone. Don't worry. Tonight, tomorrow, maybe, you hurt a little bit, like bad cramps. You get cramps?'

I nodded, mute, my teeth clenched against the pain. But her hands were busy between my legs as she looked intently at what she was doing. 'You take some aspirin, a little drink. Not too much though. When it's ready, then the tube comes back down and the bleeding comes with it. Then no more baby. Next time you take better care of yourself, darling.'

By the time Mrs Munoz had finished talking she had skilfully passed the long slender catheter through my cervix into my uterus. The pain had been acute but short. It lay coiled inside of me like a cruel benefactor, slowly hardening and turning angular as it cooled, soon to rupture the delicate lining and wash away my worries in blood.

Since to me all pain was unbearable, even this short bout seemed interminable.

'You see, now, that's all there is to it. Now that wasn't so bad, was it?'

She patted my shuddering thigh reassuringly. 'All over. Now get dressed. And wear the pad,' she cautioned, as she pulled off the rubber gloves. 'You start bleeding in a couple of hours, then you lie down. Here, you want the gloves back?'

I shook my head and handed her the money. She thanked me. 'That's a special price because you a friend of Anna's,' she smiled, helping me on with my coat. 'By this time tomorrow, it will be all over. If you have any trouble you call me. But no trouble, just a little cramps.' I stopped off on West Fourth Street and bought a bottle of Apricot Brandy for 89 cents. It was the day before my 18th birthday and I decided to celebrate my relief. Now all I had to do was hurt.

On the slow Saturday Local back to my furnished room in Brighton Beach the cramps began, steadily increasing. Everything's going to be all right now, I kept saying to myself as I leaned over slightly on the subway seat, if I can just get through the next day. I can do it. She said it was safe. The worst is over, and if anything goes wrong I can always go to the hospital. I'll tell them I don't know her name and I was blindfolded so I don't know where I was.

I wondered how bad the pain was going to get and that terrified me more than anything else. All pain was unbearable and I had no measure. But the terror was only about the pain.

I did not think about how I could die from haemorrhage, or a perforated uterus.

The subway car was almost empty.

Just last spring around this same time one Saturday

morning, I woke up in my mother's house to the smell of bacon frying in the kitchen and the abrupt realisation as I opened my eyes that the dream I had been having of having just given birth to a baby girl was in fact only a dream.

I sat bolt upright in my bed facing the little window onto the airshaft, and cried and cried and cried from disappointment until my mother came into the room to see what was wrong.

The train came up out of the tunnel over the bleak edge of South Brooklyn. The Coney Island Parachute Jump steeple and a huge grey gas storage tank were the only breaks in the leaden skyline.

I dared myself to feel any regrets.

That night about 8 p.m., I was lying curled tightly on my bed, trying to distract myself from the stabbing pains in my groin by deciding whether or not I wanted to dye my hair coal black.

I couldn't begin to think about the risks I was running. But another piece of me was being amazed at my own daring. I had done it. Even more than my leaving home, this action which was tearing my guts apart and from which I could die except I wasn't going to, this action was a kind of shift from safety towards self-preservation. It was a choice of pains. That's what living was all about. I clung to that and tried to feel only proud.

I had not given in. They hadn't gotten me. I wasn't being a pebble in somebody else's ocean, washed along by any wave that came along. I had not been the eye on the ceiling, until it was too late.

There was a tap on the alley door, and I looked out the window. My friend Blossom from school had gotten one of our old High School teachers to drive her out to see if I was 'okay' and to bring me a bottle of Peach Brandy for my birthday. She was one of the people I had consulted and she had wanted to have nothing to do with an abortion, saying I should have the baby. I didn't bother to tell her that black babies were not adopted. They were absorbed into families, abandoned, or 'given up'. But not adopted. That was just another little piece of that secret knowledge which later came to be known as cultural differences. But when I saw Blossom, nonetheless I knew she must have been worried to have come all the way from Queens to Manhattan and then to Brighton Beach.

I was touched.

We only talked about inconsequential things. Never a word about what was going on inside of me. Now it was my secret; the only way I could handle it was alone. Somewhere they were both grateful.

'You sure you're going to be okay?' Blos asked. I nodded. Blossom knew how to make anybody laugh. Miss Burman suggested we go for a walk along the boardwalk in the crisp February darkness. There was no moon. The walk helped a little and so did the brandy. But when we got back to my room, I couldn't concentrate on their conversation any more. I was too distracted by the rage gnawing at my belly. 'Do you want us to go?' Blos asked with her old characteristic bluntness. Miss Burman, sympathetic but austere, stood quietly in the doorway looking at my posters. I nodded at Blos gratefully. Miss Burman lent me $5 before she left.

The rest of the night was an agony of padding back and forth along the length of the hallway from my bedroom to the bathroom, doubled over in pain, watching clots of blood fall out of my body into the toilet and wondering if I was all right, after all. I had never seen such huge red blobs come from me before. They scared me. I was afraid I might be bleeding to death in that community bathroom in Bright Beach in the middle of the night of my 18th birthday, with a crazy old lady down the hall muttering restlessly in her sleep. But I was going to be alright. Soon this was all going to be over, and I would be safe.

I watched one greyish mucous shape disappear in the bowl, wondering if that was the embryo.

By dawn, when I went to take some more aspirin, the catheter had worked its way out of my body. I was bleeding heavily, very heavily. But my experience in the OB wards told me that I was not haemorrhaging.

I washed the long stiff catheter and laid it away in a drawer, after examining it carefully. This implement of my salvation was a wicked red, but otherwise thin and innocuous looking.

I took an amphetamine in the thin morning sun and wondered if I should spend a quarter on some coffee and a Danish. I remembered I was supposed to usher at a Hunter College Concert that same afternoon, for which I was to be paid $10, a large sum for an afternoon's work, and one that would enable me to repay my debts to Ann and Miss Burman. I made myself some sweet milky coffee and took a hot bath, even though I was bleeding. After that, the pain dimmed gradually to a dull knocking gripe.

On a sudden whim, I got up and threw on some clothes and went out into the morning. I took the bus into Coney Island to an early morning foodshop near Nathan's, and had myself a huge birthday breakfast, complete with French fries and an English muffin. I hadn't had a regular meal in a restaurant for a long time. It cost almost half of Miss Burman's $5, because it was Kosher and expensive. And delicious.

Afterwards, I returned home. I lay resting upon my bed, filled with a sense of well-being and relief from pain and terror that was almost euphoric. I really was all right.

As the morning slipped into afternoon, I realised that I

was exhausted. But the thought of making $10 for one afternoon's work got me wearily up and back onto the Weekend Local train for the one and a quarter hour's trip to Hunter College.

By mid-afternoon my legs were quivering. I walked up and down the aisles dully, hardly hearing the string quartet. In the last part of the concert, I went into the ladies' room to change my tampax and the pads I was wearing. In the stall, I was seized with a sudden wave of nausea that bent me double, and I promptly and with great force lost my $2.50-with-tip Coney Island breakfast, which I had never digested. Weakened and shivering, I sat on the stool, my head against the wall. A fit of renewed cramps swept through me so sharply that I moaned softly.

Miz Lewis, the black ladies' room attendant who had known me from the bathrooms of Hunter High School, was in the back of the room in her cubby and she had seen me come into the otherwise empty washroom.

'Is that you, Autray, moaning like that? You all right?' I saw her low-shoed feet stop outside my stall.

'Yes mam,' I gasped through the door, cursing my luck to have walked into that particular bathroom. 'It's just my period.'

I steadied myself and arranged my clothes. When I finally stepped out, bravely and my head high, Miz Lewis was still standing outside, her arms folded.

She had always maintained a steady but impersonal interest in the lives of the few black girls at the high school and she was a familiar face which I was glad to see when I met her in the washroom of the college in the autumn. I told her I was going to the college now, and that I had left home. Miz Lewis had raised her eyebrows and pursed her lips, shaking her grey head. 'You girls sure are somethin'!' she'd said. In the uncompromising harshness of the

221

fluorescent lights, Miz Lewis gazed at me intently through her proper gold spectacles which perched upon her broad brown nose like round antennae.

'Girl, you sure you all right? Don't sound all right to me.' She peered up into my face. 'Sit down here a minute. You just started? You white like some other people's chile.'

I took her seat, gratefully. 'I'm all right, Miz Lewis,' I protested. 'I just have bad cramps, that's all.'

'Jus' cramps? That bad? Then why you come here like that today for? You ought to be home in bed, the way you eyes looking. You want some coffee, honey?' She offered me her cup.

'Cause I need the money, Miz Lewis. I'll be all right, I really will.' I shook my head to the coffee and stood up. Another cramp slid up from my clenched thighs and rammed into the small of my back, but I only rested my head against the edge of the stalls. Then, taking a paper towel from the stack on the glass shelf in front of me, I wet it and wiped the cold sweat from my forehead. I wiped the rest of my face and blotted my faded lipstick carefully. I grinned at my reflection in the mirror and at Miz Lewis standing to the side behind me, her arms still folded against her broad short-waisted bosom. She sucked her teeth with a sharp intake of breath and sighed a long sigh.

'Chile, why don't you go on back home to your mama, where you be long?'

I almost burst into tears. I felt like screaming, drowning out her plaintive, kindly, old-woman's voice that kept pretending everything was so simple.

'Don't you think she's worrying about you? Do she know you in all this trouble?'

'I'm not in trouble, Miz Lewis. I just don't feel well because of my period.' Turning away, I crumpled up the used towel and dropped it in to the basket, and then sat down again, heavily. My legs were shockingly weak.

'Yeah. Well.' Miz Lewis put her hand into her apron pocket. 'Here,' she said, pulling $4 out of her purse. 'You take these and get yourself a taxi home. 'She knew I lived in Brooklyn. 'And you go right home, now. I'll cross your name off the list downstairs for you. And you can pay me back when you get it.'

I took the crumpled bills from her dark, work-wise hands. 'Thanks a lot, Miz Lewis,' I said gratefully. I stood up again, this time a little more steadily. 'But don't you worry about me, this won't last very long.' I walked shakily to the door.

'And you put your feet up, and a cold compress on your tummy, and you stay in bed for a few days, too,' she called after me, as I made my way to the elevators to the main floor.

I asked the cab to take me around to the alley entrance instead of getting out on Brighton Beach Avenue. For the first time in my life, I was afraid my legs might not take me where I wanted to go. I wondered if I had almost fainted.

Once indoors, I took three aspirin and slept for 24 hours. When I awoke Monday afternoon, the bedsheets were stained, but my bleeding had slowed to normal and the cramps were gone. I wondered if I had gotten some bad food at the foodshop Sunday morning that had made me sick. Usually I never got upset stomachs, and prided myself on my cast-iron digestion. The following day I went back to school.

On Friday after classes, before I went to work, I picked up my money for ushering. I sought out Miz Lewis in the Auditorium washroom and paid her back her $4.

'Oh, thank you, Autray,' she said, looking a little surprised. She folded the bills up neatly and tucked them back into the green snap-purse she kept in her uniform apron pocket. 'How you feeling?'

'Fine, Miz Lewis,' I said jauntily. 'I told you I was going to be all right.'

'You did not! You said you was all right and I knew you wasn't, so don't tell me none of that stuff, I don't want to hear.' Miz Lewis eyed me balefully.

'You gon' back home to your mama, yet?' she asked, dryly.

Without Apology: Abortion in Literature
Edna Bonhomme
(2023)

In 1994, when I was ten, my most reliable babysitter – a hexagonal television set with two antennae – introduced me to the concept of abortion. My cousins and I sat on the couch, our legs, clammy in the Miami heat, stuck to the plastic-covered furniture. There we watched *Dirty Dancing*. Even then, I understood the 1960s American class markers: the summer holiday resort, the pleasant cabins around a pristine lake, the employees serving the wealthy guests. But the scene I remember most was when Penny, a dance instructor, sat on the kitchen floor at night in tears and realised she had gotten into 'trouble'.

'Trouble for what?' I wondered. My older cousins explained: Penny was pregnant, and an unplanned birth was the worst tragedy. It might have been less of a problem for the wealthy guests, but for someone like Penny, it could be life-threatening. The film is set in 1963, a decade before *Roe v. Wade*. Penny can't afford to terminate the pregnancy or hold Robbie, the womaniser from Yale who impregnated her, accountable. She has to rely on the goodwill of her childhood friend and co-worker, Johnny Castle, and a guest, Frances. Penny finally gets an abortion, but viewers learn that the doctor botched the procedure, and she barely survives.

The message was straightforward: Before *Roe*, one needed money and a sympathetic doctor to get a safe abortion. If you were poor and pregnant, you might face hardship and even death if you sought out cheaper and less experienced abortion providers. For many people, this reflected reality. In 1965, according to Planned Parenthood, 17 per cent of pregnancy-related deaths were due to unsafe abortions.

Dirty Dancing illustrated why access to safe abortions is so crucial. Penny, who is white, is a likeable working-class figure. Yet the film neglected to show how working-class non-white women like me could access abortion. (My public education in Florida also wasn't helpful on that score.) Penny could not get an abortion without a coterie of friends – and she wasn't able to get a safe one.

When our parents and schools fail us, we have to rely on our personal networks and ourselves to find out what we must do to have jurisdiction over our bodies. This is why movies and books are so essential; even when the narratives are muffled or distorted, they contain lessons that circulate in our culture. And many of the most poignant stories about abortions are not on film; they're in books – novels and short stories – that show us how we can talk about women, especially working-class women, who unapologetically end their pregnancies.

The decades preceding *Roe* saw a surge in abortion narratives in literature. In some cases, abortion was presented as a potentially fatal situation, as in Richard Yates's novel *Revolutionary Road* (1961), in which a woman dies after performing an abortion on herself; Mary Astor's *A Place Called Saturday* from 1968, in which a male partner pressures the protagonist, Cora March, to have an abortion; and 1970's *Play It as It Lays* by Joan Didion, in which an actress has an abortion that contributes to her psychiatric breakdown.

Very few works portray working-class women from this period who terminate their pregnancies without regret or anguish.

There are, however, some important exceptions, including Alice Walker's short story 'The Abortion', first published in 1980, and Annie Ernaux's 1974 novel *Les Armoires vides*, or *Cleaned Out* – both of which take place before abortion was legalised in their authors' countries (the United States and France, respectively) and both of which depict abortion from the point of view of women from modest backgrounds. Perhaps more crucially, Walker and Ernaux created characters whose decisions to have abortions are unclouded by doubt. These stories hew closer to how most women describe their abortions. About 75 per cent of people who end their pregnancies are low-income. And when researchers studied the mental health and well-being of women who have had abortions, they found that 95 per cent believed that they had made the right decision.

Writing the abortion stories of working-class women with tenderness and exacting honesty, as Walker and Ernaux do, is essential to the reproductive rights movement. It helps paint realistic portraits of people who seek abortions, thwarting right-wing stereotypes and teaching readers the liberatory possibilities of making one's own reproductive choices.

In 'The Abortion', Alice Walker applies her formidable prose to the story of an African American woman seeking to terminate her pregnancy. It appears in her collection *You Can't Keep a Good Woman Down*, a reference to a Mamie Smith and Perry Bradford song. The book, a meditation on the trials and tribulations of Black women, explores love, culture, fame and despair. 'The Abortion' focuses on Imani, a young Black mother living in the South who is depressed and fatigued by marriage, motherhood, and pregnancy.

227

Facing an unwanted pregnancy, Imani lays out the toll of having and raising a Black child in America. Much of the story is devoted to what gestation does to the body: 'Imani felt her body had been assaulted by these events and was, in fact, considerably weakened, and was also, in any case, chronically anaemic and run down.' Imani already has a toddler and feels that being a parent is interfering with the life she wants to lead. 'Another child would kill me,' she says. 'I can't imagine life with two kids.' So she discusses terminating the pregnancy with her husband, a lawyer named Clarence.

In the story, Imani has two abortions – one before her marriage and the other after she had her child, a daughter. Her first abortion was a clandestine procedure that cost a 'thousand dollars, for which she would be in debt for years' and after which she haemorrhaged for weeks, while her second abortion was 'seventy-five dollars . . . safe, quick, painless'. The story, which is set before *Roe*, reflects the shifting legal landscape. Although abortion remained technically illegal in New York State, it was decriminalised in 1970 by the state legislature. The result is that Imani's second abortion is a relatively pedestrian event – a safe, standardised medical procedure.

'The Abortion' isn't just an abortion story; it's about the lives and deaths of working-class African Americans. It details Black subjugation at the height of civil unrest – in this case, on the fifth anniversary of the death of Holly Monroe, a fictional African American girl who was murdered after attending her high school graduation. Walker writes that Monroe was 'aborted on the eve of becoming herself'. For Imani – and for contemporary readers – Monroe's death is a gutting reminder that Black children's lives can be cut short. Monroe's memorial makes Imani realise that raising another Black child would only increase the probability of her having to mourn the untimely death of one of her own kids.

Walker's story echoes her own life. Like Imani, Walker had a young daughter and a lawyer husband, and she would also have two abortions in the years before *Roe*. Both Walker and her character were concerned about the cruelty that society often metes out to Black people. Decades later, writing about her second abortion, Walker explained:

We knew the children being fire-hosed were innocent of anything but being children struggling for a future. We knew the beatings, car bombings, explosions, house and church burnings and violent assassinations were intimations of a future that more and more is coming to pass. To bring anyone, especially a helpless infant, into what was clearly a destructive situation, in a world where few in power even pretended to care for children of colour, seemed the very definition of madness.

What Walker shows us is that one of the major promises of motherhood is a lie: one will not necessarily be fulfilled or content just by being a parent. Imani, however, insists on holding on to truth. She tells her toddler that white people 'think they can kill a continent – people, trees, buffalo – and then fly off to the moon and just forget about it. But you and me, we're going to remember the people, the trees and the fucking buffalo.' The toddler, mimicking her mother, responds, 'Buffwoe'. Here, Imani is attentive to oppressed people, animals, and nature, indicating that the decision to be a parent is not merely about physical care but about cultivating a political education. Walker's story is a departure from a significant portion of the abortion literature precisely because it exposes the racial hierarchies of life and the power of historical memory.

Imani is unwavering in her decision. The narrator tells the reader that 'their aborted child would have been a troublesome, 'terrible' two-year-old, a great burden on its mother, whose health was by now in excellent shape.' Parenting wears down mothers, and deciding to abort can be a decision to prioritise one's body and political integrity.

Annie Ernaux's *Les Armoires vides*, published in 1974, chronicles the experience of Denise Lesur, a twenty-year-old French scholarship student. From the description of her body and the accounts of her village, the reader quickly recognises in Denise a storyteller intent on protecting her future at any cost. The opening scene is striking:

> I was on the table, all I would see between my legs was her grey hair and the red snake she was brandishing with a pair of forceps. It disappeared. Unbearable pain. I shouted at the old woman who was stuffing in cotton wool to keep it in place. Shouldn't touch yourself down there, it'll get damaged.

The 'snake' inserted into Denise is a tube, which she has to keep inside her all day to terminate the gestation. The whole time, her body is wracked by spasms of horrific pain, a constant reminder that she has had 'a backstreet abortion'. Ernaux traces Denise's sensory journey: 'My head pressed into the smell of the blanket, the sun beating down on me from my waist to my knees, a warm tide inside me, not a wrinkle visible, everything is taking place in folds and crevices miles below the surface.'

As in Walker's short story, the illegal abortion is not only a secret affair but a costly one, requiring Denise to secure funds far beyond what she can afford. This is a central issue for Denise, the ambitious daughter of a storekeeper. Aspiring to enter the world of arts and letters, she is aware that class is determined by more than education – it is a sense of belonging that is alien to her. Denise feels 'clumsy and awkward in comparison with the private-school girls, who are confident, who know just what to do'. Similarly, the story of her abortion is not just about the physical procedure but also the disdain she feels for her upper-class classmates as she tries to move up the hierarchy. Her abortion becomes a way to secure her future, even if the post-operative symptoms cause her pain.

This novel, too, was based on the author's abortion experience and it shows the desperation of working-class French women attempting to access the procedure before it was legalised in France in 1975. In her 2000 memoir, L'Événement, Ernaux tells the story of her pursuit of an abortion. She seeks a physician. She asks her lover for money to terminate the pregnancy and he tries to have sex with her. She tries to induce an abortion herself. But the story isn't just about choice; it's about class shame, which fuels her desire to succeed. For Ernaux, having a child at that time would have prevented her from eventually becoming a Nobel Prize-winning author.

Writing to her translator, Carol Sander, Ernaux asserts, 'There is in Les Armoires vides a desire to transgress all boundaries. In its content: saying the unsayable, feeling ashamed of one's parents, humiliated, wanting to be like everyone else; speaking about the female body, menstruation, erotic pleasure, abortion.' Like Walker, Ernaux was not stifled by the stigma of abortion; instead, the procedure was a path to liberation.

Like Penny in Dirty Dancing, I grew up poor and knew what it was like to rely on friends for survival. While I never saw any reason for Penny to feel chagrin for her abortion, I internalised the film's message that an unwanted pregnancy was a life-shattering problem, especially if you were poor.

Walker and Ernaux moved past this discourse. They showed the way abortion literature could render the interests of working-class women without relegating them to mere troublemakers. Their characters didn't rely on benefactors or do as others wished; they pushed the plot forwards themselves. In Walker and Ernaux's telling, abortion is freeing. As Imani affirms, abortion can mean 'seizing of the direction of her own life'.

Today there are even more radical accounts of reproductive choices in literature. In Guadalupe Nettel's novel *Still Born*, published in 2020, Laura, the protagonist, presents an unflinching desire not to have children. When she contemplated having a kid, Laura recognised her error: 'Just as someone who, without ever having contemplated suicide, allows themselves to be seduced by the abyss from the top of a skyscraper, I felt the lure of pregnancy.' So, early in the text, Laura gets her tubes tied. Unlike the abortion plots that explore a character's troubles, Nettel's novel offers a thrilling possibility: opting out of motherhood altogether. Nettel's novel is bound to both Walker's story and Ernaux's books by a powerful sentiment: the desire to live fully.

The Abortion Stories We Tell
Maggie Doherty
(2022)

I don't talk much about my abortions. When I had my first, I was relatively young, and I did not tell my mother. When I had my second, I was older, and for a while, I did not tell my partner. I told only friends, on an as-needed basis: the one who went with me to the clinic, the one who subbed my class. I didn't 'shout my abortion' or post about it on social media or write a personal essay. My favourite magazine was selling tote bags that read 'I Had an Abortion', but I didn't purchase one.

Over the past few months, though, I've felt like I should be talking about them – like so many other people have been. Beginning last winter, when the Supreme Court heard oral arguments in *Dobbs v. Jackson Women's Health Organisation*, the case that has overturned *Roe v. Wade*, first-person abortion stories proliferated in the public sphere. I found them in newspapers, in magazines, in comments sections, on Twitter. They took the form of op-eds, anonymously authored vignettes, and moving personal essays. I read them compulsively and cried.

As moved as I was by many of these stories, I also could not help noticing something distinctive about them: they were almost never about someone who simply chose to have an abortion. Seemingly every story published in a

newspaper or magazine was narrated by a sympathetic figure – a survivor of incest, a mother of two – who became
pregnant under difficult circumstances. In many of these
stories, the abortion was granted or prescribed by a person
in a position of authority.

I knew that there were as many kinds of abortion stories
as there were people who got abortions; more than
600,000 legal abortions were reported in the United States
in 2019. But one narrative seemed to dominate – a narrative that carefully portrayed an abortion patient as virtuous
and relatable, and that proved that the patient had very
important reasons for undergoing an abortion. Very few of
the stories I read suggested that abortion is a right people
should be free to exercise, whatever the circumstances.

More people are speaking out about their own experiences because legal access to abortion is in serious
jeopardy. As restrictive bills move through state legislatures
and conservative judges multiply on the federal courts, we
tell our stories again and again, hoping that they will fall
on sympathetic ears – and help secure the right to abortion. But while it's never been easier to talk about abortion,
abortion rights are still being eroded across the country.
This paradox should make us ask: What are abortion
stories for? And might we need to tell them in a different
way?

People have been talking about their abortions for as
long as people have been terminating pregnancies (i.e.,
forever). But the abortion story – as a public narrative told
for political reasons – is only about fifty years old. We can
date its emergence in the United States to 1969, the year
the radical feminist group Redstockings organised an
abortion 'speak-out' – a public event where women spoke
about their own abortions to a crowd of assembled
strangers at a church in Washington Square.

Redstockings was part of the women's liberation movement – sometimes called 'second-wave feminism' – a crusade for sexual freedom and gender equality that erupted in the US in the late 1960s. Feminists agitated for equality under the law, a fairer division of housework and equal pay for equal work outside the home. They also tackled the topic of abortion, which was not yet legal at the federal level. But laws governing the procedure were liberalising at the state level: by the end of the 1960s, seventeen states had legalised abortion under certain conditions, such as to save the life of the mother or to spare a victim of rape or incest from carrying a pregnancy to term. In New York and several other states, a woman could obtain an abortion because of physical or mental health conditions – a so-called 'therapeutic abortion'.

But feminists, including the radical members of Redstockings, weren't satisfied. Because abortion could be legal but still inaccessible, the result was that many women – especially poor women and women of colour – were still resorting to illegal or self-induced abortion, sometimes with disastrous results: in 1972, the year before Roe, 39 women in the United States died from illegal abortions. Some feminists began pursuing change through legal channels. Others, such as the women associated with the Jane collective in Chicago, secretly connected women with abortion providers and eventually learned how to perform abortions themselves.

Redstockings, a group committed to direct action, took a different tack: in February 1969, they disrupted hearings on New York State's abortion laws. A committee of 'experts' – fourteen men and a nun – had been tasked with deciding whether the state should further liberalise its abortion laws. The debate, though, was telling: one judge suggested that women be allowed to have abortions once they had

had four children – or, as he put it, had 'paid their debt to society'. The members of Redstockings – college-educated women, some with backgrounds in the civil rights movement – believed that they didn't owe any such debt and that women were, as they put it, 'the true experts' on their own bodies and lives.

And so on the evening of March 21, 1969, they convened at the Washington Square Methodist Church to speak about abortion in public for the first time. Redstockings had been founded by, among others, the feminist writers Shulamith Firestone and Ellen Willis – women and thinkers who believed that narrative could galvanise change.

Twelve women, going only by their first names, took the stage to share their experiences obtaining both legal and illegal abortions with a crowd of several hundred people. The audience, a mix of men and women, included the abortion activist and provider Nathan Rappaport and journalists Susan Brownmiller and Gloria Steinem, both of whom would go on to become prominent feminist activists. Conscious of the historical significance of their event, the Redstockings recorded the audio for posterity.

Though the speakers were not especially diverse – most were young white women – they offered a variety of stories. The first speaker had got pregnant in college and hadn't told anyone, not even her male partner. The second had become pregnant at seventeen; she had never been told about birth control. One woman underwent an abortion without anaesthesia, then was chased out of the building by an impatient doctor while she was still recovering. Another paid $900 to a doctor who had 'pictures of crucifixes' in his operating room. One of the women was a single mother; she felt as nervous talking about having a child without a husband as she did talking about her abortion.

The women were funny, brusque and utterly unapologetic. They cracked jokes about bad boyfriends ('He told me something like, "Don't worry, when I come the second time, it washes away the sperm"'). In thick New York accents, they scorned 'liberal paternalism' and dismissed a man from the audience who asked a question about men's rights. They didn't pay lip service to the opposition or make nice with the anti-abortion listeners in the audience. They had one goal, repeated over the course of the evening: when it came to their bodies, they wanted 'ultimate control'. Brownmiller, covering the event for the *Village Voice*, wrote that the evening was marked by 'the politics of confrontation and catharsis'.

Listening to these tapes some fifty years later, I'm struck by the speakers' collective refusal to explain themselves or to justify their decisions. Other than the occasional allusion to a child 'you can't take care of', most elided the reasons why they terminated their pregnancies. Instead, they presented abortion as rational, normal. (One woman expressed frustration that obtaining a therapeutic abortion involved 'having to pretend that you're insane' even though abortion is 'the sanest thing you can do'.) As one speaker put it quite simply, 'I have no need to have a child I don't want.'

The cultural context of the late 1960s – marked by open, entrenched misogyny on the one hand and feminist militancy and optimism on the other – helps explain the form the abortion story took in 1969 at the Redstockings event. In telling their abortion stories in public, the participants weren't trying to court allies in the legislature or win the approval of sympathetic listeners. They were confronting the public and demanding their rights. They were sharing stories to name what they would no longer abide.

In the years following the Redstockings event, speaking

out about abortion became a popular tactic. In 1971, 343 French women, including Simone de Beauvoir and Catherine Deneuve, signed the Manifesto of the 343, declaring that they had sought to obtain illegal abortions. The following year, 53 prominent American women – including Nora Ephron, Billie Jean King and Susan Sontag – signed a similar document, an open letter titled 'We Have Had Abortions', which was published in Ms. magazine. Combined with legal efforts, these speak-outs worked: abortion became a constitutional right in 1973, after the Supreme Court ruled in favour of 'Jane Roe' in Roe v.Wade. The ruling, grounded in the idea that the Constitution protected a right to privacy – even if this right wasn't explicitly stated – held that a person could terminate a pregnancy before the point of viability and after that point, if the pregnancy posed a danger to that person's health.

But the victory was short-lived. The New Right, a political movement that coalesced in the 1970s, made opposition to legal abortion a central plank of its political program – one part of a broader anti-feminist backlash. In Planned Parenthood v. Casey (1992), the Supreme Court ruled that states could impose restrictions on abortion access as long as patients didn't face an 'undue burden'. GOP-controlled states quickly learned that Republican judges would consider almost any abortion restriction acceptable.

A slew of restrictions followed, and clinics across the American South and Midwest closed. Operation Rescue, a coalition of anti-choice groups that has blockaded abortion clinics, has had a chilling effect on both patients and providers; so too did the violent attacks on two Boston-area abortion clinics in 1994. The Hyde Amendment, passed in 1976, continues to prohibit the use of Medicaid funds for abortion. The upshot, for many Americans, was that abortion, though nominally legal, became as inaccessible in many parts of the country as it had in the days before *Roe* – and arguably even more stigmatised.

In the midst of these developments, both the Democratic Party (supposedly pro-choice) and mainstream reproductive rights organisations, such as Planned Parenthood and NARAL Pro-Choice America, assumed a defensive posture. Rather than championing the radical feminist slogan 'free abortion on demand', Democratic Party politicians endorsed abortions as long as they were 'safe, legal and rare', a motto coined by presidential candidate Bill Clinton in 1992. (Hillary Clinton would repeat the phrase during her own presidential run in 2008.) In the 1990s, a dystopian pro-choice ad campaign, co-sponsored by NARAL, warned of a potential return to back-alley abortions and emphasised women's vulnerability – but declined to champion abortions as such.

Not even two decades after feminists celebrated the *Roe* ruling, abortion was already seen as fraught, shameful and politically dangerous. This cultural context gave rise to a new kind of abortion story: a sympathetic, quasi-apologetic one, radically different from those told at the 1969 speak-out. In 1985, actress Ali MacGraw told the story of her illegal abortion, in excruciating detail, to a reporter for *People*. 'There is nothing casual about abortion,' she said. 'It's a horrific decision to make.' (Her story made the magazine's cover, under the headline: 'Abortion: No Easy Answers.') In 1991, Random House published *The Choices We Made*, an anthology of 25 abortion stories, including one by actress Whoopi Goldberg, who had self-induced an abortion with a coat hanger at the age of fourteen. According to the *Publishers Weekly* review, the collection emphasised the 'pain, emotional trauma and stigma' of getting an abortion.

Many of the abortion stories published today in print

and online continue this narrative tradition. Contemporary abortion stories tend to underscore traumatic circumstances and make vivid physical pain. A woman who had an abortion at 32 weeks, due to a combination of foetal and maternal health problems, describes the experience in detail: enduring genetic tests, a $10,000 shot to stop the foetus's heart (it hurt 'a little bit worse than an amnio') and a 'blindingly painful' labour to deliver the dead foetus. Another woman, writing about a 'life-threatening staph infection' she developed during pregnancy that necessitated an abortion, recounts how she awoke 'from surgery in a strange hell, spiking a fever of 105 degrees and shaking uncontrollably'. It's clear that the narrators of these stories are already suffering. How could anyone deny them the right to abortion, these stories ask, and thereby demand that they suffer more?

The contemporary abortion story seems to have two main aims: to evoke the reader's sympathy and to justify the patient's decision to get an abortion. (There are certainly exceptions to this trend.) It is often narrated by someone who slots neatly into traditional gender norms. 'I'm not some defiant firebrand hipster feminist trying to be ironic or edgy by asking for an abortion,' writes one such author. 'I'm a wife, and I am a mother of two children. And until I asked for this abortion, I had planned my family "right".' The narrator, who is almost unfailingly a responsible user of birth control, usually presents the decision to get an abortion as a difficult one. 'It was excruciating,' wrote Congresswoman Pramila Jayapal, of her decision to abort an unplanned pregnancy, after she'd had a dangerous birth with her 'miracle' first child. (She described the abortion itself as 'heartbreaking'.) Another narrator, faced with the choice of terminating a wanted pregnancy that had developed abnormally, recalled facing 'wrenching questions' about when to terminate. Narrators often emphasise that, in getting an abortion, they were following the best medical advice. They don't quite disclaim responsibility, but they suggest that the decision to terminate was mostly out of their hands.

In some ways, these sympathetic abortion stories are valuable. They educate an uninformed public about the realities of reproductive life. They point to injustices in the healthcare system and in the welfare state, and they show that hardship is unevenly distributed. Queer and trans people are more likely to encounter obstacles than straight people, and those who are Black and poor will suffer more than those who are white and rich. As reportage, they illustrate the suffering that accompanies so many attempts to access reproductive care.

But as a political tactic, they are doomed to fail. Again and again, anti-choice politicians, activists, and judges prove that they neither understand the strain of an unwanted pregnancy (recall Justice Amy Coney Barrett's suggestion that safe haven laws should eliminate the need for abortion) nor care about preventing suffering.

Even if such stories could persuade the staunchest anti-choice activist, they would still be politically and ethically flawed. Sympathetic abortion stories implicitly suggest that abortion is only warranted for certain patients, that is, the good ones. By underscoring a patient's virtues – their vulnerability, their caution, their maternal instinct – these stories imply that abortions are acceptable if they're provided to deserving patients. And just who is deserving, we might ask? Those whom the majority of readers find sympathetic and appealing: good mothers, suffering victims, poor and frightened girls.

Sympathetic abortion stories place the abortion patient in the position of the supplicant, with the narrator pleading their case to the reader. Whereas speakers at the Redstockings event were defiant and remorseless, today's narrators are conflicted and conciliatory; unlike their predecessors, they present abortion as a welcome privilege, rather than an incontrovertible moral right. When abortion stories are crafted for maximum appeal, we can only assume that the right to an abortion depends on popular approval.

In recent years, it has become popular to say that legal access to abortion is uncontroversial. This is true – up to a point. According to polls, 60 per cent to 70 per cent of Americans oppose overturning *Roe*, and a majority support abortions in the first trimester. A majority also support restrictions to abortion access, such as only allowing second-trimester abortions if the pregnancy threatens the parent's health. Katha Pollitt has referred to this contradictory majority as 'the muddled middle'. It is this audience, it seems, that sympathetic abortion stories aim to reach.

But abortion – and the world it helps create – is controversial. The unrestricted right to abortion suggests a world in which gender roles are not enforced by the state and religious beliefs are not grounds for law-making. In such a world, families can take many different forms, and caregivers, often women, might be able to participate more fully in the public sphere. This kind of world won't appeal to everyone immediately; it might poll badly today. But freedom and equality cannot be sacrificed on the altar of popular opinion. To create a more just world, we may have to start telling different stories about abortions– stories that might not move readers to tears but succeed on different terms.

When I first started writing this essay, I was tempted to tell my abortion story using one of the common scripts. It would be an elegant piece of writing, as I imagined it, self-

242

aware but nonetheless showing me in a good light. I indulged in a little fantasy in which such an essay earned me compassionate emails and friendly retweets. I would speak out against injustice and, conveniently enough, would be rewarded for doing so.

I thought I would focus on the first time I got pregnant – a first abortion is inherently more sympathetic than a second – and I would highlight my precarious position. I was a student at the time, making less than minimum wage. (I'd probably leave out the fact that I was a graduate student in English – does a more indulgent field of study exist?) I would note that my boyfriend – older, ambitious – lived in another city and that he couldn't be bothered to come to town for my visit to the clinic: it was a Tuesday, and he was teaching, and surely I understood?

If I wanted to make myself seem responsible, I would include an interlude about contraception. It had been difficult for me to find a birth control method that worked. Hormonal birth control was out due to my struggles with depression and anxiety, and at the time, gynaecologists wouldn't insert IUDs into women who had not yet had children. My boyfriend resisted condoms, a contraceptive method that was both relatively cheap and easily available. I eventually had myself fitted for a diaphragm – a generally reliable barrier method. But one, it turned out, that could fail.

I might write about how hard it was – even with health insurance, even in a state without many restrictions – to obtain timely and adequate care. I would make sure to highlight the scariest moments – an anomaly in my bloodwork, a late-night trip to the ER – and underscore my vulnerability. If I wanted to move the reader, I would probably make good use of the pathetic fallacy, describing the cold, wet spring; the slush; the bare limbs of trees.

I could end my story neatly: my abortion allowed me to form the family I have now. I would explain that my abortion was not a decision against children or parenting but a decision that allowed me to parent when I was best able to do so. I probably wouldn't say directly that I was paying my 'debt' to society, as the judge had urged women to do in 1969, but I'd imply the point all the same.

To present myself this way, however, I would have to suppress some complicating details. I couldn't reveal my own enduring horror of pregnancy, how much I hated feeling my body change. I would have to pass over all the ways I was a bad partner to my boyfriend. And I would have to remain silent about my second abortion, the story of which, as you may have already guessed, shows me to be less responsible – and therefore less sympathetic – than a deserving abortion patient should be.

As a narrator and writer, I want to be sympathetic. But as a political actor and a feminist, I want to be fearless and uncompromising. I want to read detailed narratives about people who needed abortions to escape impossible circumstances or to prevent needless suffering – but I also want to read stories about people who choose abortion freely and easily, simply because it was their right to do so.

There is another way to tell the story of my first abortion. It is a story that also covers my second abortion, which took place under very different circumstances. Here's how it goes:

Unintentionally, my partner and I conceived a pregnancy in my body. Because I did not want to be pregnant and because I did not want to carry a pregnancy to term, I terminated the pregnancy, voluntarily and without ambivalence.

This story, if we can even call it a story, is not a moving one. It is not detailed, or evocative, or horrifying, or compelling. It probably violates every rule of the creative writ-

244

ing workshop. But it's the version of the story that best communicates my understanding of what abortion is and means. It suggests that the principle of bodily autonomy applies to everyone, regardless of their circumstances; that no one should be forced to carry a pregnancy to term; that people are ends, not means.

From 'Apostrophe, Animation and Abortion'
Barbara Johnson
(1986)

Although rhetoric can be defined as something politicians often accuse each other of, the political dimensions of the scholarly study of rhetoric have gone largely
unexplored by literary critics. What, indeed, could seem
more dry and apolitical than a rhetorical treatise? What
could seem further away from budgets and guerrilla warfare than a discussion of anaphora, antithesis, prolepsis,
and preterition? Yet the notorious CIA manual on psychological operations in guerrilla warfare ends with just such
a rhetorical treatise: an appendix on techniques of oratory
which lists definitions and examples for these and many
other rhetorical figures. The manual is designed to set up
a Machiavellian campaign of propaganda, indoctrination,
and infiltration in Nicaragua, underwritten by the visible
display and selective use of weapons. Shoot softly, it implies, and carry a big schtick. If rhetoric is defined as language that says one thing and means another, then the
manual is in effect attempting to maximise the collusion
between deviousness in language and accuracy in violence,
again and again implying that targets are most effectively
hit when most indirectly aimed at. Rhetoric, clearly, has
everything to do with covert operations. But are the politics of violence already encoded in rhetorical figures as

such? In other words, can the very essence of a political issue an issue like, say, abortion hinge on the structure of a figure? Is there any inherent connection between figurative language and questions of life and death, of who will wield and who will receive violence in a given human society?

As a way of approaching this question, I will begin in a more traditional way by discussing a rhetorical device that has come to seem almost synonymous with the lyric voice: the figure of apostrophe. In an essay in *The Pursuit of Signs*, Jonathan Culler indeed sees apostrophe as an embarrassingly explicit emblem of procedures inherent, but usually better hidden, in lyric poetry. Apostrophe in the sense in which I will be using it involves the address of an absent, dead, or inanimate being by a first-person speaker: 'O wild West Wind, thou breath of Autumn's being . . .' Apostrophe is thus both direct and indirect: based etymologically on the notion of turning aside, of digressing from straight speech, it manipulates the I/Thou structure of direct address in an indirect, fictionalised way.

Baudelaire's poem 'Moesta et Errabunda', whose Latin title means 'sad and vagabond', raises questions of rhetorical animation through several different grades of apostrophe. Inanimate objects like trains and ships or abstract entities like perfumed paradises find themselves called on to attend to the needs of a plaintive and restless lyric speaker. Even the poem's title poses questions of life and death in linguistic terms: the fact that Baudelaire here temporarily resuscitates a dead language prefigures the poem's attempts to function as a finder of lost loves. But in the opening lines of the poem, the direct-address structure seems straightforwardly unfigurative: 'Tell me, Agatha.' This could be called a minimally fictionalised apostrophe, although that is of course its fiction. Nothing at first indicates that

Agatha is any more dead, absent or inanimate than the poet himself.

The poem's opening makes explicit the relation between direct address and the desire for the other's voice: 'Tell me you talk.' But something strange soon happens to the face-to-face humanness of this conversation. What Agatha is supposed to talk about starts a process of dismemberment that might have something to do with a kind of reverse anthropomorphism: 'Does your heart sometimes take flight?' Instead of conferring a human shape, this question starts to undo one.

In a poem about wandering, taking flight, getting away from 'here', it is surprising to find that, structurally, each stanza acts out not a departure but a return to its starting point, a repetition of its first line. The poem's structure is at odds with its *apparent* theme. But we soon see that the object of the voyage is precisely to return – to return to a prior state, planted in the first stanza as virginity, in the second as motherhood (through the image of the nurse and the pun on mer/mère) and finally as childhood love and furtive pleasure. The voyage outward in space is a figure for the voyage backward in time. The poem's structure of address backs up, too, most explicitly in the third stanza. The cry apostrophising train and ship to carry the speaker off leads to a seeming reprise of the opening line, but by this point the inanimate has entirely taken over: instead of addressing Agatha directly, the poem asks whether Agatha's heart ever speaks the line the poet himself has spoken four lines earlier. Agatha herself now drops out of the poem, and direct address is temporarily lost, too, in the grammar of the sentence ('Est-il vrai que . . .'). The poem seems to empty itself of all its human characters and voices, acting out a *loss* of animation which is in fact its subject: the loss of childhood aliveness brought about by the passage of time. The poem thus enacts in its own temporality the loss of animation it situates in the temporality of the speaker's life.

At this point it launches into a new apostrophe, a new direct address to an abstract, lost state: 'How far away you are, sweet paradise.' The poem reanimates, addresses an image of fullness and wholeness and perfect correspondence ('what we love is worthy of our loves'). This height of liveliness, however, culminates strangely in an image of death. The heart that formerly kept trying to fly away now drowns in the moment of reaching its destination ['Où dans la volupté pure le coeur se noie!']. There may be something to gain, therefore, by deferring arrival, as the poem next seems to do by interrupting itself before grammatically completing the fifth stanza. The poem again ceases to employ direct address and ends by asking two drawn-out, self-interrupting questions. Is that paradise now farther away than India or China? Can one call it back and animate it with a silvery voice? This last question – 'Peut-on le rappeler avec des cris plaintifs/Et l'animer encor d'une voix argentine?' is a perfect description of apostrophe itself: a trope which, by means of the silvery voice of rhetoric, calls up and animates the absent, the lost and the dead. Apostrophe itself, then, has become not just the poem's mode but also the poem's theme. In other words, what the poem ends up wanting to know is not how far away childhood is, but whether its own rhetorical strategies can be effective. The final question becomes: can this gap be bridged; can this loss be healed, through language alone?

Shelley's 'Ode to the West Wind', which is perhaps the ultimate apostrophic poem, makes even more explicit the relation between apostrophe and animation. Shelley spends the first three stanzas demonstrating that the west wind is

250

a figure for the power to animate: it is described as the breath of being, moving everywhere, blowing movement and energy through the world, waking it from its summer dream, parting the waters of the Atlantic, uncontrollable. Yet the wind animates by bringing death, winter, destruction. How do the rhetorical strategies of the poem carry out this program of animation through the giving of death?

The apostrophe structure is immediately foregrounded by the interjections, four times spelled 'O' and four times spelled 'oh'. One of the bridges this poem attempts to build is the bridge between the 'O' of the pure vocative and the 'oh' of pure subjectivity.

The first three stanzas are grammatical amplifications of the sentence 'O thou, hear, oh, hear!' All the vivid imagery, all the picture painting, come in clauses subordinate to this obsessive direct address. But the poet addresses, gives animation, gives the capacity of responsiveness, to the wind, not in order to make it speak but in order to make it listen to him in order to make it listen to him doing nothing but *address* it. It takes him three long stanzas to break out of this intense near-tautology. As the fourth stanza begins, the 'I' starts to inscribe itself grammatically (but not thematically) where the 'thou' has been. A power struggle starts up for control over the poem's grammar, a struggle which mirrors the rivalry named in such lines as: 'If I were now what I was then, I would ne'er have *striven as thus with thee* in prayer in my sore need.' This rivalry is expressed as a comparison: 'less free than thou', but then: 'One *too like thee*.' What does it mean to be 'too like'? Time has created a loss of similarity, a loss of animation that has made the sense of similarity even more hyperbolic. In other words, the poet, in becoming less than – less like the wind – somehow becomes more like the wind in his rebellion against the loss of likeness.

In the final stanza the speaker both inscribes and reverses the structure of apostrophe. In saying 'be thou me,' he is attempting to restore metaphorical exchange and equality. If apostrophe is the giving of voice, the throwing of voice, the giving of animation, then a poet using it is always in a sense saying to the addressee, 'Be thou me.' But this implies that a poet has animation to give. And *that* is what this poem is saying is not, or is no longer, the case. Shelley's speaker's own sense of animation is precisely what is in doubt, so that he is in effect saying to the wind, 'I will animate you so that you will animate, or reanimate, me.' 'Make me thy lyre . . .'

Yet the wind, which is to give animation, is also a giver of death. The opposition between life and death has to undergo another reversal, another transvaluation. If death could somehow become a positive force for animation, then the poet would thereby create hope for his own 'dead thoughts'. The animator that will blow his words around the world will also instate the power of their deadness, their deadness as power, the place of maximum potential for renewal. This is the burden of the final rhetorical question. Does death necessarily entail rebirth? If winter comes, can spring be far behind? The poem is attempting to appropriate the authority of natural logic in which spring always does follow winter – in order to clinch the authority of cyclic reversibility for its own prophetic powers. Yet because this clincher is expressed in the form of a rhetorical question, it expresses natural certainty by means of a linguistic device that mimics no natural structure and has no stable one-to-one correspondence with a meaning. The rhetorical question, in a sense, leaves the poem in a state of suspended animation. But that, according to the poem, is the state of maximum potential.

Both the Baudelaire and the Shelley, then, end with a

rhetorical question that both raises and begs the question of rhetoric. It is as though the apostrophe is ultimately directed towards the reader, to whom the poem is addressing Mayor Koch's question: 'How'm I doing?' What is at stake in both poems is, as we have seen, the fate of a lost child – the speaker's own former self and the possibility of a new birth or a reanimation. In the poems that I will discuss next, these structures of apostrophe, animation, and lost life will take on a very different cast through the foregrounding of the question of motherhood and the premise that the life that is lost may be someone else's.

In Gwendolyn Brooks's poem 'the mother', the structures of address are shifting and complex. In the first line ('Abortions will not let you forget'), there is a 'you' but there is no 'I'. Instead, the subject of the sentence is the word 'abortions', which thus assumes a position of grammatical control over the poem. As entities that disallow forgetting, the abortions are not only controlling but animate and anthropomorphic, capable of treating persons as objects. While Baudelaire and Shelley addressed the anthropomorphised other in order to repossess their lost selves, Brooks is representing the self as eternally addressed and possessed by the lost, anthropomorphised other. Yet the self that is possessed here is itself already a 'you', not an 'I'. The 'you' in the opening lines can be seen as an 'I' that has become alienated, distanced from itself, and combined with a generalised other, which includes and feminises the reader of the poem. The grammatical I/Thou starting point of traditional apostrophe has been replaced by a structure in which the speaker is simultaneously eclipsed, alienated, and confused with the addressee. It is already clear that something has happened to the possibility of establishing a clear-cut distinction in this poem between subject and object, agent and victim.

The second section of the poem with a change in the structure of address. 'I' takes up the positional place of 'abortions', and there is temporarily no second person. The first sentence narrates: 'I have heard in the voices of the wind the voices of my dim killed children.' What is interesting about this line is that the speaker situates the children's voices firmly in a traditional romantic locus of lyric apostrophe – the voices of the wind, Shelley's 'West Wind', say, or Wordsworth's 'gentle breeze'.* Gwendolyn Brooks, in other words, is here explicitly rewriting the male lyric tradition, textually placing aborted children in the spot formerly occupied by all the dead, inanimate, or absent entities previously addressed by the lyric. And the question of animation and anthropomorphism is thereby given a new and disturbing twist. For if apostrophe is said to involve language's capacity to give life and human form to something dead or inanimate, what happens when those questions are literalised? What happens when the lyric speaker assumes responsibility for producing the death in the first place, but without being sure of the precise degree of human animation that existed in the entity killed? What is the debate over abortion about, indeed, if not the question of when, precisely, a being assumes a human form?

It is not until line 14 that Brooks's speaker actually addresses the dim killed children. And she does so not direct-

---

* It is interesting to note that the 'gentle breeze', apostrophised as 'Messenger' and 'Friend' in the 1805-6 Prelude (Book 1, line 5), is, significantly, not directly addressed in the 1850 version. One might ask whether this change stands as a sign of the much-discussed waning of Wordsworth's poetic inspiration, or whether it is, rather, one of a number of strictly rhetorical shifts that give the impression of a wane, just as the shift in Gwendolyn Brooks's poetry from her early impersonal poetic narratives to her more recent direct-address poems gives the impression of a politicisation.

ly, but in the form of a self-quotation: 'I have said.' This embedding of the apostrophe appears to serve two funct-ions here, just as it did in Baudelaire: a self-distancing function, and a foregrounding of the question of the ade-quacy of language. But whereas in Baudelaire the distance between the speaker and the lost childhood is what is be-ing lamented, and a restoration of vividness and contact is what is desired, in Brooks the vividness of the contact is precisely the source of the pain. While Baudelaire suffers from the dimming of memory, Brooks suffers from an in-ability to forget. And while Baudelaire's speaker actively seeks a fusion between present self and lost child, Brooks's speaker is attempting to fight her way out of a state of confusion between self and other. This confusion is in-dicated by the shifts in the poem's structures of address. It is never clear whether the speaker sees herself as an 'I' or a 'you', an addressor or an addressee. The voices in the wind are not created by the lyric apostrophe; they rather initiate the need for one. The initiative of speech seems always to lie in the other. The poem continues to struggle to clarify the relation between 'I' and 'you', but in the end it only succeeds in expressing the inability of its language to do so. By not closing the quotation in its final line, the poem, which began by confusing the reader with the aborter, ends by implicitly including the reader among those aborted and loved. The poem can no more distinguish be-tween 'I' and 'you' than it can come up with a proper de-finition of life. For all the Yeatsian tripartite aphorisms about life as what is past or passing or to come, Brooks substitutes the impossible middle ground between 'You were born, you had body, you died' and 'It is just that you never giggled or planned or cried.'

In line 28, the poem explicitly asks, 'Oh, what shall I say, how is the truth to be said?' Surrounding this question are attempts to make impossible distinctions: got/did not get, deliberate/not deliberate, dead/never made. The uncertainty of the speaker's control as a subject mirrors the uncertainty of the children's status as an object. It is interesting that the status of the human subject here hinges on the word 'deliberate.' The association of deliberateness with human agency has a long (and very American) history. It is deliberateness, for instance, that underlies that epic of separation and self-reliant autonomy, Thoreau's *Walden*. 'I went to the woods,' writes Thoreau, 'because I wished to live deliberately, to front only the essential facts of life.' Clearly, for Thoreau, pregnancy was not an essential fact of life. Yet for him as well as for every human being that has yet existed, someone else's pregnancy is the very first fact of life. How might the plot of human subjectivity be reconceived (so to speak) if pregnancy rather than autonomy is what raises the question of deliberateness?

Much recent feminist work has been devoted to the task of rethinking the relations between subjectivity, autonomy, interconnectedness, responsibility, and gender. Carol Gilligan's book *In a Different Voice* (and this focus on 'voice' is not irrelevant here) studies gender differences in patterns of ethical thinking. The central ethical question analysed by Gilligan is precisely the decision whether to have, or not to have, an abortion. The first time I read the book, this struck me as strange. Why, I wondered, would an investigation of gender *differences* focus on one of the questions about which an even-handed comparison of the male and the female points of view is impossible? Yet this, clearly, turns out to be the point: there is difference *because* it is not always possible to make symmetrical oppositions. As long as there is symmetry, one is not dealing with difference but rather with versions of the same. Gilligan's difference arises out of the impossibility of maintaining a rigorously logical binary model for ethical choices. Female logic, as she defines it, is a way of rethinking the logic of choice in a situation in which none of the choices are good. 'Believe that even in my deliberateness I was not deliberate': believe that the agent is not entirely autonomous, believe that I can be subject and object of violence at the same time, believe that I have not chosen the conditions under which I must choose. As Gilligan writes of the abortion decision, 'the occurrence of the dilemma itself precludes nonviolent resolution'. The choice is not between violence and nonviolence, but between simple violence to a foetus and complex, less determinate violence to an involuntary mother and/or an unwanted child.

Readers of Brooks's poem have often read it as an argument against abortion. And it is certainly clear that the poem is not saying that abortion is a good thing. But to see it as making a simple case for the embryo's right to life is to assume that a woman who has chosen abortion does not have the right to mourn. It is to assume that no case for abortion can take the woman's feelings of guilt and loss into consideration, that to take those feelings into account is to deny the right to choose the act that produced them. Yet the poem makes no such claim: it attempts the impossible task of humanising both the mother and the aborted children while presenting the inadequacy of language to resolve the dilemma without violence.

What I would like to emphasise is the way in which the poem suggests that arguments for and against abortion are structured through and through by the rhetorical limits and possibilities of something akin to apostrophe. The fact that apostrophe allows one to animate the inanimate, the dead, or the absent implies that whenever a being is apostrophised, it is thereby automatically animated, anthropomorphised, 'person-ified'. (By the same token, the rhetoric of calling makes it difficult to tell the difference between the animate and the inanimate, as anyone with a telephone answering machine can attest.) Because of the ineradicable tendency of language to animate whatever it addresses, rhetoric itself can always have already answered 'yes' to the question of whether a foetus is a human being. It is no accident that the anti-abortion film most often shown in the United States should be titled 'The Silent Scream'. By activating the imagination to believe in the anthropomorphised embryo's mute responsiveness in exactly the same way that apostrophe does, the film (which is of course itself a highly rhetorical entity) is playing on rhetorical possibilities that are inherent in all linguistically-based modes of representation.

Yet the function of apostrophe in the Brooks poem is far from simple. If the fact that the speaker addresses the children at all makes them human, then she must pronounce herself guilty of murder but only if she discontinues her apostrophe. As long as she addresses the children, she can keep them alive, can keep from finishing with the act of killing them. The speaker's attempt to absolve herself of guilt depends on never forgetting, never breaking the ventriloquism of an apostrophe through which she cannot define her identity otherwise than as the mother eaten alive by the children she has never fed. Who, in the final analysis, exists by addressing whom? The children are a rhetorical extension of the mother, but she, as the poem's title indicates, has no existence apart from her relation to them. It begins to be clear that the speaker has written herself into a poem she cannot get out of without violence. The violence she commits in the end is to her own language: as the poem ends, the vocabulary shrinks away, words are repeated, nothing but 'all' rhymes with 'all'. The speaker has written herself into silence. Yet hers is not the only silence in the poem: earlier she had said, 'You will never. . . silence or buy with a sweet.' If sweets are for silencing, then by beginning her apostrophe, 'Sweets, if I sinned . . .' the speaker is already saying that the poem, which exists to memorialise those whose lack of life makes them eternally alive, is also attempting to silence once and for all the voices of the children in the wind. It becomes impossible to tell whether language is what gives life or what kills.

***

It is interesting to note the ways in which legal and moral discussions of abortion tend to employ the same terms as those we have been using to describe the figure of apostrophe. These disciplines (philosophy, theology, and civil and canon law) variously approached the question in terms of the point at which the embryo or foetus became 'formed' or recognisably human, or in terms of when a 'person' came into being, that is, infused with a 'soul' or 'animated'. The issue of 'foetal personhood' is of course a way of bringing to a state of explicit uncertainty the fundamental difficulty of defining personhood in general. Even if the question of defining the nature of 'persons' is restricted to the question of understanding what is meant by the word 'person' in the United States Constitution (since the Bill of Rights guarantees the rights only of 'persons'), there is not at present, and probably will never be, a stable legal definition. Existing discussions of the legality and morality of abortion almost invariably confront, leave unresolved, and detour around the question of the nature and boundaries of human life. As Justice Blackmun puts it in *Roe v. Wade*: 'We need not resolve the difficult question of when life begins. When those trained in the respective disciplines of medicine, philosophy, and theology are unable to arrive at any consensus, the judiciary, at this point in the development of man's knowledge, is not in a position to speculate as to the answer'. In the case of *Roe v.Wade*, the legality of abortion is derived from the pregnant couple's right to privacy – an argument which, as Catherine MacKinnon argues in '*Roe v.Wade*: A Study in Male Ideology', is itself problematic for women, since by protecting 'privacy' the courts also protect the injustices of patriarchal sexual arrangements. When the issue is an unwanted pregnancy, some sort of privacy has already, in a sense, been invaded. In order for the personal to avoid being reduced once again to the non-political, privacy, like deliberateness, needs to be rethought in terms of sexual politics. Yet even the attempt to re-gender the issues surrounding abortion is not simple. As Kristin Luker convincingly demonstrates, the debate turns around the claims not only of woman v. foetus or of woman s. patriarchal state, but also of woman v. woman.

Pro-choice and pro-life activists live in different worlds, and the scope of their lives, as both adults and children, fortifies them in their belief that their views on abortion are the more correct, more moral, and more reasonable. When added to this is the fact that should 'the other side' win, one group of women will see the very real devaluation of their lives and life resources, it is not surprising that the abortion debate has generated so much heat and so little light . . . Are pro-life activists, as they claim, actually reaching their cherished goal of 'educating the public to the humanity of the unborn child?' As we begin to seek an answer, we should recall that motherhood is a topic about which people have very complicated feelings, and because abortion has become the battleground for different definitions of motherhood, neither the pro-life nor the pro-choice movement has ever been 'representative' of how most Americans feel about abortion. More to the point, all our data suggest that neither of these groups will ever be able to be representative.

It is often said, in literary-theoretical circles, that to focus on undecidability is to be apolitical. Everything I have read about the abortion controversy in its present form in the United States leads me to suspect that, on the contrary, the undecidable is the political. There is politics precisely because there is undecidability.

And there is also poetry. There are striking and suggestive parallels between the 'different voices' involved in the abortion debate and the shifting address — structures of poems like Gwendolyn Brooks's 'the mother'. A glance at several other poems suggests that there tends indeed to be an overdetermined relation between the theme of abortion and the problematisation of structures of address. In Anne Sexton's 'The Abortion', six three-line stanzas narrate, in the first person, a trip to Pennsylvania where the 'I' has obtained an abortion. Three times the poem is interrupted by the italicised lines:

Somebody who should have been born
is gone.

Like a voice-over narrator taking super-egoistic control of the moral bottom line, this refrain (or 'burden', to use the archaic term for both 'refrain' and 'child in the womb') puts the first-person narrator's authority in question without necessarily constituting the voice of a separate entity. Then, in the seventh and final stanza, the poem extends and intensifies this split:

Yes, woman, such logic will lead
to loss without death. Or say what you meant,
you coward . . . this baby that I bleed.

Self-accusing, self-interrupting, the narrating 'I' turns on herself (or is it someone else?) as 'you', as 'woman'. The poem's speaker becomes as split as the two senses of the

261

word 'bleed'. Once again, 'saying what one means' can
only be done by ellipsis, violence, illogic, transgression,
silence. The question of who is addressing whom is once
again unresolved.

As we have seen, the question of 'when life begins' is
complicated partly because of the way in which language
blurs the boundary between life and death. In 'Menstruation at Forty', Sexton sees menstruation itself as the loss of
a child ('two days gone in blood') – a child that exists
because it can be called:

> I was thinking of a son . . .
> You! . . .
> Will you be the David or the Susan?
> . . .
> David! Susan! David! David!
> . . .
> my carrot, my cabbage,
> I would have possessed you before all women,
> calling your name,
> calling you mine.

The political consequences and complexities of addressing – of 'calling' – are made even more explicit in a poem
by Lucille Clifton entitled 'the lost baby poem'. By choosing the word 'dropped' ('i dropped your almost body
down'), Clifton renders it unclear whether the child has
been lost through abortion or through miscarriage. What
is clear, however, that that loss is both mourned and rat-
ionalised. The rationalisation occurs through the description of a life of hardship, flight and loss: the image of a
child born into winter, slipping like ice into the hands of
strangers in Canada, conflates the scene of Eliza's escape in
Uncle Tom's Cabin with the exile of draft resisters during the
Vietnam War. The guilt and mourning occur in the form of
an imperative in which the notion of 'stranger' returns in

the following lines:

> if i am ever less than a mountain
> for your definite brothers and sisters . . .
> . . . let black men call me stranger
> always   for your never named sake.

The act of 'calling' here correlates a lack of name with a loss of membership. For the sake of the one that cannot be called, the speaker invites an apostrophe that would expel her into otherness. The consequences of the death of a child ramify beyond the mother-child dyad to encompass the fate of an entire community. The world that has created conditions under which the loss of a baby becomes desirable must be resisted, not joined. For a black woman, the loss of a baby can always be perceived as a complicity with genocide. The black mother sees her own choice as one of being either a stranger or a rock. The humanisation of the lost baby addressed by the poem is thus carried out at the cost of dehumanising, even of rendering inanimate, the calling mother.

Yet each of these poems exists, finally, because a child does not. In Adrienne Rich's poem 'To a Poet', the rivalry between poems and children is made quite explicit. The 'you' in the poem is again aborted, but here it is the mother herself who could be called 'dim and killed' by the fact not of abortion but of the institution of motherhood. And again, the structures of address are complex and unstable. The deadness of the 'you' cannot be named: not suicide, not murder. The question of the life or death of the addressee is raised in an interesting way through Rich's rewriting of Keats's sonnet on his mortality. While Keats writes, 'When I have fears that I will cease to be', Rich writes 'and I have fears that you will cease to be.' If poetry is at stake in both intimations of mortality, what is the significance of this shift from 'I' to 'you'? On the one hand, the very existence of the Keats poem indicates that the pen has succeeded in gleaning something before the brain has ceased to be. No such grammatical guarantee exists for the 'you'. Death in the Keats poem is as much a source as it is a threat to writing. Hence, death, for Keats, could be called the mother of poetry while motherhood, for Rich, is precisely the death of poetry. The Western myth of the conjunction of word and flesh implied by the word 'incarnate' is undone by images of language floating and vanishing in the toilet bowl of real-flesh needs. The word is not made flesh; rather, flesh unmakes the mother-poet's word. The difficulty of retrieving the 'you' as poet is enacted by the structures of address in the following lines:

I write this   not for you
who fight to write your own
words fighting up the falls
but for another woman   dumb

In saying 'I write this not for you,' it is almost as though Rich is excluding as addressee anyone who could conceivably be reading this poem. The poem is setting aside both the 'I' and the 'you' – the pronouns Benveniste associates with personhood and reaches instead towards a 'she', which belongs in the category of 'non-person'. The poem is thus attempting the impossible task of directly addressing not a second person but a third person a person who, if she is reading the poem, cannot be the reader the poem has in mind. The poem is trying to include what is by its own grammar excluded from it – to animate through language the non-person, the 'other woman'. Therefore, this poem, too, is bursting the limits of own language, inscribing a logic that it itself reveals to be impossible but necessary. Even the divorce between writing and childbearing is less absolute than it appears: in comparing the writing of words to the spawning of fish, Rich's poem reveals itself to be trapped between the inability to combine and the inability to separate the woman's various roles.

In each of these poems, then, a kind of competition is implicitly instated between the bearing of children and the writing of poems. Something unsettling has happened to the analogy often drawn by male poets between artistic creation and procreation. For it is not true that literature contains no examples of male pregnancy. Philip Sidney, in the first sonnet from *Astrophil and Stella*, describes himself as 'great with child to speak', but the poem is ultimately produced at the expense of no literalised child. Sidney's labour pains are smoothed away by a midwifely apostrophe ('Fool,' said my Muse to me, 'look in thy heart, and write!') and by a sort of poetic Caesarean section, out springs the poem we have, in fact, already finished reading. Mallarmé, in 'Don du poème', describes himself as an enemy father seeking nourishment for his monstrous poetic child from the woman within apostrophe-shot who is busy nursing a literalised daughter. But since the woman presumably has two breasts, there seems to be enough to around. As Shakespeare assures the fair young man, 'But were some child of yours alive that time,/You should live twice in it and in my rhyme'. Apollinaire, in the play *Les Mamelles de Tirésias*, depicts woman as a de-maternalised neo-Malthusian leaving the task of childbearing to a surrealistically fertile husband. But again, nothing more disturbing than Tiresian cross-dressing seems to occur. Children are alive and well, and far more numerous than ever. Indeed, in one of the dedicatory poems, Apollinaire indicates that his drama represents a return to health from the literary reign of the *poète maudit*:

La féconde raison a jailli de ma fable,
Plus de femme sterile et non plus d'avortons . . .

[Fertile reason springs out of my fable,
No more sterile women, no aborted children]

This dig at Baudelaire, among others, reminds us that in the opening poem to Les Fleurs du Mal ('Bénédiction'), Baudelaire represents the poet himself as an abortion manqué, cursed by the poisonous words of a rejecting mother. The question of the unnatural seems more closely allied with the bad mother than with the pregnant father.

Even in the seemingly more obvious parallel provided by poems written to dead children by male poets, it is not really surprising to find that the substitution of poem for child lacks the sinister undertones and disturbed address exhibited by the abortion poems we have been discussing. Ben Jonson, in 'On My First Son', calls his dead child 'his best piece poetry', while Mallarmé, in an only semi-guilty Aufhebung, transfuses the dead Anatole to the level of an idea. More recently, Jon Silkin has written movingly of the death of a handicapped child ('something like a person') as a change of silence, not a splitting of voice. And Michael Harper, in 'Nightmare begins Responsibility', stresses the powerlessness and distrust of a black father leaving his dying son to the care of a 'white-doctor-who-breathed-for-him-all-night'. But again, whatever the complexity of the voices in that poem, the speaker does not split self-accusingly or infra-symbiotically in the ways we have noted in the abortion/motherhood poems. While one could undoubtedly find counter-examples on both sides, it is not surprising that the substitution of art for children should not be inherently transgressive for the male poet. Men have in a sense always had no choice but to substitute something for the literal process of birth. That, at least, is the belief that has long been encoded into male poetic conventions. It is as though male writing were by nature procreative, while female writing is somehow by nature infanticidal.

It is, of course, as problematic as it is tempting to draw general conclusions about differences between male and female writing on the basis of these somewhat random examples. Yet it is clear that a great many poetic effects may be coloured according to *expectations* articulated through the gender of the poetic speaker. Whether or not men and women would 'naturally' write differently about dead children, there is something about the connection between motherhood and death that refuses to remain comfortably and conventionally figurative. When a woman speaks about the death of children in any sense other than that of pure loss, a powerful taboo is being violated. The indistinguishability of miscarriage and abortion in the Clifton poem indeed points to the notion that any death of a child is perceived as a crime committed by the mother, something a mother ought by definition to be able to prevent. That these questions should be so inextricably connected to the figure of apostrophe, however, deserves further comment. For there may be a deeper link between motherhood and apostrophe than we have hitherto suspected.

The verbal development of the infant, according to Lacan, begins as a demand addressed to the mother, out of which the entire verbal universe is spun. Yet the mother addressed is somehow a personification, not a person – a personification of presence or absence, of Otherness itself.

> Demand in itself bears on something other than the satisfactions it calls for. It is demand of a presence or of an absence which is what is manifested in the primordial relation to the mother, pregnant with that Other to be situated within the needs that it can satisfy. Insofar as [man's] needs are

subjected to demand, they return to him alienated. This is not the effect of his real dependence . . . but rather the turning into signifying form as such, from the fact that it is from the locus of the Other that its message is emitted.

If demand is the originary vocative, which assures life even as it inaugurates alienation, then it is not surprising that questions of animation inhere in the rhetorical figure of apostrophe. The reversal of apostrophe we noted in the Shelley poem ('animate me') would be no reversal at all, but a reinstatement of the primal apostrophe in which, despite Lacan's disclaimer, there is precisely a link between demand and animation, between apostrophe and life-and-death dependency. If apostrophe is structured like demand, and if demand articulates the primal relation to the mother as a relation to the Other, then lyric poetry itself summed up in the figure of apostrophe – comes to look like the fantastically intricate history of endless elaborations and displacements of the single cry, 'Mama!' The question these poems are asking, then, is what happens when the poet is speaking as a mother – a mother whose cry arises out of, and is addressed to, a dead child?

It is no wonder that the distinction between addressor and addressee should become so problematic in poems about abortion. It is also no wonder that the debate about abortion should refuse to settle into a single voice. Whether or not one has ever been a mother, everyone participating in the debate has once been a child. Rhetorical, psychoanalytical and political structures are profoundly implicated in one another. The difficulty in all three would seem to reside in the attempt to achieve a full elaboration of any discursive position other than that of child.

An Irish Problem
Sally Rooney
(2018)

In 1983, a referendum was held in Ireland to establish a constitutional right to life for embryos and foetuses. Abortion was not legal in Ireland at the time; it never has been. The referendum was the result of a campaign by conservative religious groups aimed at preventing any future legislation permitting abortion in any but the most extreme, life-threatening circumstances. The Eighth Amendment passed, gaining 67 per cent of the vote. On 25 May, another referendum will be held on whether to repeal that amendment. This one won't pass so easily – if it passes at all.

So far the campaign has been distinguished by acrimony, falsehoods and a media obsession with 'balance' – an insistence that both sides must be given equal respect and consideration. Though campaign funding is strictly regulated by Irish law, there are questions about how effectively these regulations are being enforced, and in particular about the 'No' campaign's links to anti-abortion organisations in the US. A group calling itself the Irish Centre for Bio-Ethical Reform, made up largely of American volunteers, has attracted media attention by protesting outside maternity hospitals in Dublin with banners showing dismembered foetuses. The group is connected to a US organisation called the Centre for Bio-Ethical Reform, whose leader, Gregg Cunningham, visited Ireland in January.

Across the country, 'Save the Eighth' posters depict gigantic, robust babies, as if the referendum concerned the health of six-month-old infants. But the subtext is clear: no matter what's going on in a woman's life, it's always a good time to have a baby. One poster produced by the 'No' campaign shows an ultrasound image of a foetus below the caption: 'I am nine weeks old. I can yawn & kick. Don't repeal me.' The Together for Yes campaign, which crowd-funded its largely text-based posters, has opted for slogans like: 'Sometimes a private matter needs public support'.

By providing the foetus and the pregnant woman with an equal right to life, the Eighth Amendment prohibits abortion in all circumstances unless the life of the woman is at substantial risk. The threat of serious, permanent injury or illness is insufficient grounds for a termination. In 1992, a fourteen-year-old child who had been raped by a neighbour became suicidal as a consequence of the resulting pregnancy. After the attorney general issued an injunction to prevent her from travelling abroad for an abortion, the Supreme Court overturned the ruling, holding that suicidal feelings constitute a risk to life. Much of Ireland's abortion debate since then – including a referendum in 1992 and another in 2002 – has hinged on whether the possibility of suicide does in fact constitute a sufficiently immediate risk. In 1992, 35 per cent of the population believed it did not.

The criteria by which doctors gauge a risk to life, as distinct from a risk to health, are still unclear. In 2012, a woman called Savita Halappanavar developed sepsis during a miscarriage. Aware that her pregnancy was no longer medically viable, and increasingly unwell as the infection spread, she asked for a termination. The request was refused, because the risk to her life was not deemed substantial. By the time she was ill enough to be allowed a termination it was too late. Halappanavar died of a cardiac arrest caused by sepsis. The decision to hold the upcoming referendum was sparked by the public outcry that followed her death. Months after the story broke, the Protection of Life During Pregnancy Act was passed, setting out the processes by which pregnant women whose lives were endangered could access terminations – before then, no legal guidelines had existed for doctors or patients. In 2016, as demand for constitutional change continued to grow, the government set up a Citizens' Assembly to look into the issue. The Eighth Amendment was no longer just about abortion; it was now about public health. Discussion focused on the most egregious consequences of the law: the fact that pregnant women with cancer had limited rights to access treatment that might endanger the foetus; that women had to continue with pregnancies that had been deemed non-viable; that children (and adult women) who had been sexually abused were forced to bear their rapists' offspring.

Support for abortion in cases of rape or fatal foetal abnormality has been solid in Ireland since 2013. All the major political parties now advocate repeal of the amendment. And yet the outcome of the upcoming referendum looks uncertain, with a substantial cohort remaining undecided. This indecision is probably connected to worries about the government's plans for reform. If the Eighth Amendment is repealed, Fine Gael has pledged to introduce legal terminations up until twelve weeks' gestation. In other words, abortion would be available not only in the so-called 'hard cases', but also when a healthy woman in her first trimester decides she doesn't want to be pregnant. Do women who are not victims of abuse, or in mortal danger, have the right to end a pregnancy just because they feel like it?

Yes. Pregnancy, entered into willingly, is an act of generosity, a commitment to share the resources of life with another incipient being. Such generosity is in no other circumstances required by law. No matter how much you need a kidney donation, the law will not force another person to give you one. Consent, in the form of a donor card, is required even to remove organs from a dead body. If the foetus is a person, it is a person with a vastly expanded set of legal rights, rights available to no other class of citizen: the foetus may make free, non-consensual use of another living person's uterus and blood supply, and cause permanent, unwanted changes to another person's body. In the relationship between foetus and woman, the woman is granted fewer rights than a corpse. But it's possible that the ban on abortion has less to do with the rights of the unborn child than with the threat to social order represented by women in control of their reproductive lives.

Irish women's freedom to decide what happens to their bodies has been restricted by many and varied means: the prohibition on contraception until the 1980s, the legality of marital rape until 1990, the threat of incarceration in institutions like the Magdalen Laundries and Mother and Baby Homes. These legal and social practices were not arranged around the protection of unborn life, but around control of reproduction. Even now, it is the idea of female agency that separates permissible forms of abortion from those deemed unacceptable in Irish law. Traumatised or fatally ill women may be granted the right to terminate a pregnancy precisely because they are not seen to be exercising free and independent agency. Those who object to abortion, but make an exception in the case of rape, cannot be primarily concerned with the sanctity of the unborn: a foetus conceived by rape is no different from a foetus conceived by consensual sex. To make an exception for women who can be classed as victims is to display fear and anxiety of the woman who is not one, but who would simply exercise her right no longer to be pregnant.

Whatever happens on 25 May, thousands of Irish women will continue to have abortions every year. A 1992 referendum affirmed the right of pregnant women to travel abroad to access abortion. I cannot recall a major political figure ever questioning the wisdom of that amendment. If anti-abortion campaigners truly believe the foetus is a person like any other, a constitutional right to take that person abroad in order to kill them should be unacceptable; yet the 'No' campaign is united in its approval of the right to travel. The existence of accessible British abortion services has taken pressure off the issue in Ireland; most women who need to can scrape together the money for a trip to the UK. It's only those in extreme circumstances – women in severe poverty, migrant women without visas, those who are too ill to travel – who feel the full injustice of the Eighth.

In 1979, introducing a law to make contraceptives available for the first time in Ireland, the then minister for health Charles Haughey described it as 'an Irish solution to an Irish problem'. Permitting women to travel abroad for abortion is another such solution: keep the issue out of sight and out of mind. The abortion rate in Ireland will not fall if the referendum fails; it may not increase substantially if the referendum passes. But the relationship of pregnant women in Ireland to their own bodies will change, and change significantly, if the 'Yes' campaign is successful. I was born in 1991, the same year a Virgin Megastore in Dublin was raided for selling condoms without a pharmacist present. Two years before the decriminalisation of homosexuality. Four years before the legalisation of divorce. Twenty-seven years, I can only hope, before the repeal of the Eighth Amendment.

Who was Jane Roe?
Deborah Friedell
(2022)

All the Supreme Court knew of 'Jane Roe' was that she
lived in Dallas County, Texas under another name and
that she 'wished to terminate her pregnancy by an abortion performed by a competent, licensed physician, under
safe, clinical conditions'. In a notarised statement filed
with the court in May 1970, Roe affirmed that she was
over 21 and unmarried. She wanted an abortion because
of the 'economic hardship which pregnancy entailed' and
also to avoid the 'social stigma attached to the bearing of
illegitimate children'. Abortion-seeking Texans usually
travelled to states with more liberal laws, or to Mexico, but
Roe claimed, and there seemed no reason to doubt her,
that she couldn't afford to leave town. She understood that
some doctors in Dallas did perform illegal abortions, but
these were expensive and often unsafe, and she worried
that having one might kill her. In any case, she didn't want
to 'participate in an act deemed by the State of Texas to
be a felony offence'. Texas did permit a single exception
– an abortion was legal if it was 'procured or attempted
by medical advice for the purpose of saving the life of the
mother' – but this didn't apply to Roe. And even if it did,
there were no official guidelines for physicians. Could you
give an abortion to a woman who was suicidal because

of her pregnancy? What if childbirth would shorten her life, but not right away? Better not to risk it. Under the state's anti-abortion statutes, on the books since 1854, the punishment for performing an illegal abortion was two to five years in prison. If a woman in Texas died because of an illegal abortion, her abortionist could be charged with murder.

The lawyers who tried to uphold the Texas statutes – ostensibly representing the Dallas district attorney, Henry Wade – argued that whoever Roe really was, she didn't have sufficient 'standing' to bring her case to the Supreme Court. The plaintiff had to be someone who would be harmed if the law wasn't overturned. Given the 'normal 266-day human gestation period', and the fact that it had taken more than a year for *Roe v. Wade* to reach the court, Roe must already have delivered a child, or miscarried, or found a way to have an abortion after all. The court batted this challenge away. 'Pregnancy often comes more than once to the same woman,' the majority decided. 'If man is to survive, it will always be with us.' Otherwise, Roe hardly appears in the judicial opinion that granted Americans the right to abortion 'free of interference by the state'. Her anonymity, her everywomanishness, suited the court fine: Roe was just a stand-in. But Norma McCorvey – who would later say that she'd agreed to become Jane Roe in exchange 'for a piece of pizza and a beer' – never saw it that way. Estimates vary, but around 600,000 pregnancies are terminated every year in the US. McCorvey would come to think of each one of them as her own doing.

In *The Family Roe: An American Story* (2021), Joshua Prager writes that he became interested in McCorvey in 2010, while learning about the attempts of gay rights activists to bring the issue of marriage equality before the Supreme Court. Since the justices won't consider hypothetical cases, the activists needed to find real people to file suit, 'stake-holders' willing to swear that the outcome would 'con-cretely' affect their lives. Across the country, same-sex couples volunteered. But the activists were haunted by *Roe v. Wade*: they were searching for plaintiffs who wouldn't become embarrassments. An article Prager read in the *New Yorker* referred to the plaintiffs in *Loving v. Virginia*, which overturned bans on interracial marriage, as the beau idéal. The Lovings had said all the right things, then stayed out of the limelight – and stayed married. They even had the per-fect name. McCorvey was described as the 'sort of plaintiff who should have been better vetted' and Prager wanted to know more.

At first, McCorvey wouldn't talk to Prager unless he paid her $1000. Her story was her only asset, and it had sup-ported her, however modestly, for years. Sarah Wedding-ton, the lawyer who argued *Roe* at the Supreme Court and then parlayed her fame into a political career, had stopped granting interviews (possibly because of illness: she died in 2021). So Prager turned to Linda Coffee, who hardly appears in other histories: she's barely mentioned in Wed-dington's memoir, *A Question of Choice*, or in documentar-ies; unlike Weddington, she never delivered a university commencement address or appeared among the feminist luminaries who headline rallies on the Washington Mall. When Prager met Coffee, she had given only a single in-terview since 1973, and was living in an unheated house in East Texas, reliant on food banks. She had been 26 years old in 1969, when she read about the newly decided *People v. Belous*: a California gynaecologist had been found guilty of violating his state's anti-abortion laws (for passing on the details of an abortionist to a pregnant patient), only to have his conviction overturned when the state supreme court ruled that California's anti-abortion laws were unconstitutionally 'vague', in violation of the Fourteenth Amendment. Part of that amendment, which guarantees legal 'due process', had been interpreted to mean that laws must be comprehensible to the 'men of common intelligence' who have to follow them. In California, as in Texas, abortion was illegal unless it was 'necessary to preserve . . . life', but the court recognised that the meanings of 'necessary' and 'preserve' weren't always obvious, and that doctors had been forced to speculate. The court also noted that the statute had been written in 1850, before the advent of modern antibiotics. A 'great and direct interference with a woman's constitutional rights' might once have been 'warranted by considerations of the woman's health', but no longer. The circumstances had flipped: abortions now saved pregnant women from the far more dangerous experience of childbirth.

Coffee told Prager that her 'mind raced' on reading the verdict: if California's abortion laws were unconstitutional, then the Texas laws might not stand up in court either. She thought they were harmful – they 'held women back' – as well as illogical: anyone who helped a woman to get an abortion was guilty of a crime, but if a woman performed the abortion on herself, she was in the clear, not even guilty of a misdemeanour. Coffee was a Baptist, but it didn't occur to her that there might be a conflict between her faith and her feelings about abortion. She had been taught that 'life begins when breath begins,' not before. In 1970, 70 per cent of Baptist pastors 'supported abortion to protect the mental or physical health of the mother'; 90 per cent of Texas Baptists thought their state's abortion laws were too restrictive. The president of the Southern Evangelical Seminary once explained in the *Baptist Press* that, before *Roe v. Wade*, as far as his fellow seminarians had been concerned, abortion was a 'Catholic issue'. Nor had abort-

ion been a partisan cause. Many Democrats, particularly
Catholic voters in the north-east, were pro-life. Prominent
Republicans were often pro-choice – they were, after all,
meant to be the defenders of individual liberty. Many states
would probably have eventually liberalised abortion laws
on their own. In 1970, abortion was legal in two, Oregon
and California. Other states seemed to be loosening up – if
not making abortion legal outright, then at least allowing
exceptions for pregnancies that were the result of rape or
incest.

But not Texas. As Weddington explains in her memoir,
'Texas was hopeless': legislators wouldn't move abortion
bills out of committee. Coffee realised that if the Supreme
Court overruled the Texas statutes, the law could change
for everyone in the country, immediately. It seemed effic-
ient. She became 'consumed' by the idea of filing suit – it
thrilled her, unlike her day job, which was drafting bank-
ruptcy petitions. She had been an excellent law student
and had clerked for a federal judge, but Texas firms weren't
keen on hiring women. She tried to get work with Henry
Wade in the district attorney's office, but 'the only job he
had for a woman . . . was collecting child support.' (She
also couldn't get a charge card in her own name or rent
an apartment without a male co-signer.) One of her Sunday school classmates, Henry McCluskey, was attempting
to overturn the Texas sodomy statutes, which criminalised
sex acts that couldn't result in pregnancy. Coffee wrote
'some kind of brief' for him, arguing that the police who
spied on gay men in public toilets were violating constitutional protections of privacy; the court wasn't fully persuaded, but she thought that some of her arguments could
be repurposed to go after the abortion laws. Just a few
years before, in *Griswold v. Connecticut* (1965), the court had
overturned a state ban on the sale of contraceptives for use

in 'the sacred precincts of marital bedrooms'. It was the first time that the court had decided that Americans had a constitutional right to 'marital privacy', that even though no such phrase appears in the Bill of Rights, a 'right to privacy' could be 'implied' from the 'penumbras' and 'emanations' of multiple amendments. Coffee was curious to see how far the court might go: if the justices were willing to overturn laws about condoms, why not laws about abortion? She was confident that she could make a compelling legal argument – she thought that she could almost do it 'on the basis of common sense' – but she 'couldn't figure out how . . . to find a pregnant woman who was willing to come forward' as the plaintiff of record until McCluskey offered to introduce her to one of his clients.

At the start of her memoir I Am Roe, McCorvey apologises for being a 'nuisance' and 'embarrassment' to 'some in the women's movement'. She wishes that, like 'many of the women I admire', she came across as more 'gentle' and 'sophisticated' – but then, if she had been more sophisticated, she might not have been so useful. She blames her religious parents (Pentecostals turned Jehovah's Witnesses) for neglecting to tell her how babies were made. When she became pregnant at seventeen, she was 'shocked' – 'somehow what Woody and I had been doing together didn't seem to be what was needed to create a whole new life.' Woody was her husband, but the marriage was over by the time her daughter, Melissa, was born. Although she enjoyed sex with men, she thought of herself as a lesbian, and wasn't interested in living with a man, or raising children with one. For years she would claim that her own mother had 'kidnapped' Melissa – McCorvey was ashamed that she had begged her mother to take the baby away. She supported herself by working as a cleaner and by running the freak show at the Bluegrass Carnival, sometimes by selling drugs or sex. When she became pregnant for a second time, she asked a nurse if there was a 'way that they take your baby'. The nurse either misunderstood her or wouldn't break the law, and referred McCorvey to McCluskey, who arranged for the baby, another girl, to be adopted as soon as she was born. When McCorvey was 21 years old and pregnant for a third time, she went back to him: 'I didn't want to give birth to another unwanted child. I didn't want to have to give up another child. I didn't want a child to be born with me as a mother.'

When Coffee first met her potential plaintiff, McCorvey wasn't sure how far she was from giving birth. Coffee thought that she looked 'really pregnant' – at least twenty weeks along, too late to get a legal abortion anywhere in the US. Coffee knew that a lawsuit wouldn't do anything to help McCorvey terminate her pregnancy, but it's not clear whether McCorvey knew it. Coffee would admit to Prager that McCorvey had 'maybe' seemed a 'little too co-operative': her only question had been about whether she would have to pay anything (Coffee paid the $30 filing fee). Coffee told Prager she was aware that McCorvey 'didn't have a lot of education', but didn't worry that she might be taking advantage of her. Since the case would be filed under a pseudonym, almost no one would know McCorvey had been involved. Win or lose, there seemed little reason for her role in the case to affect her life – except that if they won, she might be able to get an abortion for her next unwanted pregnancy. (When Prager asked McCorvey about contraception, she told him: 'When you're in a hurry, you're in a hurry.')

McCorvey liked to say that she chose the name 'Jane Roe' herself, to honour a childhood imaginary friend, but Coffee told Prager that she knew what her plaintiff would be called before she ever met McCorvey; 'Jane Roe' was just a common pseudonym for a woman in legal proceedings, as John Roe was for a man. Coffee would probably have continued to work on the case by herself if she hadn't received a phone call from her old law school classmate Sarah Weddington. They weren't friends, but Weddington had a question about federal procedure, and knew that Coffee had clerked for a federal judge – Sarah Hughes, who was instrumental in securing Texan women the right to serve on juries, though she'll always be most famous for swearing in Lyndon Johnson as president on Air Force One after Kennedy's assassination. Weddington belonged to a network that illegally referred women to doctors willing to perform abortions, and was herself considering bringing a suit in Austin to challenge the state's anti-abortion laws. Her plaintiffs would be a group of women who weren't pregnant, but might plausibly want abortions in the future. Coffee persuaded her she'd be making a mistake – the court would almost certainly find that the women didn't have standing – and said it would be smarter to file in Dallas, not Austin, so there would be a chance of arguing in front of Judge Hughes. She invited Weddington to join her case (in her memoir, Weddington makes it seem like it was the other way around) and took her to a pizza parlour to meet their plaintiff. McCorvey was struck by how little Weddington resembled her idea of a feminist activist – 'short and blonde and a little plump', she was a former sorority girl who had led her school's chapter of the Future Homemakers of America.

When, years later, McCorvey heard Weddington say that part of the reason she had devoted herself to helping women get abortions was that she'd had one herself, in Mexico, while she was a law student, McCorvey felt betrayed – why hadn't Weddington helped her to get a Mexican abortion too? 'I thought we were all real clear on what I really want-

ed,' she told Prager. She told Coffee and Weddington she'd
been raped, but later admitted she'd only said it because
she thought it might help her case. The lawyers decided
not to mention rape in their briefs: they weren't sure they
believed McCorvey, and they didn't want the law changed
only to permit a rape exception. 'We wanted a decision
that abortion was covered by the right of privacy,' Weddington wrote. 'Our principles were not based on how
conception occurred.'

In May 1970, Coffee and Weddington represented
Jane Roe in front of a panel of three federal judges (including Judge Hughes) against the office of the Dallas district
attorney. Henry Wade had prosecuted Jack Ruby for the
murder of Lee Harvey Oswald, and was renowned in Texas
for his eager pursuit of the death penalty. According to his
son, he was a 'closeted liberal' and personally pro-choice
– but he liked to win elections in Dallas. His lawyers told
the panel that Jane Roe didn't have standing to bring a
case: the anti-abortion statutes targeted doctors, not the
women who went to them. In addition, the state had 'a
right to protect life', and the 'right of the child to life is
superior to that of a woman's right to privacy'. On 2 June
1970, McCorvey gave birth to her third child, another girl.
And on 17 June, the judicial panel ruled that the Texas
statutes were indeed unconstitutional, but stopped short of
explicitly ordering Texas officials to stop enforcing them.
Wade announced that he would appeal the decision to the
Supreme Court, and that in the meantime, nothing had
changed. Since the panel hadn't issued an injunction, he
would continue to send abortionists to prison. Coffee and
Weddington were allowed to cross-appeal, but they didn't
expect anything to come of it. Of the thousands of appeals
the Supreme Court received every year, only about 150
would be accepted. And even if the court were inclined

to hear a case on abortion law, it wouldn't necessarily be theirs: similar cases were pending in other states too.

In her memoir, McCorvey says that she had a 'moment or two of pure truth, total clarity', followed by rage, when she realised that even if she won the lawsuit, it would be too late to get an abortion herself. 'I was nothing to Sarah and Linda, nothing more than just a name on a piece of paper.' She thought that they had led her on, 'let me think that I could get an abortion – and then, when everything was going fine for them, when they had got what they wanted – they just said, "Sorry," as they told me my world had fallen in.' McCluskey arranged for her to have another closed adoption. A few days after she gave birth, she attempted suicide.

In May 1971, the Supreme Court announced that it would hear *Roe v. Wade* in December. Until then, no larger organisation of lawyers and activists had helped Coffee and Weddington plot strategy; they had relied on friends for office space and for help with research and typing. Only when *Roe* was definitely headed for the Supremes were they 'flooded', as Weddington would write in her memoir, with offers of advice and, at last, some money. At least one lawyer tried to take over the case entirely: too much was at stake, he thought, for *Roe* to be handled by neophytes. In *A Question of Choice*, Weddington admits that before her work on *Roe*, her 'total legal experience consisted of a few uncontested divorces for friends, ten or twelve uncomplicated wills for people with little property, one adoption for relatives, and a few miscellaneous matters'. Coffee stepped back from the case, but Weddington held onto it because, as she would later say, another lawyer wouldn't have understood the 'fear of pregnancy or the resentment of the limitations that the law placed on women' as well as she did. She also wanted her moment in the sun. At 26, she would be among the youngest lawyers ever to argue a case in front of the Supreme Court. The plaintiff has the last word on representation. 'To solve her problem,' McCorvey would write, 'Sarah got in touch with me, for the first time in a long time.' She gave Weddington permission to keep arguing the case, though she no longer thought much about it. 'Basically, I was no good. So that meant no good would come out of anything I ever did. The lawsuit had my signature on it – that meant it was doomed.'

In the nationwide speaking tour that would occupy much of the rest of her life – 'When people ask me where I live, I sometimes answer "Delta"' – Weddington would describe how on 13 December 1971 she dressed with studied demureness, in pearls, her hair down: feminine, likeable, not a ball-breaker. In those days there was only a men's lavatory in the Supreme Court lawyers' lounge, and someone mistook her for a secretary. During oral arguments, her inexperience was obvious: Justice Blackmun thought she barely passed (a 'C+'). In her memoir, Weddington remembers how difficult she found it to make her points when the justices kept interrupting her with questions. She tried to tell them that when the constitution was adopted, there had been 'no common law prohibition against abortion'; abortions had been available to American women from the earliest days of the republic. She didn't argue that particular constitutional amendments guaranteed a right to privacy or to an abortion – she admitted that she was 'a little reluctant to aspire to wisdom that the court was not in agreement on' – but suggested that the guarantee of 'liberty' in the Fourteenth Amendment might be relevant. And she tried to point out some of the 'variety of ways' in which a foetus wasn't a person under the law: the census doesn't count pregnant women twice; tax deductions for offspring don't kick in until after birth; the right of inheritance had always been contingent on being born alive. Her brief was heavy with affidavits from male heads of obstetrics and gynaecology departments. Weddington sensed that the justices would have a 'special respect' for them, as fellow professionals. Amicus briefs supporting *Roe* were also filed by Margaret Mead, a former Miss America, and religious groups, including Episcopalians, Jews and the United Church of Christ.

The lawyer representing Texas began his argument by saying: 'It's an old joke, but when a man argues against two beautiful ladies like this, they're going to have the last word.' When no one laughed, Weddington thought he became 'unnerved'. He went on to argue that even if a no longer pregnant Roe did have standing to sue in court (which he didn't concede), an 'unborn child' was a person with constitutional rights 'from the moment of impregnation'. A woman 'makes her choice' to become a mother 'prior to the time she becomes pregnant'; Texas was entitled to protect the lives of all its citizens. Blackmun found the defence lawyer smoother than Weddington – he gave him a B – but thought that neither lawyer had satisfactorily answered the jurisdictional question the justices had thought they were deciding: if a state law prevented a woman from getting an abortion, could she sue in federal court? The justices had initially agreed to hear *Roe v. Wade* without a full bench (two justices had recently retired) because they hadn't realised what was at stake. Once they did, they scheduled the lawyers to argue the whole case again the following year. Another reason for the delay was that Blackmun had begun his own independent research project on the history of abortion in America: he wanted more time to think things through.

Blackmun told the oldest of his three daughters that he'd give his 'eyeteeth' to write one of the opinions for *Roe v.*

Wade. Decades later, at his memorial service, she would say that he had seen at 'close range what it was like for a woman alone in the world'. His middle daughter, Sally, got pregnant in 1966, when she was nineteen; she dropped out of university and married her boyfriend, then had a miscarriage, then a divorce. An opinion was also likely to be assigned to Blackmun because of his 'medical background', the decade he'd spent as a lawyer for the Mayo Clinic in Minnesota. Blackmun wasn't certain that a woman had a right to an abortion, but he considered a doctor's judgment close to inviolable. He did believe – as he would write – that at some point in a pregnancy, 'another being becomes involved,' but he went back and forth on when that might be. His research in the Mayo Clinic's library persuaded him that until the mid-19th century, an American woman had 'enjoyed a substantially broader right to terminate a pregnancy than she does in most states today'. In colonial America, 'restoring the menses' had been a common enough domestic practice that recipes – listing abortifacient herbs – had often been included in home medical guides. Blackmun would never suggest exactly where in the constitution the right to privacy was located, but he was certain that it was in there somewhere, and that it must be 'broad enough to encompass a woman's decision whether or not to terminate her pregnancy'. He didn't think it would be necessary to 'resolve the difficult question of when life begins'. He considered the rights of fathers, and of the parents of minors who became pregnant, but so long as the defenders of the Texas laws didn't refer to them, he decided he wouldn't either.

Roe v. Wade was reargued on 11 October 1972. The court now included new Nixon appointees, including Lewis Powell. Nixon had announced that Powell 'shared' his 'judicial philosophy, which is basically a conservative

philosophy'. Although Nixon had recently supported
increased federal funding for family planning, including
abortions – 'There are times when an abortion is necessary.
I know that,' he said on one of his secret tapes – in 1971
he had been persuaded by his advisers, particularly Pat
Buchanan, that by flipping he would persuade a sizeable
number of Catholic voters to abandon the Democratic
Party. In time for his re-election campaign, Nixon announced that he could no longer 'square' abortion 'on demand' with 'my personal belief in the sanctity of human
life, including the life of the yet unborn'. He assumed that
Powell, a Southerner who in private practice had defended
Big Tobacco, would toe his new line. But although on gay
rights Powell would vote as Nixonishly as court-watchers
predicted (while upholding Georgia's anti-sodomy statutes,
Powell told a law clerk 'I don't believe I've ever met a
homosexual'), on abortion, he went the other way. Powell's
father-in-law and two brothers-in-law were all obstetricians: he'd learned from them what unsafe abortions did to
women. Powell praised Blackmun's draft opinion, which
argued that abortion should be legal during the first trimester, but persuaded him to go further, to allow for
abortions until the end of the second trimester (about 27
weeks into a pregnancy). In a note to colleagues, Blackmun agreed that there was a 'practical aspect' to allowing
for later abortions: he had learned that 'there are many
pregnant women, particularly younger girls, who may refuse to face the fact of pregnancy and who, for one reason
or another, do not get around to medical consultation until the end of the first trimester is upon them or, indeed,
has passed.'

Supreme Court clerks referred to Blackmun's draft opinion as 'Harry's abortion'; they fretted that he was acting
more like a legislator than a judge. In a note to colleagues,

Blackmun admitted that his emphasis on trimesters was 'arbitrary', but that 'perhaps any other selected point' would be 'equally arbitrary'. He wouldn't tell his daughter Sally what the decision in Roe v. Wade would be, only that she should be in the courthouse on 22 January 1973 to hear it. Weddington said later that when she found out she'd won the case, 7-2, she wanted to telephone Norma McCorvey, but hadn't been able to track her down; she 'assumed she had heard or would see press reports' – Roe was almost the top story of the day, second only to the news that Lyndon Johnson had died.

Henceforth, through the first trimester, 'the attending physician, in consultation with his patient, is free to determine, without regulation by the state, that, in his medical judgment, the patient's pregnancy should be terminated.' (This wording was the source of frustration to come: Blackmun had protected the 'woman's right, with the physician, to get an abortion', rather than the woman's right alone.) States would be free to 'regulate' abortions during the second trimester, though only to protect 'maternal health'. Once a foetus had the 'capability of meaningful life outside the mother's womb', a state would be permitted 'to proscribe abortion except where it is necessary . . . to preserve the life or health of the mother'. In Becoming Justice Blackmun (2005), Linda Greenhouse charts the immediate response to the decision from legal scholars, which 'ranged from tepid to withering'. An article in the Yale Law Journal argued that the Roe decision was 'bad because it is bad constitutional law, or rather because it is not constitutional law and gives almost no sense of an obligation to try to be'. Ruth Bader Ginsburg would say that the case had been mismanaged from the start, and that the constitutional arguments should have been based on women's equality, not privacy. (She also thought Blackmun had gone too far: 'Doctrinal limbs too swiftly shaped, experience teaches, may prove unstable.') But what mattered was the result. No one really believed that the abortion debate in America had ever been about what was in the constitution.

McCorvey began to refer to *Roe* as 'my law'; at a march in Washington she felt rebuffed – why wasn't she being invited to address the crowds? And she was hurt that Weddington 'barely acknowledged' her. In 1989, shots were fired into her house and car – the work, McCorvey knew, of a woman she had short-changed on a drug deal, but she told reporters that she'd been targeted because she was Jane Roe. A bullet had entered Justice Blackmun's house too, and abortionists were being murdered: it was a believable lie, and she was angry that she wasn't rewarded for telling it. All the women who were now benefiting from the legal abortions she had been denied – didn't they owe her something? Instead, she kept being fired from jobs answering the phones or filing papers at Texas abortion clinics. 'She had a name,' one of her bosses told Prager, 'but that's about all she had.'

In August 1995, in a televised interview with ABC News, the 'woman once known only as Jane Roe' told Ted Koppel that the feminists had never shown her the 'respect I thought I deserved'. McCorvey was now a member of Operation Rescue, an anti-abortion group with the slogan 'If you believe abortion is murder, act like it's murder.' The pro-life movement, once amorphous, had been united by a single goal since 1973 – overturn *Roe*. Now Roe was theirs: 'God has given Norma to us.' Never again would she be side-lined at a Washington rally. Now when she went to the capital, a whole event would be structured around her, a memorial service featuring a tiny casket representing all the millions of unborn children. She claimed that the first time she met Coffee and Weddington she hadn't even known the meaning of the word 'abortion'; they'd plied her with so much beer that she hadn't realised what they were up to. At other times she would admit that she was still angry with Weddington for not helping her to get a Mexican abortion. Even when she went further off script – telling interviewers that she thought that abortion should be legal in the first trimester – it didn't matter to Operation Rescue; they didn't just forgive her, they loved her, 'a miracle' and 'vessel of God'. In a new lawsuit, *McCorvey v. Hill* (2003), she argued that since her original affidavit for *Roe v. Wade* had been full of lies, the whole case should be thrown out. The court didn't agree – too much time had passed – but the attention helped Operation Rescue to raise money. Besides, *Roe* wasn't quite what it had been. In *Planned Parenthood v. Casey* (1992), the Supreme Court had thrown out Blackmun's trimester system, ruling that 'even in the earliest stages of pregnancy' states would be allowed to enact anti-abortion regulations so long as they didn't place 'substantial obstacles in the path of a woman seeking an abortion before the foetus attains viability'. When Blackmun read a draft of the opinion, he wrote in the margin: 'Wow! Pretty extreme!' It was obvious that the meaning of 'substantial' would become too open to interpretation. Impose enough regulations on an abortion clinic, and you could get it to close as surely as if you'd bombed it. Which, of course, anti-abortionists sometimes did.

At the end of her life, interviewed from a nursing home, McCorvey would say she no longer cared about the abortion wars: 'If a young woman wants to have an abortion – fine. It's no skin off my ass.' Her admission that she was no longer pro-life made headlines once again. But as much as McCorvey had been a prize, Operation Rescue hungered for an even bigger one: Baby Roe. For years, the only person who knew what had happened to the daughters

McCorvey had given up for adoption was McCluskey, but he was murdered in 1973. McCorvey never tried to find her second daughter: she knew that it was only the third one who was special. With help from a tabloid, she was able to find her – a law secretary called Shelley, living in Washington State. On the phone, McCorvey tried to persuade her to meet on camera. Shelley thought not. On another call, McCorvey demanded that Shelley thank her: 'Shelley asked why. For not aborting her, answered Norma.' As if she'd had a choice. Much as it pained her, Shelley told Prager, she thought McCorvey should have had the right to do it.

To a Poet
Adrienne Rich
(1974)

Ice splits   under the metal
shovel   another day
hazed light off fog planes
cruelty of winter   landlocked   your life
wrapped round you   in your twenties
an old bathrobe   dragged down
with milkstains   tearstains   dust

Scraping eggcrust from the child's
dried dish   skimming the skin
from cooled milk   wringing diapers
Language floats at the vanishing-point
incarnate   breathes the fluorescent bulb
primary   states the scarred grain of the floor
and on the ceiling in torn plaster laiughs   *imago*

> *and I have fears that you will cease to be*
> *before your pen has glean'd your teeming brain*

for you are not a suicide
but no one calls this murder
Small mouths, needy, suck you: *This is love*

293

I write this   not for you
who fight to write your own
words   fighting up the falls
but for another woman   dumb
with loneliness   dust   seeping plastic bags
with children   in a house
where language floats and spins
abortion   in
the bowl

After *Roe v. Wade*
Sophie Smith
(2022)

When *Triple Jeopardy*, the magazine of the Third World Women's Alliance, covered the passing of *Roe* in 1973, it pointed out that while wealthy women had 'managed for some time now to obtain these operations with little or no difficulty' it was 'the poor woman, especially third world women from low-income strata who have been at the mercy of back-alley abortionists'. In 1969, the year before abortion became legal in New York, the women of TWWA reported that 'nearly half the child-bearing deaths' in NYC were attributed to abortion. Out of these, '79 per cent were among non-white and Puerto Rican women.'

Today, thanks to medical abortion – induced by a combination of mifepristone and misoprostol pills – and improved surgical techniques, the botched procedure in a makeshift clinic is no longer the gravest threat to those seeking out illegal abortions. These will continue to happen, not least because of a lack of knowledge of safe abortion methods – one study in Ghana, where abortion is legal, showed that many women still choose risky procedures over proven alternatives. And just as poor communities of colour have been the primary targets of fake Covid 'cures', so we will no doubt see opportunistic medics peddling at best ineffectual, at worst dangerous, drugs to those seeking discreet terminations. But many harms will lie elsewhere and, again, they will be unevenly distributed. Women of colour, who are already the primary victims of maternal death in the US – and among those most likely to have abortions – will increasingly die giving birth to children they are being forced to bear. The male authority figures marginalised women already have reason to fear – cops, parole officers, judges, abusive partners – will, thanks to the many state abortion bans triggered by the fall of *Roe*, be further empowered. The position in the UK is less secure than we might like to think. Recently, a woman from Norfolk was reported to the police for taking abortion pills without the authorisation of two doctors – a legal requirement. The call was made by her social worker. (We should not forget that in 2019, 99 MPs, mainly Tories, voted to keep abortion illegal in Northern Ireland.)

For the Third World Women's Alliance and other Black feminist groups, the politics of abortion was inseparable from a broader politics of race and class. The battle for abortion, the TWWA said, was part of a larger campaign for 'free, safe (non-genocidal) healthcare', 'non-exploitative employment, controlled collectively by workers', 'an end to the racism and sexism which forces third world women into the lowest paid service jobs', and 'healthcare, housing, food, clothing, transportation and education . . . free and controlled and administered by the people who use them'.

It would be a mistake to respond to the overturning of *Roe* by fighting simply to get it, or something like it, back on the legislative books. Local abortion networks exist because the world before *Roe* was overturned was not one where abortion was everywhere safe, affordable and on demand. Legal change – while not without powerful effects – has never been sufficient for real social change.

This works in both directions. Republicans think they can legislate abortion out of existence, but they will only drive it underground, devastating lives in the process. Democrats who think that securing abortion under the law is the same as securing access to abortion have not been paying attention.

Or maybe they have. The striking down of *Roe* is a gift to anyone who wants to perform their 'woke' credentials while doing as little as possible to alter the conditions that make a progressive politics necessary. In a recent run-off, Nancy Pelosi supported Texas congressman Henry Cuellar, despite his anti-abortion stance. His challenger, Jessica Cisneros, a pro-abortion working-class woman of colour, was backed by Alexandria Ocasio-Cortez. On the day *Roe* fell, Pelosi sent out an email asking for donations to help her fight the court's ruling.

There is a coalition of actors – centrist Democrats, Republicans, corporate CEOs – who would not be unhappy if liberals and leftists spent the next decades campaigning for the reinstatement of what was there before. A flimsy protection, based on the right to privacy (the feminist irony!), eroded at state level, and with inadequate provision for the worst-off. Meanwhile, Republican legislators will step up their assaults against trans and queer people, environmental protection, and whatever simulacrum of democracy the US can still be said to have.

The only response is to meet their radicalism with our own. It is not enough to demand a woman's right to choose. We must insist, with the women of the TWWA, on full reproductive freedom, and on the conditions that make a flourishing human life possible for all.

It is worth noting that neither of today's most prominent mass feminist movements for reproductive justice – in Poland and Argentina – are trans-exclusionary. The activists in these movements know that the forces which would prohibit the right to abort a foetus are the same ones that want to pathologise trans and gay people. Trans-exclusionary feminists have a choice to make: whether to continue providing sustenance to highly organised and murderous right-wing forces, or come into coalition, however uncomfortable, with those of us looking to stop them.

Writing in *Women: A Journal of Liberation* in 1972, the year before *Roe* passed, Claudia Leight, an abortion counsellor in Baltimore, discussed her 'fears about choosing any one demand and concentrating on it exclusively'. 'I'm afraid' she predicted,

> that legal abortion could become to the current feminist movement what suffrage was to our sisters over fifty years ago. That is, that this demand could be singled out and won, nominally, with so much energy directed towards its achievement that more general issues of women's liberation may be forgotten. A similar consequence would be for our demands to be met in a minimal way so as to silence us. It is a real possibility that abortion will be legalised nationally, but will still be expensive and therefore available only to privileged women . . . If we are to work for reforms which are necessary now, we must keep in mind where we hope to be heading: that our major goal is to change the basic relationships of power in our society.

African American Women and Abortion: A Neglected History
Loretta J. Ross
(1992)

Many observers mistakenly view the African American women's struggle for abortion rights and reproductive freedom in the 1990s as a relatively recent phenomenon, rather than placing it in the context of our historical struggle against racism, sexism and poverty. Our contributions to the birth control and abortion movements in the United States have been disguised by racist and sexist assumptions about us, our sexuality and our fertility. Distilling fact from myth is difficult because so many accounts of African American history are written from perspectives that fail to acknowledge our presence.

For example, from the mid-19th century to the present, the growth rate of the African American population has been more than halved. Historians and demographers typically attribute this and other declines in African American birth rates to poverty, coercive family planning or other external factors, ignoring the possibility that African American women were in any way responsible for the change. Similarly, feminist literature often disappointingly reflects the common view that African American women's awareness regarding gender equality and abortion rights is underdeveloped. Whether these assumptions come from population experts, feminists or the African American community itself, they fail to credit the power of African American women to make responsible personal and political decisions for ourselves. A historical perspective is necessary to understand and place in context the contemporary views of African American women on abortion and birth control.

African American women were never the passive victims of eugenics (the 'improvement' of humankind through selective breeding), forced sterilisation or other medical, commercial and state policies of reproductive control. Even before slavery, African American women were intimately concerned about fertility. When legal birth control and abortion were available, African American women used them. When they were not, women resorted to dangerous methods limited only by available technology and imagination.

Abortion, in and of itself, does not automatically create freedom for African American women. But it does allow some control over our biology, freeing us from the inevitability of unwanted pregnancies, and is therefore indispensable to bodily and political self-determination. To ask whether African American women favour or oppose abortion may be currently fashionable, but it is immaterial: we obtain 24 per cent of the abortions in the United States, more than 500,000 annually. The question is not if we support abortion, but how, and when, and why. But it was neither persuasive analysis nor arguments nor ideology that influenced African American women to have abortions or to support abortion and birth control. We did so because we needed to. Necessity was the midwife to our politics.

Regrettably, African American women have been reluctant to analyse our history regarding abortion and to speak out collectively and publicly in support of abortion. To do so once seemed to further arguments of black genocide, a charge that was not unreasonable in view of a multitude of attacks on African Americans. To speak out also risked high-lighting abortion over other forms of control imposed on African American women, thus perpetuating a frequent practice of more privileged women of separating abortion rights – which concerns women of all socioeconomic strata – from the less 'popular' struggles against forced sterilisat-ion and other coercive measures – measures that privil-eged women typically failed to address. Finally, implicit in the silence is African American women's ambivalence to-wards the main-stream pro-choice movement. While 83 per cent of African Americans support abortion and birth control, little of that support translates into membership in a predominantly white feminist organisation. By explor-ing the nature of this silence, we connect ourselves to our foremothers who were activists in the cause of reproduct-ive freedom, an activism that found expression on its own terms.

Prior to the Civil War, almost 20 per cent of the US pop-ulation were African American slaves, one slave for every four whites. Controlling reproduction was important to maintain the race, class, and gender inequality of the slave economy. Plantation owners tried to withhold knowledge of birth control and abortion from both slaves and white women to maintain the caste system of white male supremacy used to justify slavery. Black women's fertility increased the owners' labour force and property value; 'slave masters wanted adolescent girls to have children, and . . . they practised a passive, though insidious kind of breeding.' Slave masters gave pregnant slave women light-er workloads and more rations to increase their willing-ness to have children. Punitive measures were also used: infertile women were treated 'like barren sows and . . . passed from one unsuspecting buyer to the next'.

African Americans used birth control and abortion to resist slavery. Abortion and infanticide were acts of desperation, motivated not by a desire to avoid birth or the burdens of parenting, but by a commitment to resist the oppressive conditions of slavery. When black women resorted to abortion, the stories they told were not so much about the desire to be free of pregnancy, but rather about the miserable social conditions which dissuaded them from bringing new lives into the world.

The midwifery culture among African American slaves maintained centuries-old African folk knowledge about contraceptives (pregnancy preventers) and abortifacients (pregnancy terminators). Unlike modern pharmaceuticals, some herbs and methods were used as both contraceptives and abortifacients, a blurred distinction that has complicated the task of reconstructing our history.

A careful reading of slave journals and narratives reveals that some Southern whites were certain that slave women knew how to use contraceptives and to terminate a pregnancy. These suspicions about slave abortions produced a limited amount of scholarly research. In an 1856 essay, Dr E.M. Pendleton claimed that planters regularly complained of whole families of women who failed to have children. Pendleton believed that 'blacks are possessed of a secret by which they destroy the foetus at an early age of gestation.' A Tennessee physician, Dr John H. Morgan, said that he was certain that slave women were aborting either by 'medicine, violent exercise or by external and internal manipulations'.

Towards the end of the 19th century, 'alum water' was one of many birth control measures used as a douche in Southern rural communities served by midwives. Women in urban areas used poultices of petroleum jelly mixed with quinine. Widely available and purchased very cheaply in stores, these ingredients were placed over the mouth of the uterus. Boiling rusty nails yielded a douche used as both a contraceptive and an abortifacient. Some women used quinine tablets or turpentine (orally or as a douche) and laxatives (orally). Such concoctions were reputed to bring about severe cramps and contractions which approximated giving birth. Plant compounds such as pennyroyal and papaya seeds were also used.

Despite their popularity, these folk methods were usually regarded as a sin by those influenced by Christianity. Nevertheless, African American women informally discussed abortion and birth control and passed along the knowledge, although written references were usually oblique. In 1894, *The Women's Era*, an African American women's newsletter, wrote that 'not all women are intended for mothers. Some of us have not the temperament for family life.' This was not an explicit endorsement of family planning, but then neither were advertisements in black newspapers for a medicated douche called 'Puf' which was reported to 'end your calendar worries' (prevent a pregnancy).

By the 1900s, black women were gaining increasing control of their fertility. 'Their grandmothers married at twelve and fifteen,' W.E.B. DuBois, one of the founders of the NAACP, observed in *The Gift of Black Folk*. In 1910, DuBois found 27 per cent of African American women still single past the age of fifteen. Women were also bearing fewer children. By the turn of the century, half of all married, educated African American women had no children. Even more revealing, one-fourth of all black women – the majority of them rural and uneducated – had no children at all.

Historians often portray the birth control movement as having been thrust upon reluctant African Americans by a population-control establishment anxious to control black fertility. But while this aim may have been part of the establishment's agenda, African Americans were clearly involved in the national birth control debate. According to researcher Jessie Rodrique, grassroots African Americans were 'active and effective participants in the establishment of local [family planning] clinics . . . and despite co-operation with white birth control groups, blacks maintained a degree of independence' that allowed the development of an African American analysis of family planning and of the role it played in racial progress.

W.E.B. DuBois wrote in 1919 that 'the future [African American] woman . . . must have the right of motherhood at her own discretion.' Joining him was historian J.A. Rogers, who wrote, 'I give the Negro woman credit if she endeavours to be something other than a mere breeding machine. Having children is by no means the sole reason for being.'

African American women saw themselves not as breeders or matriarchs, but as builders and nurturers of a race, a nation. Sojourner Truth's statement, 'I feel as if the power of a nation is within me!' affirmed the role of African American women as 'seminal forces of the endurance and creativity needed by future generations of Blacks not merely to survive, but to thrive, produce, and progress.' The Coloured Women's Club Movement, the organised voice of African American women during the late 19th and early 20th centuries, addressed directly issues of black women's sexuality. This movement sought to 'confront and redefine morality and assess its relationship to 'true womanhood'. 'Stereotypes about black women's alleged sexual immorality prompted many African American women to 'make the virtues as well as the wants of the coloured women known to the American people . . . to put a new social value on themselves.' The Club Movement was integral to networks among African American women who shared information about contraception.

The Club Movement also denounced the rampant sterilisation of black women and supported the establishment of family planning clinics in black communities. In 1918, the Women's Political Association of Harlem, among dozens of other black women's organisations, held lectures on birth control. The National Urban League asked the Birth Control Federation of America (the forerunner to Planned Parenthood) that a clinic be opened in the predominantly black Columbus Hill section of the Bronx in 1925. Several ministers discussed birth control at their churches and in 1932, Rev. Adam Clayton Powell of Abyssinian Baptist Church spoke publicly in support of family planning.

African American organisations, including the NAACP, the National Urban League and such leading black newspapers as the *San Francisco Spokesman* and the *Pittsburgh Courier*, promoted family planning. The African American newspapers of the period also reported the mortality rates of women who had had septic abortions and championed the causes of black doctors who were arrested for performing illegal abortions.

The *Baltimore Afro-American* wrote that pencils, nails, and hat pins were instruments commonly used for self-induced abortions and that abortions among black women were deliberate, not the result of poor health or sexually transmitted diseases. Although statistics on abortions among African American women are scarce, 28 per cent of black women surveyed by an African American doctor in Nashville in 1940 said they had had at least one abortion.

In the early 20th century, as racism, lynchings and poverty took their heavy toll on African Americans, fears of depopulation, articulated by a rising black nationalist movement, produced a pronatalist shift. Prominent blacks who were concerned about the long-term survival of the race began to speak out against measures that reduced African Americans' numbers. Opposition to fertility control for African American women came not only from black nationalist leaders such as Marcus Garvey, who believed in increasing the black population in response to racial oppression, but also from the Catholic Church for religious and political reasons, and from white conservatives who feared the availability of birth control for white women. This change from African Americans' relative indifference about population size to using population growth as a form of political currency presaged the inevitable conflict between the right of women to exercise bodily self-determination and the need of African Americans for political and economic self-determination.

The opposition to fertility control ran headlong into a new social movement in support of birth control. When the movement for birth control began, organisers such as Margaret Sanger insisted that women's controlling their own fertility led to upward social mobility. This argument persuaded middle-class women, both black and white, to use birth control when available. Sanger's successful campaign benefited middle-class women of all races. But because it focused on legal rights alone, it did little to guarantee poor women access to care. Indeed, the early feminism of the movement collapsed under the weight of support offered by the growing number of white eugenicists who decried the growing numbers of people of colour, and immigrants. Birth control advocacy was co-opted as Sanger opportunistically built alliances with eugenicists at the expense of people of colour. This co-optation resulted in racist depopulation policies and doctor-controlled birth control technology.

Many of these birth control advocates believed it was important to 'prevent the American people from being replaced by alien or Negro stock, whether it be by immigration or by overly high birth rates.' To promote the reproduction of self-defined 'racially superior' people, eugenicists argued both for rewards (such as tax incentives and education) for 'desirable' racial stocks, and penalties (such as sterilisation, involuntary confinement, and immigration restrictions) for the 'undesirable'. While birth control was demanded as a right for privileged women, it became a duty for the poor.

African American women supported birth control and abortion, but they offered a strong critique of the eugenicists. A clear sense of dual values emerged among African American women: to want individual control over their bodies while simultaneously resisting government and private depopulation policies that blurred the distinction between incentives and coercion. The *Pittsburgh Courier*, which favoured family planning, suggested in 1936 that African Americans should oppose sterilisation programmes being advanced by eugenicists because the burden would 'fall upon coloured people and it behoves us to watch the law and stop the spread of [eugenic sterilisation].'

The majority of abortions available to African American women in the 1950s and early 1960s were provided by doctors and midwives operating illegally. For example, Dr Edgar Keemer, a black physician in Detroit, practised outside the law for more than thirty years until his arrest in 1956. Women also travelled to Mexico to have abortions. Dr Dorothy Brown, the first black female general surgeon in the United States, graduated from Meharry Medical College in 1948 and while in the Tennessee state legislature in the 1950s, became the first state legislator in the United States to introduce a bill to legalise abortion.

Long after most 'granny' midwives in other ethnic groups had been replaced by hospital practices, hundreds of black lay midwives in the deep South continued to provide most of the abortion and contraceptive services for black Southern women. Middle-class women sometimes persuaded doctors to arrange a clandestine abortion or to provide a referral. Poor women either carried their unplanned children to term or went to 'the lady down the street' – either a midwife or partially trained medical worker. Abortions from these illegal providers cost between $50 and $75, which was expensive considering that a pregnant woman might earn $10 a day. Many white women came to black neighbourhoods to obtain abortions this way.

In the mid-1950s, population 'time bomb' theories from demographers offered a newer approach to eugenics. These theories, still in vogue today, created an ideological link between population growth in non-industrialised nations and the United States' ability to govern world affairs. Brochures from groups such as the Draper Fund and the Population Council showed 'hordes of black and brown faces spilling over a tiny earth.' By the early 1960s, the United States government began supporting population control policies overseas and linked foreign aid with de-population policies. Time-bomb theorists sanctimoniously argued that they were simply saving the poor from themselves.

In response to the racism of the population control establishment, black nationalist campaigns against family planning re-emerged. Several birth control clinics were invaded by Black Muslims associated with the Nation of Islam, who published cartoons in *Muhammad Speaks* that depicted bottles of birth control pills marked with skull and crossbones, or graves of unborn black infants. The Pittsburgh branch of the NAACP declared that the local family planning clinic was an instrument of genocide. William 'Bouie' Haden, leader of the militant United Movement for Progress, went one step further and threatened to fire-bomb the Pittsburgh clinic.

Similarly, Whitney Young, leader of the Urban League, reversed his organisation's support for family planning in 1962. Marvin Davies, head of the Florida NAACP, said, 'Our women need to produce more babies, not less . . . and until we comprise 30 to 35 per cent of the population, we won't really be able to affect the power structure in this country.' This represented a major ideological shift from the early days of the NAACP and the Urban League, when both organisations supported women's reproductive rights as a means of racial progress. The NAACP of the 1920s would have been stunned to find itself in the 1960s sounding more like nationalist Marcus Garvey, who urged population expansion, than NAACP co-founder W.E.B. DuBois, who praised reproductive rights.

The time-bomb theories emerged at the time of America's growing civil rights movement. Perhaps in response to the militancy of the movement and its potential for sweeping social change, members of the white elite and middle-class suggested that black population growth should be curbed. White Americans held inordinate fears that a growing welfare class of African Americans concentrated in the inner cities would not only create rampant crime, but exacerbate the national debt, and eventually produce a political threat from majority-black voting blocs in urban areas.

This new 'politics of population' that emerged in the mid-1960s gave rise to family planning programmes directed at predominantly black urban areas in the South. At the same time, some African American leaders expressed interest in 'taking over' the big cities and 'holding them as enclaves against increasing repression'. Congress pressured the newly created Office of Economic Opportunity (OEO) to wage war on poverty by emphasising family planning programmes for African Americans in the year after passage of the 1965 Voting Rights Act. Family planning, which offered a wide range of maternal and childcare services to poor women, was included in Medicaid coverage after a series of state-level fights with Catholics and conservatives. Family planning also won passage over the objections of some medical experts, who were convinced that African American women 'wanted to be pregnant and have all those children and that even if they did not want repeated pregnancies, they could not possibly understand the principles of birth control because they were not bright enough and lacked behavioural control.' By the late 1960s, family planning became 'synonymous with the civil rights of poor women to medical care.'

Although abortion was still illegal, some public health agencies operated an 'underground railroad' of referrals for women to have illegal abortions. A major strength of the abortion-rights activism was the informal networks of African American women who spread the news about the availability of services and became activists in support of birth control, better healthcare, and abortion rights, and against sterilisation abuse. In the 1960s, underground abortions were facilitated by church and community-based referral services and co-operative doctors' networks in cities and states. An estimated 200,000 to one million illegal abortions occurred annually in the late 1960s.

Women were not blind to the incongruity of the government plan to make contraceptives free and accessible to African American communities that lacked basic health care. African American women warily watched state legislatures propose to sterilise poor women who had too many 'illegitimate' children. None of the proposals succeeded, largely because of the militancy of women such as civil-rights leader Fannie Lou Hamer, who told an interviewer that 'six out of every ten Negro women were . . . sterilised for no reason at all. Often the women were not told that they had been sterilised until they were released from the hospital.' A Princeton University fertility study found that 20 per cent of all married African American women had been sterilised.

African Americans and other women of colour also bore the brunt of the tragic consequences of illegal abortions. Before 1973, when *Roe v. Wade* legalised abortion, 80 per cent of deaths caused by illegal abortions in New York in the 1960s involved black and Puerto Rican women. In Georgia between 1965 and 1967, the black maternal death rate due to illegal abortion was fourteen times that of white women.

Partly as a consequence, the Black Power conference held in Newark in 1967, organised by poet Amiri Baraka, passed an anti-birth-control resolution. Two years later, the May 1969 issue of the *Liberator* warned, 'For us to speak in favour of birth control for Afro-Americans would be comparable to speaking in favour of genocide.' Opposition to family planning came to dominate the black freedom movement, which, interestingly, had mostly male spokespersons.

Thus, the assault on birth control and abortion came from both the left and the right. Conservatives saw family planning as an assault on traditional values of motherhood, while some radicals saw it as a race and class-directed eugenics programme. In contrast, African American women exerted a dynamic and aggressive influence on the family planning movement. They constituted the largest single bloc of support for family planning and were so visible that politicians in some states began to see them as a potential political force. African American women fully understood that there were no Planned Parenthood clinics in poor white neighbourhoods, but they still perceived the free services to be in their own best interests. Quoting from DuBois, they declared, 'We're not interested in the quantity of our race. We're interested in the quality of it.' Shirley Chisolm, a black Congresswoman from Brooklyn, dismissed the genocide argument with these words:

> To label family planning and legal abortion programmes 'genocide' is male rhetoric, for male ears. It falls flat to female listeners and to thoughtful male ones. Women know, and so do many men, that two or three children who are wanted, prepared for, reared amid love and stability, and educated to the limit of their ability will mean more for the future of the black and brown races from which they come than any number of neglected, hungry, ill-housed and ill-clothed youngsters.

A distinct black feminist consciousness countered opponents to family planning. In 1969, Frances Beal, then head of the Student Nonviolent Coordinating Committee's Black Women's Liberation Committee, wrote, 'Black women have the right and the responsibility to determine when it is in the interest of the struggle to have children or not to have them and this right must not be relinquished to any . . . to determine when it is in her own best interests to have children'[emphasis in original]. This sentiment was echoed by Toni Cade Bambara in 1970 when she wrote, 'I've been made aware of the national call to Sisters to abandon birth control . . . to picket family planning centres and abortion-referral groups and to raise revolutionaries. What plans do you have for the care of me and the child?'

Black feminists argued that birth control and abortion were, in themselves, revolutionary – and that black liberation in any sense could not be won without women controlling their lives. The birth control pill, in and of itself, could not liberate African American women, but it 'gives her the time to fight for liberation in those other areas.'

African American women thought it absurd to face coercion to limit their family size through sterilisation when they were willing to do so voluntarily if safe methods were accessible. This combined support for birth control and abortion and opposition to sterilisation, a view unique to African American women at the time, did much to inform both the feminist and the civil rights movement in later decades. African American women rejected the single-issue focus of the women's movement on abortion, which excluded other issues surrounding reproductive freedom. They also opposed the myopic racial focus of the male-dominated civil rights movement, which ignored gender equality.

The Black Panther Party was the only nationalist group to support free abortions and contraceptives on demand, although not without considerable controversy within its ranks. 'Half of the women in the Party used birth control and we supported it because of our free health care programme. We understood the conditions of the Black community,' remembers Nkenge Toure, a former member, who also recalls that there were no formal political education discussions around the issue, but there was support from many party women. This view of many women within the Black Panther Party often collided with male opposition to abortion and birth control. Some male members tried to shut down family planning clinics in New Orleans and Pittsburgh. As Angela Davis concluded, the late 1960s and early 1970s were 'a period in which one of the unfortunate hallmarks of some nationalist groups was their determination to push women into the background. The brothers opposing us leaned heavily on the male supremacist trends which were winding their way through the movement.'

Abortion Involves Killing –
and that's OK
Sophie Lewis
(2022)

In 2019, I published a kind of manifesto, *Full Surrogacy Now*, whose opening line is 'It is a wonder we let foetuses inside us.' The opening pages are entirely given over to my extended paean to the process of gestating in all its shockingly grisly biology, its everyday sublimity. Whereas, in other species, a female can often discard or expel a pregnancy at will, in our species, a hyper-invasive placenta puts the gestator at risk of lethal haemorrhage. Locked down, our body becomes a daredevil participant in a wrestling match (or similar extreme sport) we cannot easily quit. From this starting point, I make a case for rethinking human gestation as real and often deadly dangerous labour, deserving of maximal support. The controversial part is that a key correlate of viewing gestating as labour is that forcing someone to gestate against their will is forced labour.

Furthermore, if the labour of pregnancy is productive of life, then interrupting that labour is – logically speaking – productive of death. Rather than shy away from this, I believe we should embrace it as part of an effort to give gestating the respect it deserves. In the intervening years since publishing my book, I have received dozens of reports of women who experienced the ideas in it as deeply salutary during pregnancy. Strangers have sent me photos of *Full Surrogacy Now* lying face-down in maternity wards. By the same token, I had drawn on heterodox pregnancy memoirs to bolster my claims.

'Never in my life have I felt more pro-choice than when I was pregnant,' Maggie Nelson wrote in *The Argonauts* in 2015,

> And never in my life have I understood more thoroughly, and been more excited about, a life that began at conception. Feminists may never make a bumper sticker that says IT'S A CHOICE AND A CHILD, but of course that's what it is, and we know it. We're not idiots; we understand the stakes. Sometimes we choose death . . . Harry and I sometimes joke that women should get way beyond twenty weeks – maybe even up to two days after birth – to decide if they want to keep the baby. (Joke, OK?)

I agree with Nelson. There is something infantilising about denying the fact that embryos die when we scrape them out of the bodies of which they are a part. It sentimentalises pregnant or potentially pregnant humans as fundamentally non-violent creatures to imply that we can't handle the truth about what we are up to when we opt out. And it patronises abortion-getters to insist that we are only making a healthcare choice, rather than (also) extinguishing a future child. In my view, recognising that gestating manufactures a proto-person requires acknowledging that abortion kills a proto-person. A baby is completely dependent on human care in order to stay alive, but its needs could be filled by any person – whereas a foetus, a proto-person, is ineluctably dependent on specific person.

We humans do kill, when necessary: victims of assault sometimes kill in self-defence, targets of persecution sometimes kill for justice – or just to reduce the number of their persecutors – and the colonised sometimes kill for liberation. Mothers living in unspeakable conditions (including chattel slavery) have been documented to kill their children as an act of mercy. Of course, these examples are instances of necessary violence, generated by the conditions for which we struggle to render extinct. When it comes to abortions, it seems possible that the conditions that necessitate them may never be wholly eliminated, even if vasectomies become generalised and perfected ectogenetic technologies become universally accessible. As long as people are performing pregnancy on this earth, they must be free to change their minds about seeing it through. The adoption industry could be revolutionised and child welfare lavishly subsidised; regardless of the available supports, no one should be pregnant involuntarily. The science of medicine dictates that when foreign organisms inhabit the human body unwelcomely, we tend to eject them.

When a beloved nonhuman member of the family is sick and elderly, many pet owners decide not to pay for medical care and opt for euthanasia instead. It is a mark of moral seriousness to acknowledge what it is that we're doing when we butcher a cow, put a pet 'to sleep' or, for that matter, euthanise a human relative. According to the philosopher of science Donna Haraway, we must 'stay with the trouble' of the violence we inevitably mete out in our everyday traffic with forms of life, be it at the dinner table, the battlefield or in the scientific laboratory. Rather than squaring our acts of killing away according to a moral calculus, or pretending that we aren't really killing, multispecies feminists should subscribe, suggests Haraway, to the ethical imperative, 'Thou shalt not make killable.'

This might seem counterintuitive in the context of an argument in favour of abortion-as-killing, but the distinction between making foetuses killable, and making it easy and stigma-free for people to take the decision to kill a foetus, is significant. The former refers to casting something (a lab rat, for example) out of the sphere of the grievable, thanks to a tidy and final verdict on the permissibility of systematically sacrificing its life to a greater cause. The latter, while expanding access to the means of feticide, does not necessarily require any such sanitisation of violence.

For millennia, those of us who have helped a friend terminate a pregnancy – be it with herbal abortifacients, progesterone blockers and ulcer tablets or vacuum extraction devices – are well situated to understand that something is killed during a uterine evacuation, much as a flower dies when it is plucked.

But what's the point of acknowledging this now, at a time when abortion rights are so imperilled? For one thing, it would seem hard to deny that the euphemistic, apologetic, placatory 'pro-choice' strategy hasn't worked out thus far. So, why not risk coming out for what we actually want, namely, abortion – a clearly documented public good? The Supreme Court decision thrusts us into a situation in which we have little left to lose. Rather than cleave in desperation to the rear-guard missions of defending the rights (to privacy, rather than abortion) enshrined in *Roe v. Wade*, we could consider this moment a chance to reset the terms on which abortion is fought.

What would it mean to acknowledge that a death is involved in an abortion? Above all, it would allow for a fairer fight against the proponents of forced gestating. When 'pro-life' forces agitate against foeticide on the basis that it is killing, pro-abortion feminists should be able to acknowledge, without shame, that yes, of course it is. When we withdraw from gestating, we stop the life of the product of our gestational labour. And it's a good thing we do, too, for otherwise the world would sag under the weight of forced life. It is a hard pill to swallow for a misogynist society, sentimentally attached to its ideology of patriarchal motherhood, but the truth is that gestators should get to decide which bodies to give form to. This choosing is our prerogative. A desire not to be pregnant is sufficient reason in and of itself to terminate a gestatee.

When we force anti-abortionists to disagree explicitly with this, we bring their logic of female subordination into the open: those with uteruses must serve patiently as the vessels through which life passes. We lay bare the calculus at the heart of their worldview, which they only sometimes spell out in so many words, as does the Mississippi pro-life leader Barbara Beaver: 'Mothers should die for their babies, not the other way around.'

Women are human, and as such can never be as innocent as the unborn. But innocence (as we see every time a police victim is described as 'no angel' by the press) is a fundamentally inhumane category in politics, deriving from the most punitive interpretations of Christianity. According to this imaginary, non-innocence is the core characteristic of everything 'fallen', which is to say, everything that has ever lived.

That's why the ghoulish natalism of those lobbying to give embryos the rights of patients and persons in law is, in the end, an anti-life position. It cares solely for the quantitative rather than qualitative dimensions of life, chasing life in the abstract and missing everything that matters about life as it is actually lived: life in particular. Fetishising newness and sentimentalising helplessness, pro-lifers pit themselves ruthlessly against the overwhelming majority of human life-in particular. In their minds, foetuses deserve every protection, while we actually existing human beings belong to a completely different species. We are on our own, self-responsible; fatally compromised, because anti-abortionists routinely sacrifice the health and happiness of actual persons in defence of the forced survival of potential ones. It is high time we went on the offensive against their sickening, sacrificial version of vitalism. Ours is the mature pro-life politics. I don't want to live in a world that valorises life for its own sake. I want to live in a world that prioritises the life chosen and wanted. Peoples' lives are worth more than foetuses' lives.

Jane Does
Judith Arcana, Heather Booth,
Jeanne Galatzer-Levy, Laura Kaplan
(2018)

From conversations between Madeleine Schwartz and members of the Abortion Counselling Service of Women's Liberation, later known as Jane, an underground railroad for reproductive care that was started in Chicago in 1969. According to 'The Story of Jane' by Laura Kaplan, the service provided eleven thousand abortions before it was shut down in 1973.

HEATHER BOOTH: In 1965, I was a college student at the University of Chicago. My friend's sister was pregnant and not prepared to have a child. She was nearly suicidal, didn't know what to do. My friend asked if I could help.

I turned to the Medical Committee for Human Rights, which was the medical arm of the civil-rights movement and was directed to Dr T.R.M. Howard. I called him up and discussed the situation. My friend's sister was treated. It worked out well. I didn't think about it again. Then someone else called. Word must have spread. I made the next arrangement too. And then someone else called. At that point I realised, well, there really must be a problem. So I called Dr Howard and set up a system. I was living in a dormitory, so I told people to call and ask for Jane.

I asked Dr Howard for detailed descriptions of what was involved, how the procedure went – I had never had the experience myself – what I should do to advise the women in advance, what I should do as a follow-up, what signs I should look for, if there was trouble that might develop.

That went on until 1968, when I got pregnant with my first child and realised that I needed to recruit other people to take on the work. I would go to political meetings and at the end I would say, 'If anyone wants to work on this issue and provide counselling for women, come see me.' I recruited a number of women and trained them in the process I had set up for the counselling. I turned it over to them and they became 'Jane'.

LAURA KAPLAN: We are often called a collective. But we weren't really a collective. The group was organised as a series of concentric circles: the closer you were to the centre, the more you knew, the more responsibility you had.

JEANNE GALATZER-LEVY: Everybody counselled. It was the backbone of the service.

JUDITH ARCANA: When I started, I was assigned to an experienced Jane and sat with her through a couple of counselling sessions.

GALATZER-LEVY: We had an ad in various little underground newspapers that said, 'Pregnant? Worried? Call Jane.'

ARCANA: I became the person who would pick up the phone messages and call women back and ask them crucial medical questions. We kept all their information on index cards.

GALATZER-LEVY: We met every two weeks or so. We rotated through people's apartments.

KAPLAN: We always had lots of food at meetings. There was a social quality to it.

GALATZER-LEVY: You would sit on the floor or on chairs, if there were chairs. There generally weren't enough. When I was in the group, at its height, there were about thirty women. We would pass around index cards with information on them about the women seeking abortions.

ARCANA: Some of them had terrible stories. There was a fifteen-year-old, for example, who had been raped and was in her second trimester.

GALATZER-LEVY: You'd usually set up an evening appointment. You'd give everybody a cup of tea, talk for a half hour or so. We would explain exactly what the procedure was, how it worked, what the instruments were that would be used and what they could expect.

ARCANA: People would come to what we called the Front and then be taken from there to what we called the Place, where the procedure would be performed.

GALATZER-LEVY: I worked the Front a good deal. We'd give people an address, and there would be someone there to greet them. We always had snacks – pretzels, cookies, coffee, tea, soda. People could bring a sister, brother, boyfriend. Sometimes they brought their kids. And the person at the Front would talk to them. Some of the women would be nervous.

ARCANA: We were working from people's homes, usually an apartment. So if you were a friend of the service, but not a Jane, and if you were willing to let us use your place, you would take your cats or your kid and you would leave for eight or nine hours.

KAPLAN: One of the women in the group was in her forties, so to us she seemed much older – we were mostly in our twenties and early thirties. She lived in a Frank Lloyd Wright house in Oak Park. We loved that.

GALATZER-LEVY: We had our own sheets, which were very pretty. We were into Marimekko. We wanted it to be comfortable and not feel like a medical setting.

BOOTH: Dr Howard died when I was still involved. I found another person. He was doing the procedures in a northwestern suburb.

ARCANA: When I met him at the end of 1970 or 1971, he had already, under pressure from the Janes, sacrificed his original m.o., which was to blindfold women throughout the procedure. He didn't wish to be recognised.

With abortionists, these guys either had to pay off the mob or hide from the mob. Our guy was in that latter category.

GALATZER-LEVY: He and one of the women became quite close, and she discovered that he wasn't a doctor. In fact, somebody had just trained him to do the procedure.

ARCANA: I had heard that he learned when he was in the medical corps in the Korean War. That was the going tale.

GALATZER-LEVY: She thought, 'Well, if he can do it, I can do it.' And she talked him into training her. And then she trained a different woman. And then they stopped using him.

KAPLAN: There was a point – nobody remembers exactly what happened – when someone decided to let the group at large know that he wasn't a doctor. Of course, once she did, people flipped out. Women were crying and saying, 'We're just like the back alleys. We have to fold!'

Calmer heads prevailed and people said, 'We've been using this guy for a year and a half. We only get the most fabulous feedback from ob-gyns who see the women for post-abortion exams. So clearly you don't have to be a doctor to do this.' At that meeting one woman said, 'If he can do it and he's not a doctor, then we can do it, too.'

GALATZER-LEVY: You were gradually trained. There was an assistant and an abortionist. The assistant would sit next to the woman and hold her hand if she wanted us to, which she often did. We talked to them. We would be at their head while the person who actually did the abortion finished it up. Sometimes people would squeeze your hand so hard – you'd be amazed. You were there to talk to them and get them through it. It's not a particularly pleasant procedure, but it's not particularly long either. And it was – I know this sounds weird – but it was quite festive.

KAPLAN: I don't think you can underplay the sense of personal power that the members of Jane felt. We were doing something so radical, breaking so many taboos and changing women's lives as a result.

GALATZER-LEVY: Most political work is very, very slow. You have to keep telling yourself that things will get better. It's one step forward and half a step back. This was not like that. We could just do it. There was a problem and we could solve it.

ARCANA: Of course, we recommended to all the women that if they got a fever, if they had any unusual bleeding, if anything happened, if they had a doctor they trusted, go deal with that doc. If not, we had a back-up. There were a few guys who knew they might get a call from a Jane.

KAPLAN: We were all annoyed at the medical profession for not being more willing to help. We'd ask women how they heard about us. And if we got a particular doctor's name from a few of them, one of us would call that doctor up and say, 'Hi, this is Jane, you've been referring women to us and we wanted to talk to you about how you can help us.' Nine times out of ten they would say, 'Don't ever call me again.'

BOOTH: Once there was a police raid at one of the homes. Seven women were arrested, but no one would testify against them.

GALATZER-LEVY: I was working that day. One of the women in the service had come by the Front to check on something. It was one of those apartments with a long hallway. Everybody was in the back and there were a lot of kids that day, which made it fairly chaotic. The woman who had visited the apartment had just left when I heard a knock at the door. I thought she was coming back, that she had forgotten her scarf or whatever. So I walked back to the door. There were two homicide detectives. They were enormous – these two really tall men. I'm five feet two inches.

I looked at them. I turned around. I walked in front of them into the living room and said to everyone, 'These are the police, you do not have to say anything.' The police were angry about that and I was arrested. We were smart enough to know that you don't have to talk to the police and that policemen are not your friends.

We were arrested in May 1972. The Supreme Court decision came down in January 1973. Everybody knew that the Supreme Court was debating the case. It was then a question of waiting to hear the verdict.

After the *Roe* decision, the courts cut a deal with us that if we didn't ask for our instruments back – they had grabbed all the stuff – they would not charge us for practising medicine without a licence. We said OK – we didn't need the instruments anymore – and that was it.

KAPLAN: The first clinics opened in early spring. A few months later, we had a party. Everybody who had been involved was invited. The guy who wasn't a doctor – he was there. All of us were there. By then we were fed up with one another. I think we were mostly burned out and happy to step back from the project. So we had our end-of-Jane party. And we all went our separate ways.

The Logic of Abortion
Bernard Williams
(1977)

One thing to be said about this debate right away is that it is, at no point, distinctively a debate about religion. It is, indeed, a fact that, among those who oppose the deliberate termination of pregnancy, many are Christians, and, in particular, Roman Catholics; but the views that they bring to bear on the issue are not uniquely Roman Catholic views. You do not have to have religious beliefs to be against murder, and it is not peculiar to Catholics to classify abortion as murder. Since the issues are not essentially connected with religious beliefs, I shall not make any special reference to religion from now on.

The shortest moral argument against abortion is the one I just mentioned – that abortion is, simply, murder. This very traditional line of argument will say: murder is the deliberate killing of an innocent human being; that is exactly what abortion is; it is therefore wrong. Let us call this the 'murder argument'. It is a very simple argument. To those who offer it, that seems part of its virtue – it is a mark of its truth, which sophisticated qualifications are only designed to evade. To other eyes, its extreme simplicity seems to be bought just by assuming the answers to all the important questions before one begins to look at them.

Among those who want to crack the smooth surface of

the murder argument, there are, of course, many different approaches. They can be usefully divided, I think, into two camps. The first camp shares a certain belief with the murder argument itself: that the central question here is a *definitional* question, in the sense that the important point lies in defining what class of beings the rule against deliberate killing applies to, and whether the foetus belongs to that class. This approach agrees with the murder argument in method, by treating the issue rather like a legal question about the application of a law, though it disagrees, of course, about what the verdict should be. The second camp of those who reject the murder argument want to get away from that type of debate altogether.

The main definitional issue has been whether the foetus is, within the terms of the moral law against murder, a human being or not. In one way, the answer to this question seems to be 'yes', and, indeed, obviously 'yes'. The foetus is, after all, a living thing, and it does not belong to any other species. But then we are faced with the familiar fact that the foetus is, up to a certain point, not a formed human being, and, even after that point, it is not a fully formed human being. If one pursues that kind of consideration, one can naturally arrive at the conclusion that it is when the foetus is viable that it is properly or fully a human being; and drawing the line at this point will, of course, yield a more permissive abortion policy than the murder argument originally anticipated.

If the murder argument is going to insist absolutely on the humanity of the foetus before viability – its humanity, that is to say, in the sense relevant to how it is to be treated – then certainly it will yield a quite strikingly conservative abortion policy. If you consider a separate, already born, human being – consider, for instance, one who is are, already grown – it would be generally agreed that one can-

not just kill him because he is likely to contract some dis-
abling disease, or, again, because his mother runs a risk of
death or injury if he is not killed; and since the point of the
murder argument is to insist on the equal humanity of all
human beings, it could not permit even very early termination, even in cases where deformity or disablement of
the infant is indicated, or, again, serious harm to the
mother.

The murder argument, then, in its use of the concept,
'human being', seems to yield either a very permissive
abortion policy or an absolutely rigidly negative one: a
permissive policy if 'human being' implies viability, and a
negative one if it does not. In this second, rigidly negative
version, the argument is using one undoubted biological
fact – that the foetus is a developing member of the species
– to do all the work, while many will feel that their problem starts from that fact and cannot simply be solved by
referring to it.

A different definitional question arises if one applies the
prohibition on murder not to human beings as such, but
to *persons*. Even if the foetus is a human being, it seems easy
to deny that it is a person, where this implies faculties of
communication, relations to others, consciousness of a
fairly complex kind, and so on. Some philosophers argue
that it is not human beings as such, merely biologically
determined, that we should be particularly concerned
with, but rather with persons; and the foetus is not yet a
person.

The trouble about this – or, rather, what I find the trouble
about this, since the philosophers in question seem to be
pretty unconcerned about these consequences – is that, if
the foetus is not yet a person, then neither is the newborn
baby; nor again, if the requirements of personhood are
made sophisticated enough, will small children be per-

331

sons. What is more, the senile, and other adults in a defective condition, will be, on this sort of showing, ex-persons
or sub-persons. Of course, those who think in this way
will urge other rules with respect to non-persons, and will
doubtless urge us not to cause unnecessary suffering to
any sentient thing. But if failure to qualify in the person
stakes is enough, as this argument would have it, to eliminate restrictions on killing the foetus, it is presumably
enough to remove restrictions on killing those other
non-persons as well, and the results of taking this line will
be wide-ranging indeed.

There is a deep fault with the notion of a person, as used
in these connections. It sounds like an all-or-nothing
matter, whether a given creature is a person or not, but, in
fact, the term turns out just to mean that the creature dis-
plays, to some extent – it seems, an arbitrary extent – some
psychological and social characteristics which lie on a
sliding scale. Unlike the matter of degree presented by the
physical development of the foetus, questions raised by
the variable scale of psychological characteristics arise all
over the place.

The 'person' approach to abortion presents, perhaps
more than any other, the danger of the slippery slope, by
which one's decisions about abortion leave one with no
way of resisting other policies about killing and death
about which one would have the gravest qualms. Some
tough philosophers would say that this merely shows that
we should not have qualms about those policies, such as
infanticide, suppression of the senile, and so on. I find it
quite unclear, however, what is supposed to give their
arguments more authority with us than is possessed by
our sense of humanity, as it is significantly called.

I have already touched, implicitly, on the notion of a
right, and the language of 'rights' is indeed involved quite

deeply in this debate. It is invoked, of course, by both sides. Thus, on the one hand, there is talk of the rights of the unborn child; on the other, one hears, sometimes, of the right of the woman to do what she likes with her own body. These particular ways of talking about rights very obviously presuppose, each in its own way, answers to the definitional questions I have just been discussing. If you can dispose of the issue by saying that it is just an issue of the woman's right to do what she likes with her own body, then you are implying that the foetus is to be regarded just as part of the woman's body, which is to answer the definitional question one way. If you treat the matter in terms of the rights of the unborn child, then you are answering the definitional question the other way, seeing the foetus as a human being, like any other, with rights. So these particular ways of bringing in rights are very closely tied to the definitional issues.

Another line of argument, however, makes an effort to get away from the definitional issue, and belongs rather to what I called, earlier, the second camp of those who resist the murder argument: the camp of those who try to get away from the question of defining the foetus, whether as a human being or a person. They may say: 'Let us agree, if you like, that the foetus is a human being, and killing the foetus is a case of killing a human being, The question is, in what circumstances one is justified in doing that.'

One way of trying to answer that question has, again, invoked the idea of a right. It asks whether we can think of circumstances analogous enough to the situation in which abortion is at issue, to help us decide whether we could have the right to kill a human being in such a situation. A bold argument on these lines has been advanced by the American philosopher, Judith Jarvis Thomson. She suggests that, if one woke up one day and found oneself strapped to another adult human being, with his life-systems dependent on one's own, so that the only way to get rid of him was to kill him, then one could have the right to kill him – even if one was partly responsible for his being there. I have presented the example very baldly, without Ms Thomson's striking and chilling elaboration, which makes it more plausible than perhaps I have done, that one would have the right to kill this incubus.

But even if one were persuaded that one had the right to kill the incubus, it is hard to see how that conclusion could merely carry over to the abortion case. One difference between the cases is that pregnancy is normal and not freakish. Another is that, in itself, it only lasts nine months. Another is that, because it is normal, and normally issues in a baby, it has sentiments and reactions attached to it which could not be attached to the freakish case of the incubus. These differences do not all cut the same way with regard to the abortion issue, but, in my view, they do discourage the idea that we are going to get much insight into the rights and wrongs of abortion by considering what we might say about rights in such imaginary situations – situations which may have some structural resemblance to the pregnancy situation, but are, at the same time, freakishly unlike it.

This brings out a question which has been gradually pressing itself on us all the time: whether pregnancy, the situation in which abortion is in question, is enough like anything else at all for us to reach answers about it by analogy from other situations. While the definitional approach was faced with the problem that the foetus is neither just like nor just unlike an independently existing human being, argument by moral analogy faces the problem that pregnancy is, at once, highly familiar and also very unlike any other situation.

334

There is one school of thought which, at any rate, is better placed to acknowledge that fact than the others I have mentioned. This is the utilitarian approach, which considers the issue entirely in terms of consequences, the consequences being measured in terms of happiness and unhappiness. This approach does not need to get involved in the definitional issues; nor does it find it helpful to think in terms of rights.

That it does not have to worry about the issues of definition comes out clearly when one reflects that, if we can think about social questions in terms of consequences at all adequately, we must, in general, be able to think in terms of the consequences of various policies for merely possible people, people who may not exist at all. In thinking about birth control and population policies, for instance, we have to think about how things would be for people who, if those policies are adopted, will never be conceived. All the more, then, we should be able to think about the possible welfare of someone who, if a pregnancy is terminated, will never be born, and it does not matter for this consequentialist argument how the foetus itself is classified.

Those who feel strongly that the foetus is an actual human being, with actual rights, will, of course, reject the utilitarian approach, which attaches little weight to whether this is an actual human being, and, in general, is not very concerned with rights. Utilitarians tend to regard the language of rights as an obscure and unhelpful way of discussing matters better considered in the light of the all-round consequences.

If we reject the view that the foetus is unqualifiedly a human being who has rights like any other – and I suggested, earlier, that the consequences of accepting that could be very conservative indeed – we will, to that extent, agree with the utilitarians about the abortion issue (though we may well not agree with them more generally in their unconcern for rights). But even those who agree thus far with the utilitarians may well have other worries about the utilitarian approach. Does utilitarianism pursue its study of consequences far enough?

Obviously, in a matter such as abortion, we must be concerned not just with the consequences of each particular case, for the particular mother and the particular child, if it is born. The more general consequences of having certain sorts of laws and practices also come into it. Here, it is a valid question to ask what sort of society the practice of abortion on a wide and liberal basis would fit into; what general outlooks would naturally go with it; what attitudes to birth and to killing you would have to teach young people if they were to live easily in such a society. Moreover, in asking that sort of question, we need to look to a wider range of values than utilitarianism admits – values which go beyond happiness, or, at any rate, involve a deeper conception of happiness than utilitarianism usually admits.

The situation we actually have now, it seems to me, is that this wide range of questions is most characteristically raised by opponents of freer abortion, who answer it by predicting a society indifferent to human life and to human values if abortion is widely sanctioned. Those on the other side often seem indifferent to the issues of how a certain practice demands an appropriate outlook and set of values to go with it, and what that outlook might, in the case of abortion, be. They urge the particular miseries of the particular cases, which is forceful enough, but this, often conjoined with an emphasis on individual freedom, does not meet the anxieties of the other side. Thus, each of these opponents feels that the other side is indifferent to what should most be cared about.

This leads to something characteristic of this controversy: that each side honestly regards the other as heartless. Clearly, the larger question must be raised. What sort of society would it be that had got thoroughly used to the institution of relatively liberal abortion? What kind of life goes with that? Would it threaten other values, such as the rights of the senile not to be tidied away? The question must be raised, but I do not see why the answer to it has to be hostile to a liberal abortion policy. I pointed earlier, to the fact that the pregnancy situation, the situation which raises the question of abortion, just is markedly different from others, in particular from others that involve life and death. This is not a problem which has to invite the slippery slope even – though it easily can do so if this is wrongly treated. A social context in which liberal abortion laws are both in effect and easily accepted may not have to be one in which there is general indifference to human life.

Whether it is actually possible, in the long run, to have a society which combines full acceptance of liberal abortion institutions with humane attitudes to such things as birth, death and killing depends, in part, on whether it is genuinely possible for most people, without either self-deception or brutality, to feel that the killing of a foetus is something basically different from the killing of a separate human being: to feel that, not just to think it. Whether that is possible for most people I do not claim to know. But there is one significant piece of evidence on the subject which does not seem to be often mentioned: that there is a difference between the death of a foetus in early pregnancy, and the death of a separate human being.

This is a difference, above all, in the experience of women. A genuine psychological distinction, for most women, exists with regard to spontaneous abortion: for

337

most women, to miscarry at two or three months is not at all the same experience as a stillbirth, or an infant dying in its first weeks. I speak of the emotional or psychological difference, not just of the obvious physical difference, though that itself no doubt contributes. If there is that difference with regard to spontaneous abortion, it is no good, on the question of induced abortion, advancing theories or fears which involve the consequence that the difference should not exist, that miscarriage and stillbirth should seem the same. Yet many moral theories about abortion do seem to have that consequence.

This is a point about the experience of women. In the end, this issue can only come back to the experience of women. This is not because the experiences are the only thing that count. It is because their experiences are the only realistic and honest guide we have to what the unique phenomenon of abortion genuinely is, as opposed to what moralists, philosophers and legislators say it is. It follows that their experience is the only realistic guide to what the deepest consequences will be of our social attitudes to abortion.

From
'The Heart of Maternal Darkness'
Adrienne Rich
(1976)

We know the judgments from within the psychiatric establishment against women who do not wish to become mothers. We have to connect these voices with others reaching far back in history. Soranus of Ephesus, the Greek gynaecologist, would have had abortion permitted for only three reasons: 1) 'to maintain feminine beauty'; 2) to avoid danger to the mother's life if her uterus should be 'too small' for the foetus; 3) to control population as urged by Plato in the *Republic* and Aristotle in the *Politics*. St Augustine regarded abortion as 'the work of minds characterised by lustful cruelty or cruel lust'. Christian theologians through the ages have engaged in hair-splitting debates. If a pregnant woman is attacked by a bull, may she run for her life even though running may cause her to abort? Yes, said the 16th-century Jesuit Tomás Sánchez. If a woman conceives out of wedlock, and her male relatives would kill her if they found out, may she destroy the foetus to save her life? Yes, again, said Sánchez. Within the Catholic Church opinion has swayed back and forth as to when a foetus is a controversy which began with Tertullian, a self-confessed loather of female sexuality and also the first to say in effect that 'abortion is murder.' The early Christian theologians, still cleaving to Aristotle, believed that abortion was only murder if the foetus (if male) was within forty days of conception and (if female) within eighty to ninety – the time when 'ensoulment' was presumed to occur for each sex. (We can only guess at how the gender of the foetus was supposed to be determined.) By 1588, Pope Sixtus V, a fanatic Counter-Reformation cleanser of the Church, declared all abortion murder, with excommunication as its punishment. His successor, finding the sanctions unworkable, revoked them in 1591, except for abortions performed later than forty days from conception. By 1869, Pius IX decided the time was ripe to swing back to the decision of Sixtus V: All abortion was again declared murder. This is at present the official, majority Catholic position. In spite of it, Catholic women comprise over 20 per cent of all abortion patients.

The arguments against and for abortion range from attempts to determine biologically or legally when the foetus becomes a 'person' to exercises in the most abstract logic and ethics. I shall not attempt here to enumerate the range of arguments; Mary Daly has already provided an overview from a feminist perspective. She notes that

> abortion is hardly the 'final triumph' envisaged by all or the final stage of the revolution. There are deep questions beneath and beyond this, such as: Why should women be in situations of unwanted pregnancy at all? Some women see abortion as a necessary measure for themselves but no one sees it as the fulfilment of her highest dreams. Many would see abortion as a humiliating procedure. Even the abortifacient pills, when perfected can be seen as a protective measure, a means to an end, but hardly as the total embodiment of liberation.

Few if any feminists are deceived in this matter, although male proponents of the repeal of abortion laws tend often to be short-sighted in this respect, confusing the feminist revolution with the sexual revolution.

The demand for legalised abortion, like the demand for contraception, has been represented as a form of irresponsibility, a refusal by women to confront their moral destiny, a trivialisation or evasion of great issues of life and death. The human facts, however, are hardly frivolous. Here are some of the methods resorted to by women who have been denied legal, safe, low-cost abortion: self-abortion by wire coat-hangers, knitting needles, goose quills dipped in turpentine, celery stalks, drenching the cervix with detergent, lye, soap, Ultra-Jel (a commercial preparation of castor oil, soap, and iodine), drinking purgatives or mercury, applying hot coals to the body. The underworld 'cut-rate' abortionists, often alcoholic, disenfranchised members of the medical profession, besides operating in septic surroundings and performing unnecessary curettages on poor women who cannot afford a pregnancy test, frequently molest their patients; well-to-do women have been raped or sexually molested, forced to travel thousands of miles to receive a medically safe abortion.

Clearly, the first violence done in abortion is on the body and mind of the pregnant woman herself. Most people, women and men alike, find it difficult to perform even a minor operation upon themselves, from giving themselves an injection to lancing an infected finger or removing a splinter. It is nothing less than grim, driven desperation which can impel a woman to insert an unbent coat-hanger into her most sensitive parts, to place her body in the hands of a strange man with unverified credentials or to lie down without anaesthesia on a filthy kitchen table, knowing that in so doing she risks illness, grilling by the police, and death. Some women are able to speak later of such experiences in a measured, almost indifferent way; no one should be deceived by this attempt to distance or minimise the trauma. An illegal or self-induced abortion is no casual experience. It is painful, dangerous and cloaked in the guilt of criminality.

Even when performed in a hospital, under the law, abortion is often packaged with sterilisation as a kind of punishment for the crime of wishing not to be pregnant, just as women who request simple tubal ligation as sterilisation are frequently given only the option of hysterectomy. The sadism of the underworld abortionist and that of the hospital to which a haemorrhaging woman turns herself in a fter an incomplete self-inflicted abortion are not so different after all.

To become pregnant with an unwanted child is itself no light experience. There have been efforts to show that abortion, legal or not, is harder psychically on women who have borne children than on a woman who has borne none. A recent Swedish study of nearly five hundred women concluded, however, that no such generalisation was possible. Each woman reacts to pregnancy, wanted or not, and to abortion, even the easiest and most legal, in her own way. Guilt about abortion can serve as the channel for other, older feelings of guilt, of needing to atone; it can also be the result of lifelong exposure to the idea that abortion is murder. If a woman feels her guilt or depression as a kind of punishment, she may try to disavow such feelings. It is crucial, however, in abortion as in every other experience (especially in the realm of sexuality and reproduction) that women take seriously the enterprise of finding out what we do feel, instead of accepting what we have been told we must feel. One woman's depression may actually be anger at the man who got her pregnant; angry at her treatment by the abortionist or the hospital; another may wish to have a child, know her situation renders it impossible, and genuinely mourn the loss.

No free woman, with 100 per cent effective, non-harmful birth control readily available, would 'choose' abortion. At present, it is certainly likely that a woman can – through many causes – become so demoralised as to use abortion as a form of violence against herself – a penance, an expiation. But this needs to be viewed against the ecology of guilt and victimisation in which so many women grow up. In a society where women always entered heterosexual intercourse willingly, where adequate contraception was a genuine social priority, there would be no 'abortion issue'. And in such a society there would be a vast diminishment of female self-hatred – a psychic source of many unwanted pregnancies.

Abortion is violence: a deep, desperate violence inflicted by a woman upon, first of all, herself. It is the offspring, and will continue to be the accuser of, a more pervasive and prevalent violence, the violence of rapism.

The Long, Disgraceful History
Natasha Lennard
(2020)

Rightful public fury has followed allegations this week that hysterectomies were performed on numerous women imprisoned at US Immigration and Customs Enforcement's Irwin County Detention Centre. According to a whistle-blower, a nurse at the facility, the women 'reacted confused' when they learned what had been done to their bodies.

The allegations produced a flood of commentary. Some drew comparisons to Nazi Germany's eugenic sterilisation programs. These commentators, however, did not need to reach so far across the globe: Some of the most extreme allegations echo a long and disgraceful history right here in America.

The accounts of ongoing brutalities at ICE concentration camps may be a direct consequence of fascistic Trumpian excess, but, if the whistle-blower claims are proven true, they would be extensions of – not aberrations from – a wholly American practice of sterilising populations deemed 'undesirable'. President Donald Trump's administration did not bring white supremacist eugenic practices to US soil: They have always been inherent to a country fixated on its 'borders' and locking certain people away. It does an injustice to centuries of victims of sterilisation to pretend otherwise.

Like almost every report on detainee treatment at ICE concentration camps, the whistle-blower complaint filed this week makes accusations of routine dehumanisation. Dawn Wooten, a licensed practical nurse at a Georgia-based detention centre, filed a whistle-blower complaint to the Department of Homeland Security's Office of Inspector General that a doctor contracted to treat detained women had performed a seemingly high rate of hysterectomies. Wooten and one of the groups representing her, Project South, raised issues about the women giving what the complaint called a lack of 'proper informed consent' before procedures. The Intercept was able to gather independent allegations from detainees and lawyers that were consistent with Project South's complaints. In the complaint to the Office of Inspector General, the whistle-blower called the doctor 'the uterus collector'– a moniker seemingly ripped from the annals of notorious eugenicists.

And such annals are part of a very American legacy. The man dubbed the 'father of modern gynaecology', J. Marion Sims, conducted experiments on enslaved Black women without anaesthesia, but was nonetheless lionised in the 19th century with statues around the country. Only now are some of them being taken down – the mere beginning of a long overdue reckoning.

Eugenics programs directed at decimating the lives of Black, Indigenous, and other people of colour, particularly poor and immigrant communities, as well as people with disabilities, were an explicit part of US policy in the 20th century. Thirty-two states maintained federally funded eugenics boards, tasked with ordering sterilisations of women – and sometimes men – deemed 'undesirable.' Tens of thousands of forced sterilisations were carried out nationwide last century. California's so-called Asexualis-

346

ation Acts, which led to 20,000 men and women losing reproductive capacity, were a direct inspiration to Nazi eugenicists. 'There is today one state,' Adolf Hitler wrote, 'in which at least weak beginnings towards a better conception [of citizenship] are noticeable. Of course, it is not our model German Republic, but the United States.'

A 1965 survey found that one-third of Puerto Rican women between 20 and 49 years old had been sterilised, a result of US population control programs enforced on the territory. So common were coerced sterilisations in the American South that they became referred to as 'Mississippi appendectomies'. The extent to which these practices fit within a genocidal, white supremacist ideology cannot be underestimated. Between 1930 to 1970, 65 per cent of the 7600-plus sterilisations ordered by the state of North Carolina were carried out on Black women.

And as Angelin Chaplin noted recently in the Cut, 'During the same time that *Roe v.Wade* granted mostly white women more bodily autonomy in the 1970s, approximately 25,000 Native American women were forcibly sterilised by the US government – between 25 and 50 per cent of the female population.'

By the end of 1970s, thanks in part to the organising efforts of women of Mexican origin in California, programs of state-ordered sterilisations had ended and guidelines were put in place to better ensure informed consent around sterilisation procedures (although numerous laws enabling state-forced sterilisation remain on the books).

But the absence of explicit eugenics policies did not end eugenicist practices. The denial of reproductive choice to poor people of colour, though sterilisation, forced birth, and mass incarceration – alongside every form of necropolitical governance that leaves communities to suffer and die – is an assertion of which lives get to matter in the US

As recently as 2013, an investigation found that at least 148 female inmates in two California prisons were sterilised between 2006 to 2010; many of the women said they were coerced into the procedure.

The whistle-blower and detainee's allegations from current US concentration camps sit squarely in this American legacy. 'The fact that Black and brown immigrant women are held in an extremely vulnerable position at this prison where they have no control over their bodies and no say what is done to them is sickening,' said Azadeh Shahshahani, legal and advocacy director of Project South. 'Irwin should be shut down immediately and people should be freed. The United States government, as well as the private prison corporation running this prison, should be held accountable.'

She is right. But holding the United States accountable in any robust sense requires a reckoning with the ways it has been defined by the control of Black and brown bodies: domestically, at its borders, and internationally. There need be no explicit policy of forced sterilisation for a eugenicist system to exist. Normalised neglect and dehumanisation are sufficient. These are Trumpian specialties, yes, but as American as apple pie.

Songs of Praise II
Amelia Loulli
(2023)

release as holding cell
coffee mornings with other mums from school

as holding cell

imagine a secret   *we all have secrets* says Laraine who talks

openly about her divorce   body like an early text
discarded   Gina is a Christian who believes in love

but someone has to speak up for the babies   imagine the taste
of 25 hand-iced fairy cakes   my vagina as fairy cake

Tinkerbell my mother called it   hundreds and thousands
                                        what if
I said it
there is an abortion counter online   tick tick tick
                                        what if

I said I watch it   I'm not asking you to answer   Jesus
don't you know anything about the rhetorical   what if you
                                couldn't
what if you had to   what if you wanted to   think liberation

think feminism   I am bleeding into my office chair
soaking occurs post trauma

can you really say you're intimate with someone if you don't know
what they look like in the company of death

                              back to the fairy cakes
        you wish this was sexier   if you want a ghost

to leave you alone   become as insignificant as a grey stone
jump   hit your heels against your tail bone   a controlled fall
into a hot bath   the frog was covered with a white cheesecloth

then put inside my mouth   *hold it there*   *until it dies*   they said
              how will I know

you will feel its heart thumping between your lips   when it stops   you
will know   you have been cured

I left the clinic
a brick of padding between my legs

                    I left my body
to the grey stone steps

        became a way in
and a way out

Abortions Are for Everyone
Annabel Sowemimo
(2020)

A conversation about the way we think about abortion access and the inclusivity of our services is long overdue. For far too long, the abortion movement has championed access for all those that require abortion care with little acknowledgement of the wider structures that govern our reproductive health. The idea that abortion is always a straightforward choice is far too simplistic and minimises the experiences of many of those seeking abortion care.

Black women are more likely to report a consecutive abortion than their white and Asian counterparts. While the difference is small, there are many reasons for this that typical pro-choice narratives simply fail to address. Those racialised as non-white are likely to be paid 10 per cent less than their white counterparts even when educational attainment is adjusted for. Black women are at heightened risk of experiencing intimate partner violence and less likely to receive adequate support when they do report it.

Black motherhood is plagued with stereotypes, including that of the teenage mother, who is usually incompetent or dependent on government welfare. A recent report into maternal deaths in the UK revealed that black women are five times more likely than their white counterparts to die in childbirth and black babies are more likely to be stillborn. These statistics are not clearly explained by increased comorbidities (the presence of more than one disorder in the same person) or socio-economic conditions. For many black women, becoming pregnant goes beyond traditional anxieties such as 'How will I cope?' Instead, some consider the rather question, 'Could I die?'

The circumstances for gender non-conforming black people are likely to be even more bleak. Very few medical studies address their experiences of accessing healthcare. In one small study, the majority of respondents were not using contraception, incorrectly believing that gender affirming hormones would protect them from unplanned pregnancy. Data from the US show that reproductive health is poorer among black trans and non-binary people, with significant rates of sexually transmitted infections and HIV, but there is very little information on their experiences of accessing healthcare within a UK context. Department of Health reporting forms do not collect gender information, yet the same form still includes a section on marital status. Our institutions still treat this population as if they do not exist. How can you advocate for service improvement for populations that are not recorded as existing in the first place?

Arguments against trans-inclusive facilities often position trans people as a threat to women's safety, even though the evidence shows that cis-gender people continue to be much more of a threat to theirs. For those trans men and non-binary people who do continue with their pregnancy, there is little medical information available. All pregnant people are at increased risk of intimate partner violence. As medical providers, we should not forget the additional mental burden that continuing with a pregnancy may place on those who live in a world already hostile to their survival.

Many American healthcare providers are familiar with

terms such as 'reproductive justice', coined by women of colour to highlight the way that structural oppression affects reproductive health. Its application in the UK continues to lag behind. During the Black Lives Matter protests, images of black pregnant women holding signs expressing concern for the safety of their unborn child were shared widely. Issues of safety and healthcare, access and recognition, overlap and intersect; we can no longer address them in isolation.

Mara Clarke, founder of the Abortion Support Network, says, 'We know that many of our clients have been migrants, refugees, asylum seekers, members of the Irish traveller community. We don't ask our clients who they are or how they got pregnant. We don't ask if they are women or what their gender identity is. We don't care, and we know that women and pregnant people with money can access services without having to explain or justify themselves. As an abortion fund, we want any person who needs an abortion to have that same experience.'

While many in the sector are starting to understand the importance of acknowledging the diverse experiences of abortion, it is integral to providing good quality care that we go a step further and demand better research, data collection and information on the experiences of those most marginalised by society.

It is time that we build our movements with diverse experiences in mind, that our abortion services reflect the stories of the communities that we serve.

From *Why Women Have Better Sex Under Socialism*
Kristen Ghodsee
(2018)

One of my childhood friends, whom I will call Jake, hungered for financial success in a society where financial success reflected a kind of moral superiority. Jake valorised the idea of the American Dream. He saw goodness in the kind of Horatio Alger, pull-yourself-up-by-the-bootstraps hard work required to 'make something' of yourself. Back then, I was already a feminist with concerns about economic inequality, while Jake, true to the spirit of the 1980s, believed that whoever dies with the most toys wins. We spent hours debating the pros and cons of capitalism, and the ways that Thatcherism and Reaganomics sucked or didn't suck. Jake embraced the Gordon Gekko zeitgeist of the age: 'Greed is good.' I wasn't buying it. But back in those days when domestic politics weren't so polarised, we managed to maintain our friendship throughout our college years. In the 1990s, while I was off teaching English and reading Karl Polanyi in Japan, Jake was hustling his way up the corporate ladder at a tech start-up.

One day in 1997, Jake informed me with great pleasure that he'd hired a promising young woman for a strategic position in his firm. She'd been a finalist with two other men, and with my voice ringing in his ears, he decided to take a chance on her. 'They were all equally qualified on paper,' he told me, 'But after years of listening to your feminist rants, I convinced my boss that since women face so many barriers in tech, she had actually worked harder to get where she was than the men in the pool.' I was struggling through my first year of graduate school at the time, and Jake's news warmed my heart; I'd made a little difference in the world.

Over the next few years, the woman proved herself clever, competent and hard-working. Jake's company gave her a three-month paid sabbatical for some additional training, grooming her for a promotion. Then she announced she was pregnant. The start-up had no formal maternity leave policy, but Jake asked his boss to give her twelve paid weeks to stay home with her baby and make child care arrangements. Jake argued that they had already invested so much money in her training that a twelve-week leave would pay for itself in the long run. His boss reluctantly agreed. The woman returned to work after the birth of her baby and tried her best to keep up with the demands of a small start-up. But she was nursing. And the baby kept her up at night. She would attend meetings bleary-eyed and unprepared. She called in sick when the nanny didn't show. She found a place in a good nursery, but if her son got sick, they sent him home. Her husband travelled for business, and she had no family in the area. Jake, always the optimist, believed things would improve once the child was older. He even offered to babysit in a pinch. His star employee managed to hold on for six months. Then she quit.

That night Jake called me to share the news. Dejected and frustrated, he told me: 'I'm never hiring a woman again.'

'But she's just one woman,' I said. 'Not every woman is going to make her choice.'

'There's no way my boss will let me,' he said. His voice was low. 'And it's the baby thing. I can't be sure of anything about any employee, but I can be certain that a man won't have a baby.'

I think I hung up on him. But it really wasn't Jake's fault. What could he do in a system that provides no support for women when they become mothers, that forces women to choose between their careers and their families? Economists call this 'statistical discrimination.' The basic idea is that since employers can't directly observe the productivity of individual workers, they can make observations about demographic characteristics that are correlated with worker productivity. They make decisions based on the averages: if women are more likely to quit than men for personal reasons, employers assume that any given woman is more likely to quit than a man. Economists observe that the theory of statistical discrimination can create a vicious cycle. If women are (or used to be) more likely to quit, they will be paid less. If they are paid less, they are more likely to quit. This vicious cycle provides a very good justification for government intervention.

The perception of women's comparative inferiority as workers is linked to their biological capacity for child-bearing and nursing, and the concomitant social expectation that women will be the primary caregivers for babies and young children. And in some patriarchal fantasy world, our supposedly innate caring nature also makes us perfectly suited for nursing other sick, weak or aged relatives. And since women are at home anyway, so the argument goes, we might as well do all of the shopping, cooking, cleaning, and emotional labour required to maintain a household, right? Someone has to do it, and that someone is almost always a woman, in part because the location of the tasks aligns, but also because she has been socialised from infancy to believe that it's her natural role. Baby dolls, EZ Bake ovens, and toy vacuum cleaners allow girls to play-practice the labours they will perform when they grow up.

Employers discriminate against those whose bodies can produce children because society attributes certain characteristics to the owners of those bodies. When scholars talk about men and women, they often make a distinction between the terms 'sex' and 'gender'. The word 'sex' means the biological difference between males and females and the word 'gender' connotes the social roles that cultures expect to match the biology. For example, by sex I am a woman because I have the physiological equipment necessary for baby manufacturing, but my gender is also female because in many ways I conform to contemporary American society's imagination of what a woman should be: I have long hair; I wear skirts, jewellery, and makeup; I enjoy romantic comedies and nice bath products; and although I might claim it's for my general health, I do a daily hour on the elliptical trainer because I worry about my weight (okay, well, maybe it's only 45 minutes, and it's not every day, but you get the idea). In other ways, however, my gender identity is more masculine: I have always worked full-time and earned my own money; I enjoy watching soccer, science fiction, and action movies; I love a good beer; and although I try to be polite about it, I always speak my mind even if my thoughts and opinions may offend. I suffer no fools, while according to some, real women tolerate gropers, mansplainers, and plain old idiots with a smile.

Gender discrimination arises because society constructs archetypes of the ideal man and the ideal woman based on their supposedly natural biological differences. This is not to say that men and women are the same – they are not –

but only that our beliefs about how men and women behave are a figment of our collective imaginations – a powerful figment, yes, but a figment nonetheless. When a student ranks a professor with a female name lower than a professor with a male name, the student may assume that the male professor has more time and energy to dedicate to his teaching because he is not distracted by his care obligations outside of work. When employers like my friend Jake's boss see a woman's name on a job applicat- ion, they immediately think that 'woman' equals potential mother with priorities in life that take precedence over their careers. Employers also assume that men will put their careers over their families because they are supposed- ly less biologically attached to children. It doesn't matter if individual men decide to stay home with their children or if individual women sterilise themselves to overcome the challenges of work/family balance; our gender stereotypes of how men and women behave are rooted in our ideas about the 'natural' link between biological sex and how this informs our life choices.

I used to do a classroom exercise with my students to get them to think about the relationship between sex and gender. I borrowed a scenario from Ursula K. Le Guin's *The Left Hand of Darkness*, where a man from earth is sent to work on a planet of 'bisexual hermaphrodites'. This means that all people have both male and female sexual organs and hormones. Throughout the month, there are seven-day periods when a portion of the population experiences a form of heat: an irresistible desire to copulate. At the init- iation of sexual contact, one of the members of the pair becomes the male, and the other person becomes the female. In any given sexual encounter, an individual will randomly become either the male or the female. The mem- ber of the pair who becomes female can become pregnant and will then have a nine-month gestation period before giving birth. When an individual is not copulating or pregnant, they revert to a neutral state until their next sexual encounter, when the process repeats. Any one individual can therefore be both a father and a mother, and everyone is equally 'at risk' for pregnancy and childbirth.

I asked my students to try to imagine how the society on this fictional planet would be arranged compared to our society in the United States. The first thing to go would be sex discrimination, since everyone would be biologically identical. All people are 'hermaphrodites,' so you couldn't use biological sex to create hierarchies. Of course, more attractive 'bisexual hermaphrodites' might enjoy more privileges than the ugly ones, and the old might have more power over the young, but discrimination would not be based on whether you can make babies. Similarly, the social roles linked to biology would be the same for everyone, since most members of this society would be both mothers and fathers to multiple children. My students also imagined that the society on this fictional planet would be organised to accommodate the demands of pregnancy and childbirth, since every member of that society would benefit from collectively organised forms of support. Socialists have long understood that creating equity between men and women despite their biological sex differences requires collective forms of support for child rearing. By the mid-19th century, as women flooded into the industrial labour force of Europe, socialists theorised that you could not build strong worker's movements without the participation of women. The German feminist Lily Braun promoted the idea of a state-funded 'maternity insurance' as early as 1897. In this scheme, working women would enjoy paid furloughs from their jobs both before and after delivery, with guarantees that their jobs would be held in

their absence. As late as 1891, in Germany female industrial workers toiled for a minimum of 65 hours per week,
even if they were with child. Under these circumstances,
pregnant women and girls stayed at the assembly line until
they gave birth, and if they had no husband or family to
support them, they returned to work soon afterwards. The
infant and maternal mortality rate for working women
was more than double that of middle-class women because of the harsh conditions.

Although British and American feminists wanted to support working mothers through non-state charities, Braun
proposed that funds for the maternity insurance be raised
through a progressive income tax. The German government could then pay a woman's wages for a fixed period
before and after the birth of her child. Everyone would
contribute to a special pot of money that new mothers
could draw on, much like unemployment insurance or a
state pension. Braun asserted that since society benefited
from children, it should help bear the costs of raising
them. Children are future soldiers, workers, and taxpayers.
They are a benefit to all, not just to the parents who bring
them into the world (and some parents of teenagers might
argue that they are more of a benefit to society than they
are to their parents). This is especially true in ethnically
homogeneous states, where societies place a premium on
preserving a particular national identity.

But Braun's proposal was expensive. It required new
taxes and would redistribute wealth to the working classes,
an idea that many middle-class men and women opposed.
Braun's ideas also faced initial opposition from the Left.
Because Braun was a reformer and believed that her maternity scheme could be implemented under capitalism,
more radical German socialists like Clara Zetkin initially
rejected her ideas, claiming they could only be realised

361

under a socialist economy. Braun also favoured communal living arrangements (communes) over state-funded nurseries and kindergartens, whereas Zetkin believed that housework and childcare should be socialised. Nonetheless, Braun's proposals, in watered down form at least, were passed into law as early as 1899. And by the Second International Conference of Socialist Women in 1910, Braun's ideas were incorporated into the official socialist platform with the support of Clara Zetkin and the Russian Alexandra Kollontai.

The fourth point on the 1910 socialist platform laid the foundation for all subsequent socialist policies regarding state responsibilities towards women workers. Under the title 'Social Protection and Provision for Motherhood and Infants,' the women of the Second International demanded an eight-hour working day. They proposed that pregnant women stop working (without previous notice) for eight weeks prior to the expected delivery date, and that women be granted a paid 'motherhood insurance' of eight weeks if the child lived, which could be extended to thirteen weeks if the mother was willing and able to nurse the infant.

Women would get a six-week leave for stillborn children, and all working women would enjoy these benefits, 'including agricultural laborers, home workers and maid servants'. These policies would be paid for by the permanent establishment of a special maternity fund out of tax revenues. Seven years later, Kollontai attempted to implement some of these policies in the Soviet Union after the Bolshevik revolution. Instead of burdening individual women with household chores and childcare in addition to their industrial labour, the young Soviet state proposed to build kindergartens, crèches, children's homes, and public cafeterias and laundries. By 1919, the Eighth Congress of the Communist Party handed Kollontai a mandate to expand her work for Soviet women, and she secured state commitments to expend the funds necessary to build a wide network of social services. The year 1919 also saw the creation of an organisation called the Zhenotdel, the Women's Section, which would oversee the work of implementing the radical program of social reform that would lead to women's full emancipation. But Soviet enthusiasm for women's emancipation soon evaporated in the face of more pressing demographic, economic, and political concerns. After the country was devastated by the brutal years of the First World War, followed by the Civil War and the horrendous famine of 1921 and 1922, Lenin and the Bolsheviks did not have the funds to support Kollontai's plan. Hundreds of thousands of war orphans roamed the major cities, plaguing residents with petty crime and theft. The state lacked the resources to care for them; children's homes were overburdened and under-staffed. Liberalisation of divorce laws meant that fathers abandoned their pregnant wives, and poor enforcement of child support and alimony laws meant that those men who had survived the First World War, the Civil War, and the famine routinely skipped out on their responsibilities. Working women couldn't look after their children and hoped the state would step in and help, as Kollontai and the other women's activists had promised. In 1920, the Soviet Union had also become the first country in Europe to legalise abortion on demand during the first twelve weeks of pregnancy. Birth-rates plummeted as women sought to limit the size of their families. Eventually there was fear that the falling birth-rate combined with the devastations of war and famine would derail the country's plans for rapid modernisation.

No one ever wanted women's economic independence

to come at the cost of motherhood, but this is what happened. As the demands on Soviet women's time increased, they chose to delay or limit childbearing. Eventually, Stalin disbanded the Zhenotdel, declaring that the 'woman question' had been solved. In 1936, he reversed most liberal policies, banned abortion, and reinstated the traditional family, on top of his sustained program of state terror and arbitrary purges. The rapidly industrialising Soviet state needed women to work, have babies, and do all of the care work the world's first socialist state could not yet afford to pay for. Soviet women were far from emancipated, and Alexandra Kollontai spent most of her remaining years in diplomatic exile.

Visioning New Futures for Reproductive Justice SisterSong (2023)

22 January 2023 should have been the fiftieth anniversary of *Roe v. Wade*. Instead it was our first January in fifty years without federal protection to the right to an abortion. The SisterSong Women of Color Reproductive Justice Collective convened leaders at the forefront of the Reproductive Justice movement from 20-22 January 2023 in Atlanta, Georgia to discuss the future of the movement and articulate a new vision for Reproductive Justice. This convening was co-anchored by Collective Power for Reproductive Justice, Unite for Reproductive and Gender Equity, and Forward Together.

This vision statement illustrates the intersectional framework, rooted in human rights, that makes up Reproductive Justice. The statement calls on a range of communities to fight for liberation and centres the BIPOC leaders who are ready to bring us into new futures.

In the wake of the *Dobbs v. Jackson Women's Health Organisation* decision, Reproductive Justice is the solution we must fight for. Reproductive Justice is about more than protecting the right to an abortion; it affirms the human right to have children, to not have children, and to raise our children in safe and sustainable communities.

The group envisioned a new future for Reproductive Justice to address our post-*Roe* world and dismantle the white supremacy that threatens our ability to live freely. The right to an abortion was never enough as economic barriers, police brutality, environmental racism, and medical violence have all prevented us from truly having control over our bodies and our families.

This statement envisions a loftier goal than the status quo under *Roe*. It ushers in a new era in this fight that centres Black women and people of colour who have never stopped fighting for bodily autonomy and liberation.

We Declare:

We choose us. We invoke the spirit of our ancestors who cleared the path for us, the comrades who fight alongside us today, and those who will fight beyond us, who will become our greatest dreams.

We reclaim the demands of Reproductive Justice that our Black foremothers named nearly thirty years ago:

The human right to own our bodies and control our future

The human right to have children

The human right to not have children, and

The human right to parent the children we have in safe and sustainable communities.

We are still fighting for these rights to be real in our lives;

we know things are not okay. We have a lot of work to do.

We need you to join our fight so we can make this dream a reality.

How do you know if this movement is for you?
- If you've ever felt shamed during conversations about sex, sexuality, or pregnancy instead of receiving the support and information you desired – this movement is for you.
- If you have ever had abortions, thought about having an abortion, supported someone having an abortion, loved someone who has had abortions – this movement is for you.
- If you've ever felt targeted or criminalised for your labor, including doing sex work for pay – this movement is for you.
- If you're a parent, a mama, an auntie, an abuela, a transgender dad – this movement is for you.
- If you love to have sex and pleasure with consent – this movement is for you.
- If you are a man, cisgender, straight, queer or transgender, who is ready to move with us and trust Black Women – this movement is for you.
- If you've survived state, sexual, interpersonal, or other violence, and exploitation – this movement is for you.
- If you are a person of faith – this movement is for you.
- If you are undocumented – this movement is for you.
- If you are queer, transgender, nonbinary, or gender-expansive – this movement is for you.
- If you are a young person, if you are an elder, or anywhere in between – this movement is for you.
- If you are a healthcare provider who supports all the tenets of reproductive justice – this movement is for you.

- If you are disabled or have not had your accessibility needs met in your community or in a medical space – this movement is for you.
- If you know, from experience, how important it is to be able to vote, feed our families, be paid a liveable wage, drink safe water, and live in safe and affordable housing – this movement is for you.

The right to have kids (or not), to survive, and thrive is universal, and one of the basic building blocks of liberation. When we fight for reproductive justice – we show up for people who are harmed the most. Reproductive justice builds economic, social, and political power for our communities, *even as we struggle in systems that were never meant for us to survive.* This movement saves lives.

Many fundamental rights have been snatched away from us. This isn't new—but it is getting worse. With the rise of white nationalism, people who want more white babies born and to control and end the lives of Black and Brown ones are using every tool in their arsenal to advance their hate.

The truth is, ending white supremacy and racism is going to be hard and messy. That's exactly why we can't run from the fight, especially since our opposition won't stop. They will keep trying to break up our families, lock up our loved ones, and take us out in the streets. Too many of our beloved community, including Indigenous children and transgender women and femmes have been harmed, kidnapped, or killed by patriarchal or state violence.

We are fighting for an end to anti-Blackness, misogynoir, machismo, white supremacy, patriarchy and colonialism, capitalism, xenophobia, transphobia, harmful religious fundamentalism, and all other systems of oppression that are the foundational harms of this country and much of the world.

We need to keep our communities safe against the rising tide of hate and violence. We need to join in a global uprising for global liberation.

Our Vision and What We Are Fighting For

We are dreaming ourselves into the future, fighting like revolutionaries.

Our vision is a future rooted in human dignity and worth, bodily autonomy, joy, love, and rest.

Reproductive justice is our framework, intersectionality is our lens, and liberation is the goal.

Reproductive justice leads to futures we do not yet know but dare to imagine:

- Liberation is giving the land back to Indigenous people who stewarded and protected it for generations before colonisation, and who live on it today.
- Liberation is having what you need to keep your kids, care for your kids, and keep your family safe and together.
- Liberation is being able to have healthy and supported pregnancy options, and prenatal, birth, and postpartum care. This is birth justice.
- Liberation is choosing your family, and being able to care for yourself and your community.

369

- Liberation is an end to police, prisons, family surveillance, and detention centres which are designed to harm Black and Brown bodies and break up our families.
- Liberation is building communities where we all feel safe, able to experience joy, and live together with our loved ones.
- Liberation is ending the war on drugs and providing physical and mental health care, help and support for everyone who needs it.
- Liberation is reparations.
- Liberation is abortion care for any person who needs it.
- Liberation is sexual consent, pleasure, and joy.

We will not be silenced. We will take up all the space we need. We will lead with love. We will reclaim our power for ourselves, our beautiful families, our children, and the generations to come.

Women and Abortion in
Victorian and Edwardian England
Patricia Knight
(1977)

It is always the case that when abortion is illegal, it is
driven underground and a great deal of backstreet abortion occurs. The period before 1914 was no exception. In
spite of being illegal, abortion was widespread. It was
probably the most prevalent form of contraception for
working-class women. The evidence of such women and
of their medical and other opponents, shows not only that
abortion was common but that it was an accepted part of
working-class life.

The exact extent of abortion before 1914 is impossible
to estimate, since only a small percentage of cases came to
the attention of doctors and an even smaller number before the courts. Abortion had first been made illegal in
1803 and the law was tightened up in the 1861 Offences
against the Person Act. Abortionists could be given harsh
sentences ranging from several years imprisonment to
death, but prosecutions usually only took place if the
woman died or became seriously ill. Women were, of
course, very reluctant to proclaim that they had attempted
abortion which was regarded by respectable opinion with
the same horror as infanticide. Since birth control (though
widely used by 1914) was still not an acceptable subject
for open discussion, it is not surprising that no one before

1914 publicly supported abortion. Officially there was some doubt as to whether safe abortion was medically possible though doctors did apparently sometimes abort women suffering from tuberculosis or syphilis.

Abortion was of course already practised before the beginning of the century. Francis Place, who published one of the first leaflets advocating birth control, wrote to Richard Carlile in 1822, that 'means to destroy the foetus had been practised by many married women' – wives of his acquaintances among skilled craftsmen such as tailors and plumbers – and that they would be used more often if they were not dangerous to health.

In the 1860s abortion was often mentioned in the debate in the press on the 'flight from maternity' and the trend towards smaller families in the middle class. Henry Mayhew in 1862 noted 'the immense number of embryo children who are made away with by drugs and other devices' and associated this phenomenon with prostitutes, for whom getting pregnant was an occupational hazard and for whom the alternative was baby farming – the farming out of illegitimate children for a lump sum or weekly fee.

In the 1890s, however, there were frequent assertions in the medical press that abortion, especially by ingestion of drugs and chemicals, was increasing. The same period saw increased use of contraception and it is likely that birth control and abortion increased at the same time, both being due to pressures on standards of living. From the mid-1870s through the period of the Great Depression, while money wages stagnated and unemployment rose in many trades, the more literate and urbanised working class demanded a better standard of living. They did not agree with the individualist and anti-trade union propaganda spread by the Malthusian League. The league saw birth control as an overall social solution to poverty and unemployment rather than a solution to individual problems. Its attitude to the working class tended to be condescending and patronising. It opposed state intervention and social reforms, and insisted that the only good strike was a strike against large families. This meant that it had little direct influence on the working class. Nevertheless, wider discussion of contraception did lead to greater awareness of the advantages of small families. As a labour representative on Huddersfield Trades Council commented shortly before the First World War, 'the time's gone when we'll breed soldiers to be shot at for 1/- a day, or workers to addle brass for manufacturers and starve thersen'. At the same time, contraceptives were expensive and had a high failure rate, leaving abortion as the only means of birth control.

In many ways birth control and abortion were less sharply separated than they are today. Abortion was illegal, but those who published information on birth control or sent appliances through the post were also liable to prosecution. Opponents of contraception often, deliberately or accidentally, confused it with abortion, and some pamphlets recommended both – a leaflet of 1868, along with the safe period and withdrawal, advised abortion methods of 'coughing, sneezing, jumping and violent exercise'. Birth control appliances and abortifacients could be purchased at the same chemists' shops – quinine, for example, could be used either as a spermicide or as a drug to procure abortion.

Though there was probably a good deal of discreet middle-class abortion, indicated by the extensive sale of the more expensive abortion remedies, contemporaries persisted in seeing abortion as a working-class phenomenon. It was not confined, however, to the very poor, as some opponents liked to imagine, but was prevalent in the skilled and semi-skilled groups. In a survey carried out by

373

Ethel Elderton on the decline of the birth-rate in Northern England between 1876 and 1906, abortion was said to be common in 26 of the 104 registration districts covered in Lancashire, Cheshire, Yorkshire, Northumberland, Durham, Westmorland and Cumberland. All 26 were urban working-class areas – like birth control, abortion was less frequently attempted in rural districts, partly because of problems obtaining information and remedies. Eleven of the 26 districts were Lancashire textile towns, where the decline in the birth-rate was higher than average, and where small families were considered to be partly due to the large numbers of married women working in cotton factories. (Higher than average falls in the birth-rate were noted in all areas where industrial employment for women was available.) In Burnley for instance, 'there is more than a suspicion that abortion is freely practised in the working class.' In Bolton it was said to be 'a favourite form of birth control among the working class'. In Bradford there was 'a great deal of abortion, only a small percentage of which was detected by the police'. Estimates of the percentage of women using abortion varied, but all were high. A working-class woman in York told an interviewer, 'six out of ten working women take something.' Two other 'respectable working women' in the same town said that 70 to 80 per cent of all women took drugs. A social worker told the National Birth-Rate Commission in 1913 that in Birmingham, 25 per cent of poor women attempted abortion at some point in their lives, adding, 'women will do a great deal in order to avoid being pregnant.' Certainly one mail order business alone sold drugs to 12,000 women in the two years from 1896 to 1898.

After 1906, doctors anxious at the increased use of lead to procure abortions began to carry out their own surveys. A circular sent to every doctor within 30 miles' radius of

374

Sheffield produced two hundred replies, fifty of which were from doctors who had attended cases of lead poisoning due to abortion attempts. Between one hundred and two hundred cases of lead poisoning were observed in Sheffield in two years. In York in 1904, thirty women were treated for lead poisoning, and in Derby one doctor alone had seen one hundred cases between 1896 and 1905. These figures of course were only the tip of the iceberg since they did not include the great majority of women who did not become ill enough to require medical attention (or who went direct to hospital) or who used other methods of abortion.

All the evidence points to abortion being very widespread, and most women who attempted it, like those who used birth control, seem not to have been young unmarried girls, but married women who already had two or more children. Abortion was often resorted to in desperation after the birth of a number of children.

The use of abortion is not surprising, since the main methods of birth control available to the working class were abstention, the 'safe' period (anything but safe since it was thought to occur mid-way between periods, the very time of maximum fertility) and withdrawal. These all depended on the co-operation of the man, as did the sheath, the cheapest mechanical method, which could be bought for 6d per dozen, though 3/− per dozen was the usual price. Since even skilled workers could expect to earn only 30/− per week, and one-third of families existed below the poverty line on less than 21/- per week, it is evident that sheaths, even at the lowest prices, were for many an unattainable luxury. Female methods of contraception were even more expensive and complicated, so that apart from use of abortion, working-class women were unable to control their own fertility. Accurate information on birth control was difficult to acquire, was rarely provided by doctors, and was available only in chemists' catalogues, or tucked away in a few pages of books with abstruse and intimidatingly long titles, dealing with Malthusian economics. By the 1880s sponges, soluble pessaries, rubber diaphragms and syringes were sold by chemists, but success was not guaranteed unless two methods were combined. Spermicidal solutions for use with sponges or syringes had to be mixed by the woman herself, using quinine and other ingredients in a process resembling a chemical experiment. Successful female contraception required time, space, perseverance and above all, money. The minimum outlay required was 5/– to 6/– for which one could buy a cheap syringe, a dozen soluble pessaries and a box of quinine powder. Abortion on the other hand was much less expensive, since only a few 'pennyworths' of drugs needed to be bought; and it required no previous planning, organisation or forethought, nor co-operation from the man. It was not, however, any more reliable than birth control and was often much more dangerous to health.

Women who attempted abortion generally used drugs in preference to instruments. Use of knitting needles and other implements was more likely to require assistance from abortionists and therefore to be more expensive, and the results were likely to be more traumatic and painful. Many women, however, tried more than one method if the first did not work – for example, one woman who already had several children took herbs, and when these had no effect scraped out her womb with a hairpin: she finally aborted some weeks later, when she was delivered of a five-month-old dead foetus (. A wide variety of drugs and herbs were tried, singly or combined, which were easily and cheaply available without prescription, from herbalists and chemists' shops. They included colocynth (commonly known as 'bitter apples'), hiera picra ('hikey pikey' in popular terminology), tansy, pennyroyal, apiol (combined with steel), gin and gunpowder (the latter bought from the ironmongers), gin and salts, iron and aloes, caraway seeds, turpentine, washing soda and quinine. A Birmingham midwife noted one unusual method which consisted of boiling copper coins and drinking the liquid which resulted. These drugs if taken in sufficient quantities could produce vomiting, muscular contractions and convulsions, which might cause abortion as a side-effect, though apparently in many cases abortion failed to occur. Knowledge of drugs likely to produce abortion was part of local folklore, handed down from generation to generation, and passed on from one woman to another. Most women obtained advice from friends and neighbours. By the 1800s a relatively new method, consumption of lead pills, was becoming popular, and was believed to be more successful than other methods. It had been observed that women who worked in factories where white lead was used often had miscarriages and spread of this knowledge was no doubt responsible for the growing use of lead as an abortifacient. Use of lead was traced from the Midlands in the early 1890s to Sheffield by 1900, and Manchester, Newcastle and London by 1906. It was easy to obtain, since lead plaster (diachylon) was sold by chemists for the treatment of bruises and fractured ribs, and could be mixed with aloes or boric acid to form pills ('black stick' in popular jargon). Many women took large doses of these pills. One woman aged forty, who already had eleven children, ate forty pills without avail. Another woman took 144 pills, before she miscarried seventeen days later. In some working-class streets in Newcastle it was said, 'women take the drug regularly before each expected monthly period so as to be sure that the event is realised'. The use of lead became so common that one doctor 'when called in to see a woman who has aborted, invariably examined the gums for lead poisoning'. Lead poisoning or plumbism was easy to detect since a distinguishing symptom was a blue line round the gums.

The numerous women who resorted to abortion frequently had to face illness and sometimes death. Abortion, especially by use of instruments, was often painful and dangerous. A typical example in 1866 concerned a woman with seven children, who was five months pregnant, and who paid a midwife to abort her: her uterus was lacerated, punctured and inflamed and she died a fortnight later from peritonitis and gangrene. There were many pathetic court cases reported in the press. For example, in 1868 there was an inquest on Louisa Thomas aged 24, who was two months pregnant and died from an attempt made by a doctor (who was the father of her child) to abort her. The doctor had committed suicide by throwing himself under a train. Death sometimes occurred from lead poisoning, and women who took lead pills frequently suffered from sickness, abdominal pains, headaches, paralysis of the hands, and occasionally blindness. In Newcastle in 1913, a woman who had aborted after consuming large quantities of lead pills for seven days suffered severe headaches and vomiting; a month later her hands and legs were paralysed: and she was still ill five months afterwards. More commonplace drugs could also have ill-effects: a doctor in Thornton Heath treated a woman who had become very ill with 'hands and legs stone cold and clammy', after eating large amounts of crushed nutmeg.

BIOGRAPHICAL NOTES

LAUREN BERLANT's books include *The Female Complaint*, *Cruel Optimism* and the 'national sentimentality trilogy'. They taught English at Chicago for many years.

JOANNA BIGGS is a senior editor at *Harper's* and the author of *A Life of One's Own: Nine Women Writers Begin Again*.

EDNA BONHOMME is a historian of science and culture writer based in Berlin. Her first book is *A History of the World in Six Plagues*.

GWENDOLYN BROOKS was the author of more than twenty collections of poetry.

BEVERLEY BRYAN, STELLA DADZIE AND SUZANNE SCAFE were members of Brixton Black Women's Group. Many of the group's members contributed to *The Heart of the Race*.

STORM CECILE is a spoken word poet.

LUCILLE CLIFTON wrote many volumes of poetry as well as books for children and a memoir, *Generations*.

RACHEL CONNOLLY is a journalist. Her first novel, *Lazy City*, was published in 2023.

T.L. COWAN is a writer, performer, activist and professor based in Toronto.

MAGGIE DOHERTY is the author of *The Equivalents: A Story of Art, Female Friendship and Liberation in the 1960s*.

NELL DUNN's books include *Up the Junction*, *Talking to Women* and *Poor Cow*, which was made into a film.

ANDREA DWORKIN was a radical feminist and the author of a number of books, including *Women Hating* and *Intercourse*.

ANNE ENRIGHT's *The Gathering* won the 2007 Booker Prize.

DEBORAH FRIEDELL is a contributing editor at the *London Review of Books*.

TRACY FUAD's second collection, *PORTAL*, will be published in 2024.

KRISTEN GHODSEE is professor of Russian and East European Studies at the University of Pennsylvania.

VIVIAN GORNICK is a critic and memoirist.

URSULA K. LE GUIN's works of speculative fiction include *The Left Hand of Darkness* and the *Earthsea* series.

DONNA HARAWAY is professor emerita in the history of consciousness and feminist studies departments at the University of California, Santa Cruz.

BELL HOOKS wrote extensively on race, feminism and class.

BARBARA JOHNSON taught English at Harvard for many years.

JAYNE KAVANAGH, LISA HALLGARTEN AND ANGELA POULTER's documentary *Kind to Women: How the 1967 Abortion Act Changed Our Lives* came out in 2017.

JAMAICA KINCAID is the author of five novels and many works of non-fiction, including *A Small Place*.

PATRICIA KNIGHT's essay in this collection was originally published in fourth issue of the History Workshop Journal.

R.O. KWON's The Incendiaries was shortlisted for the National Book Critics Circle first book award.

NATASHA LENNARD is a columnist for the Intercept and the author of a book of essays, Being Numerous.

SOPHIE LEWIS teaches at the Brooklyn Institute for Social Research. She is working on a book about 'enemy feminisms'.

AUDRE LORDE described herself as a 'black, lesbian, feminist, socialist, mother, warrior, poet'. Your Silence Will Not Protect You, a collection of essays and poems, is published by Silver Press.

AMELIA LOULLI's collection Slip will be published in 2024.

ERIN MAGLAQUE is a historian of gender in early modern Europe. She teaches at the University of Sheffield.

HOLLY PESTER's first collection, Comic Timing, came out in 2021.

ADRIENNE RICH was a poet and essayist. Diving into the Wreck won the National Book Award in 1973.

DENISE RILEY lives in London. Her books include 'Am I That Name?' Feminism and the Category of 'Women' in History, Impersonal Passion: Language as Affect and Time Lived, Without Its Flow. Her most recent poetry collection, Lurex, came out last year.

SALLY ROONEY is the author of Conversations with Friends, Normal People and Beautiful World, Where Are You?

LORETTA J. ROSS is a reproductive justice activist and a co-founder of SisterSong.

MADELEINE SCHWARTZ is journalist and editor-in-chief of the *Dial*.

SISTERSONG was formed in 1997 as a women of colour reproductive justice collective. They work to improve policies and systems that impact the reproductive lives of marginalised communities.

SOPHIE SMITH is a historian of political thought at Oxford. She is finishing a book on feminist history for Harvard University Press.

ANNABEL SOWEMIMO is an NHS community sexual and reproductive health registrar and the founder and co-director of the Reproductive Justice Initiative. *Divided: Racism, Medicine and Decolonising Healthcare* was published in 2023.

AMIA SRINIVASAN is Chichele Professor of Social and Political Theory at All Souls College, Oxford and the author of *The Right to Sex*.

KEEANGA-YAMAHTTA TAYLOR teaches African American studies at Northwestern University.

JUDITH JARVIS THOMSON, a professor of philosophy at MIT, wrote widely on ethics and metaphysics.

ALICE WALKER is the author of seventeen novels and short story collections.

BERNARD WILLIAMS was an English moral philosopher.

ACKNOWLEDGEMENTS

We thank the contributors to this book and their collaborators, publishers and executors. This collection has been made possible by the efforts of many, and we acknowledge in particular Marleen Boschen, Sarah Shin, Jay Drinkall, Leila Edelsztein, Ailsa McNicol, Jayne Kavanagh and Lisa Hallgarten, Denise Riley, Luiza Prado, Christine Kakaire, Charmaine Li, Fran Spawls and Michael Crabtree. We are grateful for the financial support of Arts Council England.

SILVER PRESS

THE DEBUTANTE AND OTHER STORIES
LEONORA CARRINGTON
With an introduction by Sheila Heti
and an afterword by Marina Warner
ISBN: 978-0-9957162-0-9
£11.99

TALKING TO WOMEN
NELL DUNN
With an introduction by Ali Smith
and a new afterword by Nell Dunn
ISBN: 978-0-995716-21-6
£13.99

YOUR SILENCE WILL NOT PROTECT YOU
AUDRE LORDE
With a preface by Reni Eddo-Lodge
and an introduction by Sara Ahmed
ISBN: 978-0-9957162-2-3
£13.99

MY MOTHER LAUGHS
CHANTAL AKERMAN
Translated by Daniella Shreir
With an introduction by Eileen Myles
and afterword by Frances Morgan
ISBN: 978-0-9957162-3-0
£14.99

REVOLUTIONARY LETTERS
DIANE DI PRIMA
With a foreword by Francesca Wade
and an introduction by Sophie Lewis
ISBN: 978-0-9957162-6-1
£13.99

FUGITIVE FEMINISM
AKWUGO EMEJULU
With a foreword by Edna Bonhomme
ISBN: 978-0-9957162-8-5
£12.99

SPACE CRONE
URSULA K. LE GUIN
Edited and introduced by So Mayer and Sarah Shin
ISBN: 978-0-9957162-7-8
£13.99

ZONG!
M. NOURBESE PHILIP
With a new preface by M. NourbeSe Philip
and essays by Katherine McKittrick and Saidiya Hartman
ISBN: 978-0-9957162-4-7
£13.99

This selection first published by Silver Press in 2023
silverpress.org

978 0 9957162 9 2

1 2 3 4 5 6 7 8 9 10
Design by Rose Nordin
Typeset in Joanna

Printed and bound by CPI in England.

Supported using public funding by
**ARTS COUNCIL
ENGLAND**

LOTTERY FUNDED